Teknon
AND THE
Champion
Warriors

Mentor Guide

AN INTERACTIVE ADVENTURE TO EXPLORE COURAGEOUS MANHOOD

A companion leader's guide for *Teknon and the Champion Warriors*

A *Mission Guide* for sons is also available

Teknon and the CHAMPION Warriors Mentor Guide—Father

Published by FamilyLife, a division of Campus Crusade for Christ.

Author: Brent Sapp
Senior Editor: Ben Colter
Editorial Team: Stephen W. Sorenson, Anne Wooten, Fran Taylor, David Sims,
           and Bob Anderson
Illustrator: Sergio Cariello
Designer: Jerry McCall

ISBN 1-57229-246-6
Printed in the United States of America.

NOTE: This book is intended for boys ages 11 to 16. However, it contains some mature subject matter addressing dating, sexual temptation, and pornography.

Dennis Rainey, Executive Director
3900 N. Rodney Parham Road
Little Rock, AR 72212-2441
(501) 223-8663
1-800-FL-TODAY
www.familylife.com

A division of Campus Crusade for Christ

*The CHAMPION Training
adventure program
is dedicated to a pair of champions—
my mom and dad*

TEKNON
AND THE
CHAMPION
WARRIORS

MENTOR GUIDE–FATHER

An Interactive Adventure to Explore Courageous Manhood

TABLE OF CONTENTS

AIMING YOUR ARROW
FOREWORD BY DENNIS RAINEY

MENTOR PREPARATION

PLANNING YOUR SON'S CHAMPION TRAINING

Chapter One M8

WHAT IS CHAMPION TRAINING?

Overview
Timetable

Chapter Two M10

I'M WAITING FOR YOU, DAD

My Wake-up Call
Dive Into His Life
My Son's Response to the CHAMPION Training

Chapter Three **M14**

THREE WAYS TO APPROACH THE CHAMPION ADVENTURE

Levels of Commitment
Adapting to Unique Situations
(mentors, small groups, mothers)

Chapter Four **M18**

HOW TO USE THE CHAMPION TRAINING PROGRAM

Pre-training and Preparation M18
Night of Challenge M22
CHAMPION Sessions M24
Celebration Ceremony M26
Ongoing Involvement M29

Chapter Five **M31**

THINK TANK

Chapter Six **M62**

FATHER'S ARSENAL

CHAMPION Training Commitment Form M63
Understanding Your Son's Bent M64
Media Evaluation Report Form M70
Fiction Glossary M71
Greek Terms in the Story M78
Guiding Insights Request Letter (Sample) M79
Summary of Success (Sample Presentation) M80
CHAMPION Symbol and Gift Ideas M82

Mission Guide

This section follows the Mentor Preparation section, giving you a page-by-page copy of your son's Mission Guide. You will be working from the same material as your son except that we have given you the answers to the questions as well as notes and tips in the margins.

Sessions 1-15 and Appendices . . . . .1 through 202
Acknowledgements and Notes 203
About the Author and Illustrator 204

AIMING YOUR ARROW

Congratulations! You hold in your hands a powerful, life-changing tool—a way to impact your son for a lifetime and leave a mighty legacy for future generations.

The psalmist tells us that our children are like "arrows in the hands of a warrior" (Psalm 127:4). Our culture is in dire need of young men who know *who* they are and *where* they're going. What better way to launch your son into young adulthood than with a planned adventure resource like this one? It's a great way to direct your son toward godly character and convictions.

You're in for a few months of dynamic interaction with your son. It may be hard at times and you might feel you're in over your head, but you'll find all the resources you need in your *Mentor Guide*. Your son will probably tire from time to time, and you may, too. But stay with it! You can't help but draw closer to God and closer to each other through the course of this study.

Men, the time is now. You can do it! With the proper preparation and a planned trajectory, you can watch your "arrow" take flight.

Dennis Rainey
Executive Director, FamilyLife

Mentor Preparation

Planning Your Son's Champion Training

Chapter One

What Is CHAMPION Training?

Overview

CHAMPION Training is an interactive adventure designed to encourage a young man to embrace the process of developing godly character and convictions in his life, under the guidance of his father or a mentor.

This adventure program is designed to instill specific character traits in your son with the ultimate goal of preparing him for young adulthood. The eight qualities, built around an acrostic of the word "CHAMPION," are defined in the CHAMPION Code (see page 6 in the *Mission Guide* section). Once a solid foundation of character is laid, your son will continue to build upon it through his teen years and into adulthood.

For the purpose of this program, "character" is defined as moral strength that grows out of our relationship with God. Personal growth is expressed through the physical, emotional, social, mental, and especially spiritual areas of our lives.

CHAMPION Training also provides an opportunity to formally celebrate your son's transition into young manhood through a ceremony assembled to honor him. Robert Lewis, in his excellent book *Raising a Modern Day Knight*, writes about a young manhood ceremony: "Ceremony should be one of the crown jewels for helping a boy become a man. In many cultures throughout history, a teenage boy is taken through some type of ritual to mark his official passage into manhood. I believe one of the great tragedies of the western culture today is the absence of this type of ceremony."[1]

It is our privilege and responsibility to prepare our sons for young adulthood and to celebrate their transition into this important stage of life. You will interact regularly with your son on issues that are important to him. This process will help to open lines of meaningful communication, deepen your relationship, and launch a life-long friendship.

The CHAMPION Training program consists of three fully integrated resources:

▲ *Teknon and the CHAMPION Warriors* fiction book—15 action-packed episodes

▲ *Mission Guide* for your son—16 CHAMPION Sessions linked to the fiction episodes

▲ *Mentor Guide* for you—Everything you need to plan and carry out the program, including the contents of the *Mission Guide* with answers, tips, and hands-on projects

TIMETABLE

There are three different approaches that you can take with your son's CHAMPION Training: casual, concise, or complete (see chapter 3). The complete strategy level is fairly intensive, but highly recommended. Plan for you and your son to meet every other week for the CHAMPION Sessions. With this approach, you should plan up to 10 months to complete the entire program: one month for preparation, eight months for the 16 sessions, and one month to arrange for the celebration ceremony. If you meet weekly and scale down your program to reduce the level of time investment, it could take as little as four months.

> *Example is not the main thing in influencing others. It is the only thing.*
>
> Albert Schweitzer

Chapter Two

I'm Waiting for You, Dad

My Wake-up Call

It happened for me (Brent) in June 1995. At the time, my life was probably a lot like yours. Day after day I hit the floor running, making sure I was responding adequately to the noisemakers of society. You've heard them before, haven't you? The noisemakers are those urgent messengers that pummel us from all directions, and at all hours of the day. They continually try to tempt us away from our important priorities, and throw us headlong into a frantic, perpetual treadmill of busyness.

I have heard that workers in some parts of Asia during the early 20th century were sent into the fields and jungles, armed with an unusual objective. They positioned themselves under a group of trees filled with birds, and then they began banging noisemakers together until the birds flew away. After a while the birds came back and tried to light again on the branches; but the noisemakers sounded again, and the birds scattered. This process occurred over and over, until finally the birds couldn't fly anymore. Eventually they dropped dead from exhaustion.

Does this scenario sound familiar? The noisemakers of society try to hit us three ways: hard, fast, and continuously. They keep banging away, and we keep flying from the "branch," away from our important priorities. Every time we get to a position where we can evaluate our personal mission and subsequently make wise, long-term decisions, the noisemakers immediately try to get us back on the treadmill.

Have you heard the noisemakers lately?

"What do you mean, you're going home at 5:30? Don't you know we have a report due in two weeks?!" BANG, BANG, BANG!!

"Go ahead and buy that house. It's just a few hundred more per month, and besides, you'll be living close to the 'movers and shakers'!" BANG, BANG, BANG!!

"Your voice mailbox is full. Please delete those messages that are not needed. You have 25 new messages; 15 are urgent." BANG, BANG, BANG!!

Even though we're not supposed to burn the candle at both ends, we spend a lot of time trying to do it. But there is a price to pay for that kind of "dance 'til you drop" type of living. Like the birds in Asia, we often experience fatigue and become preoccupied to the point that we forget, or postpone, those things that are most important to us. That is, until we get a wake-up call.

My call came in 1995, when I paused momentarily from the normal frantic pace of life to experience one of those, "When in the world did this happen?" revelations. I glanced across our living room to see a mature-looking 11-year-old boy. He was 5' 6" tall, with feet almost as big as mine. His voice sounded a little lower than I remembered. It seemed like yesterday when he rode a miniature fire truck around the driveway, yelling at me to watch him. Now he was reading novels, taking more showers, and excelling in basketball. My son, Casey, was becoming a young man.

I really didn't see it coming. *Wait a minute*, I thought to myself, *I'm not ready for this*! In two years Casey would be a teenager. What had I done to prepare him for such a major transition? Did he have the foundation of knowledge and skills to enter young manhood? Had he heard me verbalize my priorities and values? Was he ready to face the inevitable temptations that society and his peers would offer him?

I have long admired the Jewish tradition of the bar mitzvah. As a Jewish boy approaches his teenage years, he engages in a program of rigorous academic training based on Jewish tradition and beliefs. At the end of his training, the boy recites some difficult Hebrew passages and reads a speech he's prepared describing why he is ready to become a young man. Then, a ceremony occurs.

At the ceremony the boy's father formally acknowledges to his friends and family that his son is a young man. In essence, the father communicates to everyone present that the boy is ready to assume the privileges and responsibilities that come with his new stage in life. It's a powerful moment!

The more I thought about the richness of tradition involved with the bar mitzvah, the more I wanted Casey to experience a transition like that. I wanted him to enter young adulthood with a sense of direction and purpose. The description of Jesus in his early years provided the ultimate example for my son: "And Jesus grew in wisdom and stature, and in favor with God and men." (Luke 2:52).

According to this passage of Scripture, Jesus set the pattern for us to follow as He grew in wisdom (mentally), in stature (physically), in favor with God (spiritually), and in favor with man (socially/emotionally). As Casey entered his early teen years I also wanted him to establish a foundation of skills and principles to utilize in the years ahead—socially, mentally, physically, emotionally, and most importantly, spiritually. Finally, I wanted Casey to experience a formal celebration of his young adulthood. Not that he would become a man at 12 or 13, but that he would recognize that he was no longer a child and that he must start learning what it means to be a godly man.

I decided to write down all of the elements I felt Casey needed to make his training complete. I detailed character qualities to develop, activities to accomplish, books to read, movies to watch, and cassette tapes to listen to. I also wrote down the names of men, individuals I knew and trusted, whom I wanted to play a role in Casey's development.

You are probably experiencing the same type of wake-up call that I experienced a few years ago. You may feel, as I did, that you need a practical guide to help you think through the issues of guiding your son as he transitions into young manhood. It is my hope that the *Teknon and the CHAMPION Warriors* adventure materials will help you in this process. I commend you for caring enough about your son to take the proactive step of completing this training adventure with him.

Dive Into His Life

There is a true story of a family who owned a cottage on a lake in Michigan. One day the father and his two young sons (one 5 years old, the other almost 3) enjoyed a great boat trip together. Upon returning, they docked the boat and headed for the house. The man did not notice that the younger boy had stayed behind, stretching over the water to get back into the boat. Suddenly, the father heard a splash and he realized only one of his sons was with him.

He rushed back to the dock, frantically looked around, but saw nothing in the dark water. He dived in and swam around underneath the dock searching for his son. Finally, he burst to the surface, took another deep breath and dove back down. He found his young son several feet under the surface, desperately gripping one of the pilings. The father helped his son release his grip, and then pulled him to the surface. The youngster was frightened, but unharmed.

For the remainder of that day the father carried his young son around and held him close. After some time he asked the boy, "Son, what were you doing down there?" The young boy looked up at his father and replied, "I was waiting for you, Dad. I was waiting for you."

Our sons are waiting for us to dive into their lives and help to pull them through the dark, uncertain waters of adolescence. They want to grow up and embrace independence from our authority, and yet they still need our guidance and involvement in their lives. Regardless of this tension, we as fathers must keep reaching and taking the initiative to help our sons prepare for the years ahead. *Teknon and the CHAMPION Warriors* is designed to offer a transition program (for young men ages 11 to 16) that will strengthen your son's character and equip him to face the challenges during his teen years and into adulthood.

My Son's Response
to the CHAMPION Adventure

Here is what my son, Casey, had to say at age 13 about our CHAMPION adventure together:

> When I started the CHAMPION Training, I was really looking forward to doing it with my dad because I knew it would be a way for us to spend time together. Although we had a very strong relationship before, we were even closer after the training was finished. It was a great experience for me to learn what being a "real man" meant. During the week, we would share and discuss articles from our local newspaper, or Time magazine just to discuss our feelings on different topics. Sometimes we would watch a movie like "Ben Hur" or "Sergeant York" or listen to a tape by Dennis Rainey or Chuck Colson. Every time I watched or listened to what Dad suggested, I got a lot out of it. I learned a lot about my dad and myself during that time.
>
> After the training was finished, I looked back on the previous year and thought about what I had learned from discussing those articles and watching those movies with my dad. It was unbelievable to look back and realize that I had changed spiritually and mentally. If I had to go back and do it all over again, I would not change one thing.

Several years ago, I (Brent) met Dr. Donald Joy, author and seminary professor, to gain his opinion of the CHAMPION Training program. After looking it over he turned to me and said, "This really boils down to involved parenting." Dr. Joy was absolutely right. We can become "difference makers" in our son's lives by becoming involved enough to guide them into maturity.

> *No man will ever rise above the opinion his children have of him.*
>
> Dennis Rainey

Chapter Three

THREE WAYS TO APPROACH THE CHAMPION ADVENTURE

LEVELS OF COMMITMENT

There are three different levels of commitment you can take in approaching the *Teknon and the CHAMPION Warriors* adventure with your son. Although the complete strategy requires the most time and energy, the results are definitely worth the investment. The other two levels are offered for those people who cannot commit the time and energy for the complete strategy, but still want to build into the lives of their sons in some way. See chapter 4 for "how to" instructions.

A. Casual Strategy

▲ Read the fiction book yourself.

▲ Give your son the fiction book to read.

▲ Informally discuss the story and life applications with your son.

▲ Glean discussion ideas from the *Mentor Guide*.

B. Concise Strategy

▲ Introduce the idea of reading through the fiction book and meeting regularly to discuss it.

▲ Read the fiction book yourself.

▲ Give your son the fiction book to read.

▲ Set up regular times to meet for CHAMPION Sessions.

▲ Before each session, prepare by reviewing that session in this *Mentor Guide*; select key elements you want to focus on.

▲ Try to have your son work through the sessions in advance.

▲ Note: this approach would typically eliminate some discussion questions (at your discretion) plus omit projects, Bible power verses, inclusion of mentors, and the celebration ceremony.

C. Complete Strategy

This recommended strategy involves five basic steps for preparation and training. Of course, the CHAMPION Sessions (step 3) are the central focus. Listed below are the highlights of each step, with more detailed instructions provided in chapter 4.

1. Pre-training and Preparation (instructions in chapter 4)

▲ Pray regularly for a month in preparation.

▲ Identify goals and expectations for the experience.

▲ Read the fiction book and review all the program elements and helps in your *Mentor Guide*.

▲ Enlist two or three adult mentors to be involved.

▲ Begin to create a desire in your son to pursue this training adventure with you.

2. Night of Challenge (instructions in chapter 4)

▲ Have a kick-off dinner with your son.

▲ Challenge and motivate your son to commit to the CHAMPION Training.

▲ Give your son the fiction book to read and ask him to read through it (set a target date).

▲ Set a date for your first CHAMPION Session and ask your son to re-read episode 1 and to complete the session 1 questions in his *Mission Guide* before your session together.

3. CHAMPION Sessions (instructions in chapter 4)

▲ Pray before each session.

▲ Prepare before each session by reviewing that session in this *Mentor Guide*.

▲ Have your son prepare before each session using his *Mission Guide*.

▲ Meet with your son every other week for your CHAMPION Sessions (one to two hours).

▲ Have your son complete special hands-on projects between sessions and join him in these projects.

4. Celebration Ceremony (instructions in chapter 4)

▲ Prepare for your son's celebration.

▲ Conduct your son's celebration after he has completed all the sessions with you.

5. Ongoing Involvement (instructions in chapter 4)

▲ Encourage him to continue executing the action points on his Sheet of Deeds.

▲ Continue informal coaching.

▲ Create opportunities for further training.

▲ Continue to seek out and involve mentors in your son's life.

Adapting to Unique Situations

While this program is designed to be used by a father and son in a one-on-one mentoring situation, it can be adapted and used effectively in other settings.

Other Male Relatives or Mentors

There will be boys who do not have a father that can take them through the CHAMPION Training. This is a significant ministry opportunity for an uncle, grandfather, or other male relative to step in and mentor this boy. In addition, godly men who are friends of the family could also take the challenge of mentoring a young man in this situation. You will need to explain to the young man that the *Mission Guide* uses the words "son" and "father" often, but that you are adapting this material so that you can participate with him and invest in his life.

A special word for adoptive fathers or stepfathers: There are additional relational challenges for you as an adoptive father or stepfather in using the CHAMPION Training with your boy. Even if you do not refer to each other as father and son, remind the young man that God has a special plan for your family and has blessed your life and your home with him. Communicate how much you care about him and that you are using this CHAMPION Training to help him to be all God intended for him to be. God Himself set the model for adoption (or step-fathering). It's one of His greatest gifts (see Galatians 4:5-7).

Small Groups/Church

Option #1: Father/son teams linked together through your church

Consider coinciding your CHAMPION Training start date with other men in your church or community. You could meet with the other fathers on a monthly basis for the purposes of prayer, brainstorming, encouragement, and accountability. You can decide whether your sons should come to your meetings or not. It is important, however, that you keep the celebration ceremonies separate and special for each young man.

Option #2: Single leader with a group of boys

With some extra planning and creativity, boys without fathers to take them through the program could be trained in a small group setting. Each of the young men will need a copy of the fiction book *Teknon and the CHAMPION Warriors* and their own copy of the *Mission Guide*. You will need to explain to the boys that the *Mission Guide* uses the words "son" and "father" often, but that you are adapting this material for use in your group. It would be very advantageous to enlist a group of godly men to act in a role as mentors or discussion leaders for individual boys or very small groups.

MOTHERS

Mothers truly deserve respect and encouragement in the task of raising a son. If you are mother who wishes to provide the CHAMPION Training to her son but lacks adequate adult male participation due to divorce, the death of a spouse, or some other reason, your desire to invest in your son's life is to be applauded.

There are three basic alternatives available to expose your son to this training:

▲ Approach a spiritually mature adult man in your church or community about leading your son through the program. Perhaps a relative meets this criterion. Pray that God would provide someone to whom your son can relate and whom he respects. (See the Other Male Relatives or Mentors section above.)

▲ Facilitate the training program yourself. If you choose this option, it might be best if you approach it somewhat like a homeschool teacher. A lot will depend upon the level of openness that you have with your son on male issues. Concentrate on the content, presenting the material to your son as an academic project that you and he can discuss together. Understand ahead of time, however, that the story line is decidedly male-oriented, with a science fiction flavor. Work to deepen your relationship with your son, but try to enlist male mentors to befriend him and augment your efforts as needed. You will need to explain to your son that the *Mission Guide* uses the word "father" often, but that you are adapting this material so that you can participate with him and invest in his life.

▲ Approach your pastor or a spiritually mature adult man in your church who would be willing to invest in the lives of several young men. With some extra planning and creativity, these boys could be trained in a group setting. (See the Small Groups/Church section above.)

Remember, above all, that God is capable of providing for your needs in this area. He will honor your love for your son and your obedience to Him!

CHAPTER FOUR

HOW TO USE THE CHAMPION TRAINING PROGRAM

The following instructions are provided to help you to succeed in every facet of the CHAMPION Training program with your son. Instructions are provided for the complete training strategy, but you can extract elements for use with the concise or casual strategies outlined in chapter 3. Although the complete strategy requires the most time and energy, the results are definitely worth the investment.

PRE-TRAINING AND PREPARATION

PRAY REGULARLY FOR A MONTH IN PREPARATION

Prayer is the first and most important step in your preparation. It will also be essential throughout the course of the CHAMPION Training. Psalm 127:1a tells us, "Unless the Lord builds the house, they labor in vain who build it."

IDENTIFY THE TARGETS FOR YOUR SON'S ADVENTURE

Ask yourself one question: "What do I want to accomplish?"

What would it take for you to say, at the end of the program, that your son's training was a solid success? Visualize your son on the night of his celebration ceremony. What has he learned? What's different about him ... about you ... about your relationship? Does your son understand your convictions in life? Are you modeling those convictions? Is he developing or deepening his own convictions?

> *Build me a son, O Lord, who will be strong enough to know when he is weak, and brave enough to face himself when he is afraid, one who will be proud and unbending in honest defeat, and humble and gentle in victory.*
>
> General Douglas MacArthur

If you understand what you want to accomplish with your son through the CHAMPION Training ahead of time, your target will become more clear and your efforts more directed.

Take a few minutes and write down key targets you want to set for your son:

_____

_____

_____

_____

_____

_____

_____

Understand Your Son's Bent

"Understanding Your Son's Bent" is an assessment tool found in chapter 6 to help you determine your son's temperament and motivational "hot buttons." The more you understand about his temperament before you begin, the easier it will be to motivate your son during the training. Your son will have an opportunity to interact with this material and explore his bent as a part of session 14 in his *Mission Guide*. Four key characters from the fiction story (Tor, Epps, Arti, and Matty) illustrate the four temperment types.

Set Your Expectations

Take the time to set expectations for your son in preparation for the CHAMPION Training. As you prepare, consider the training method perfected by the eagle.

When an eaglet is young, the mother eagle carefully lines her nest with an ample supply of her own down feathers. This allows the young bird to live comfortably in the warmth and security of its mother's care. As the eaglet grows, however, the mother begins taking the down out of the nest, so the eaglet gets more and more uncomfortable from the cold air. Then one day, a swift push from the mother's wing forces it out of the nest.

The small bird plummets down the side of the mountain, frantically flapping its wings to no avail. Almost immediately, the mother eagle swoops underneath her youth and carries it safely back to the nest. Then she tenderly puts her massive wing around the fledgling to soothe it, its heart now beating to the breaking point.   When the eaglet becomes calm and comfortable again, the mother promptly nudges it out of the nest again. This difficult process continues until one day the eaglet decides to fly on its own. On that day, the young bird is no longer an eaglet, but an eagle ready to soar like its parents.

One of our jobs as fathers is to make our sons progressively more uncomfortable by challenging them to step out of their comfort zones. By providing an occasional "loving push" out of the nest, we help them to increase their confidence in facing and overcoming obstacles. Just remember, as you set expectations for your son, do not challenge him with too much, but don't challenge him with too little either.

Read the fiction book and review your Mentor Guide

Read through the story *Teknon and the CHAMPION Warriors*. Then carefully review the process, adventure ideas, and program tools provided in your *Mentor Guide*.

Enlist two to three adult mentors to be involved

For the purpose of the CHAMPION Training, a mentor is defined as an adult male who takes an active interest in your son's development. He commits to your son's success by offering his experience, resources, time, skills, and emotional support during the young man's teen years. He models godly character and/or specific skills for your son.

Choosing Mentors

Mentors should be men whom your son has had the opportunity to observe ahead of time, so that he understands your level of respect for them. First consider specific attributes or abilities you want modeled for your son, and then match those attributes or abilities to potential mentors.

These two or three select individuals must have some essential characteristics:

- ▲ You have great respect for them—socially, morally, and especially spiritually.
- ▲ They have specific attributes or skills you would like your son to learn.
- ▲ They live in close proximity to you so that they can regularly get together with your son.

Mentor Responsibilities

Begin early to identify several men whom you would like to have contributing to your son's CHAMPION Training. A few of these men will have the opportunity to provide "guiding insights" to your son for his celebration ceremony. Other men may attend the celebration and participate in the festivities. But only two or three will become his mentors. You should limit the number of mentors to three at most. Typically, one man will emerge as the primary mentor.

Ask one of these mentors to:

▲ Pray regularly for you and your son.

▲ Call your son occasionally to check his progress.

▲ Encourage your son.

▲ Attend an athletic event now and then.

▲ Be available in times of struggle.

▲ Join you (if possible) for the Night of Challenge dinner with your son and for witnessing the signing of your CHAMPION Training Commitment form.

Communicate your specific expectations with each of the potential mentors for your son. Brainstorm with each man about what activities he might expose your son to in order to enhance the attributes and skills you are seeking to develop. Discuss and agree upon the level of involvement he will have during and after the CHAMPION Training.

Create a Desire

In Proverbs 22:6, Solomon gives us our marching orders as fathers: "Train up a child in the way he should go, even when he is old he will not depart from it."

The Hebrew verb for "to train" refers to the act of the Hebrew midwife, who at the time of birth would plunge her finger into a bowl of dates or olive oil, and then place her finger into the baby's mouth to stimulate the palate and encourage sucking. Through this training, the child would learn to take nourishment and live. Thus, the verb "to train" in Proverbs 22:6 can translate, "to create a desire."[2]

You will need to create a desire in your son to pursue this training adventure with you. Start the process of "pre-selling" him at least one month before your projected start date to spark his interest. You might periodically ask him if he would like to engage in an adventure with you that will be challenging, yet fun and rewarding. If he expresses interest, tell him how excited you are, and that you will give him more details soon. Then set up date to meet with him at his favorite restaurant.

To build more anticipation, call him from work occasionally or leave him a note, reminding him of your excitement to meet with him on the Night of Challenge.

NIGHT OF CHALLENGE

Create a Night of Challenge to kick off your son's CHAMPION Training in a special way. If possible, have one of the mentors you selected join you. Think carefully through the challenge you will present to your son. Here are some tips for this important evening:

▲ Explain to your son the importance of training boys to become young men.

▲ Tell your son that he has a unique opportunity to undertake a training adventure with you that will prepare him for his teenage and young adult years.

▲ Give him the fiction book *Teknon and the CHAMPION Warriors* and ask him to read through it.

▲ Show him the *Mission Guide* and explain the contents and format (highlight the direct tie to the fiction book, the interactive discussion questions, and the fun "maneuvers").

▲ Discuss with him how often you would meet and the length of time it would take to complete the CHAMPION Training (up to eight months).

▲ Remind him that this will be a joint project between the two of you.

▲ Make it clear that completing his training will be hard work, but it will be a lot of fun and worth the effort.

▲ Explain that if he completes the training you will honor his accomplishment with a special celebration and a CHAMPION Symbol (a pendant or ring representing his accomplishment and recognition of his becoming a young man; see chapter 5 for more ideas).

Ask your son to think and pray about your challenge for a few days before making a decision. Even if he wants to say "yes" immediately, insist on the delay to affirm to him that you see this as an important undertaking.

If your son declines the challenge, ask him why, but don't press him or become discouraged. He may not understand his need yet or he may feel he isn't ready. Bide your time, continue to pray for him, and revisit your proposal at a later date. If your son accepts the challenge, both of you should sign the CHAMPION Training Commitment form (in chapter 5). Ask one of your son's mentors to witness the signing. This agreement will provide your son with a visible reference to the commitment he is making.

At this time, schedule your first CHAMPION Session together and ask your son to read or re-read the first episode of *Teknon and the CHAMPION Warriors*. Give him his *Mission Guide* and ask him to complete the questions as best he can in session 1 before your first CHAMPION Session. Explain that it will probably take him a couple of hours to complete each session.

Take this opportunity to explain to him that both of you are making a significant commitment of time and energy. Describe how Green Berets, fighter pilots, Olympic athletes, or even the mythical Jedi Knights of "Star Wars" fame labor diligently to attain the distinction of their rank. Describe to him that no worthy prize is gained without significant effort.

NOTE: The primary premise of selling anything to anybody is that only an unmet need will motivate him to act. We must create a desire in our sons by motivating them and helping them to identify their need for the CHAMPION Training. Communicate your interest in this adventure to your son by:

▲ **Enthusiasm**—Your excitement about your son engaging in the CHAMPION Training will become contagious.

▲ **Encouragement**—Reinforce your belief in him and your belief that he can complete his training.

▲ **Example**—As your son sees your desire to live the life of a CHAMPION yourself, he will also want to become a CHAMPION.

Brent and Casey's Story

We went to one of our favorite restaurants and chose a table in the corner. I pulled out the materials and walked him through the concept of CHAMPION Training. To my surprise (and relief) he was thrilled with the idea. I knew Casey wouldn't completely understand what was ahead in his training. But what he did understand excited him, and that excited me.

I promised Casey that if he finished the training I would put together a celebration that would honor his accomplishment. I also committed to give him a CHAMPION Symbol, a pendant or ring, representing his accomplishment and recognizing his becoming a young man.

CHAMPION Sessions are the heart of the CHAMPION Training. Plan to meet together for CHAMPION Sessions every other week, if possible.

Read: Before starting the CHAMPION Training, both you and your son should read the entire story of *Teknon and the CHAMPION Warriors*. This story chronicles the adventures of a young man as he learns to develop the CHAMPION characteristics in his life.

Pray: Be sure to pray before each session that God will work through your time together to develop Christ-like character in your son.

Meet regularly: Meet with your son every other week for your CHAMPION Sessions. Plan for at least one hour and no more than two.

Make it your own: Customize and make this training your own. Holidays, vacations, and occasional business trips can make it difficult to maintain a rigid schedule for our meetings. Your son may grow weary. If so, take a break! This training is about character development and relationship building, not completing a project. Be flexible and creative with the location and setting.

Remember that the suggestions offered in this book concerning how to conduct your son's training are just that—suggestions. You can customize your son's training to meet his particular needs and temperament. If you have an idea for an activity or a tool to use in your son's training, by all means use it.

Elements of a CHAMPION Session

▲ **CHAMPION Characteristics**—One or two key character traits are highlighted for each session.

▲ **Story Summary**—The fiction episode is summarized only in your *Mentor Guide*, not in your son's *Mission Guide*.

▲ **Discussion Topics**—Key subjects are summarized in both guides, with extra explanation only in your *Mentor Guide*.

▲ **Mission Debrief**—Debriefing is a military practice where a soldier recaps his previous mission activities. This section provides you and your son an opportunity to review the mission assigned at the previous session. You will debrief on your critical maneuver, his action point from the Sheet of Deeds, and his newly memorized power verse.

▲ **Reconnaissance**—Reconnaissance (or "recon") is also a military activity in which a soldier explores an area to gather important information for the mission ahead. In this section you and your son will discuss an episode from *Teknon and the CHAMPION Warriors*.

▲ **Strategy and Tactics**—Strategy refers to the overall planning of a mission. Tactics refers to the methods used to secure the objectives planned out in the strategy. In this section you and your son will discuss specific CHAMPION characteristics, investigate strategies and tactics from the Bible, and discover how to apply them in your son's life.

▲ **Your Mission**—At the end of each CHAMPION Session, you will assign a mission to your son to be completed before the next session. Each mission includes:

■ **Power Verse:** A new Bible verse related to this session is given to your son to memorize.

■ **Critical Maneuver:** A hands-on project or activity for you and your son to do together *to reinforce* what you discussed during your session (movies, interviews, tally surveys, Bible discovery, books, and more movies!). Well-chosen movies are an excellent tool to illustrate principles and provide a springboard for discussions.

■ **CHAMPION Sheet of Deeds:** At the end of the Strategy and Tactics section, you and your son will agree on an action point that he will begin *to apply* before the next session and will carry on as he develops these deeds for a lifetime as a CHAMPION.

Think Tank (SEE CHAPTER 5)

This is a key section containing recommended action points for the Sheet of Deeds and for the critical maneuvers, designed specifically for each CHAMPION Session. There is also an index of other movies, tapes, and book resources to select from.

Equipment in the Father's Arsenal (SEE CHAPTER 6)

A storehouse of equipment is provided for you in the Father's Arsenal (chapter 6) to help you effectively carry out your CHAMPION Training adventure.

▲ CHAMPION Training Commitment Form—A sample agreement between you and your son to complete the CHAMPION Training

▲ Understanding Your Son's Bent—An exercise to help you determine your son's temperament (based around temperaments of four key characters from the story) and what motivates him

▲ Media Evaluation Report Form—A suggested format for your son to use as he reports on lessons learned from his critical maneuvers

▲ Fiction Glossary—A list of words, pronunciations, and definitions for characters and terms used in the story

▲ Greek Terms in the Story—A summary of the character and location names derived from Greek terms and their meanings

▲ Guiding Insights Request Letter—A sample letter for soliciting special participation from people for your son's celebration ceremony

▲ Summary of Success—A sample presentation for your son's celebration ceremony that summarizes key points of accomplishment through the CHAMPION Training

▲ CHAMPION Symbol and Gift Ideas—A list of meaningful symbols or gift ideas

ADDITIONAL SUGGESTIONS

The following suggestions will increase the effectiveness of your CHAMPION Sessions.

▲ Provide your son with a yellow highlighter to underscore important phrases in each episode of the story. Key phrases are referenced in the *Mission Guide* to launch into discussions on important issues.

▲ Use a wide range of approaches and technologies to bring varied and creative elements to your son's application projects. You are encouraged to use your own creativity and solicit ideas from other people and sources.

▲ Use the real-life quotes in the margins of his *Mission Guide* to stimulate discussion.

▲ Most of the character and location names in the story are Greek words that represent the unique qualities of that person or place. For example, the Greek word kratos means "power or strength," a distinctive trait that Teknon's father possesses. Refer to the Father's Arsenal for a summary of the names and their Greek meanings.

▲ Consider discussing the questions while doing something active, such as basketball, bowling, swimming, hiking, yard work, or washing the car.

▲ Have a CHAMPION Session over dessert after a fun outing such as a movie or sports event.

▲ Read the story out loud together.

▲ Whenever possible, share an event or story from your own life that reinforces the CHAMPION characteristic or principles in the session.

CELEBRATION CEREMONY

At the end of your CHAMPION Training, take time to plan an appropriate celebration ceremony for your son. This event is essential in the training process, and it will be one of those key markers in his life that he will never

> ## BRENT AND CASEY'S STORY
>
> *Sometimes we took our CHAMPION Sessions on the road. One memorable night, we went to a diner after an Orlando Magic basketball game. We pulled out our Mission Guide at 11:00 p.m. in a booth at the back of the restaurant. The waitress noticed that Casey had polished off his milkshake in short order. In an unprecedented gesture, she offered to let Casey drink as many shakes as he could for the price of one. What a night! Basketball, milkshakes, CHAMPION Training, and lots of laughs ...*
>
> *Casey and I had potholes to navigate on the road to the final celebration. Holidays, vacations, and occasional business trips made it difficult to maintain a rigid schedule for our meetings. And, as is the case with most lengthy projects, there came a time when Casey grew weary and resistant to completing his task. At one point, we decided to take a break for a few weeks. However, because of the value he saw in the training, the fun we were having, and his previous commitment to finish, he pressed on and completed his CHAMPION Training. I was very proud of him! We began to plan for his celebration ceremony.*

forget. Author and speaker Robert Lewis says, "A man is not a man until his father says that he is." This is your opportunity to announce to your son, and to those who attend his ceremony, that he has now made the transition into young manhood and that you are proud of him.

Consider the following factors when planning your son's celebration ceremony:

▲ Setting—Where will the ceremony take place? Will you have food, and if so, what will it be? What atmosphere do you want to create for the ceremony?

▲ Script—Determine the format of the ceremony. What events will you include and in what order?

▲ Speakers—Who will speak? What will they say? In what manner will they say it—in person, on video, on audio cassette, in writing? (Refer to the Guiding Insights Letter in chapter 5.)

▲ Summary of Success—Take time to write a short speech documenting some of the highlights of your son's training. (Refer to the Summary of Success sample in chapter 5.)

▲ Symbol—Will his CHAMPION Symbol be a ring, pendant, plaque, or some other gift? (Refer to CHAMPION Symbol and Gift Ideas in chapter 5.)

▲ Special Finale—What fun, memorable activity will you do together to top off the celebration? What would your son really enjoy? (Don't just choose something that you would enjoy doing with him.)

Brainstorm with your son about his celebration about halfway through his training. Let him have input into the format to heighten his enthusiasm, but make sure you leave enough room for the element of surprise. If you plan to give him a CHAMPION Symbol at the celebration, let your son know that you plan to have it and what it will be. This CHAMPION Symbol can become a significant motivator for your son to complete the program.

Brent and Casey's Story

Even though it took extensive preparation, Casey's celebration was an event we will never forget. First, I sent blank videotapes a few months ahead of time to close friends and relatives around the country. Casey either knew these men, or had heard me talk about them. On these tapes, Casey heard from the men that had the greatest impact on his father's life. I asked them to film themselves answering these three questions for Casey:

1. If you were Casey's age again, what would you do differently?

2. What skills would you recommend that Casey begin to develop?

3. What is the single most important thing for Casey to remember as a young adult?

When I received the completed videos, I copied them to one master tape. The next step was to find a location for the celebration. One of my friends told me about a wilderness ranch owned by another friend. We were able to secure the ranch for the date I set.

On the night of the celebration, I kept Casey unaware of the details. I picked him up at 7:00 p.m. from a youth meeting and took him out to the ranch. On the way out, I began to play the videotape containing insights and encouragement from my friends on a small VCR/TV in the van. Casey enjoyed their talks immensely. First, a friend of 20 years spoke. Next came Casey's uncle. As we entered the ranch, we turned off the television and got out to greet the godly men I had invited to join us. We feasted on Casey's favorite foods: barbecue, brownies, and IBC root beer.

After dinner I played another video, and this time Casey heard from the man who led me to Christ more than two decades before. Then, each man in turn took Casey on a short walk to share his specific insights and encouragement. One of the men gave him a compass to remind him to keep his focus on the "True North" of the Word. Another gave him a pocketknife. All gave him the pearls of their experience. As the last walk finished, we gathered around the fire, and I asked Casey to recite the characteristics of a CHAMPION Warrior. I followed with a short prepared speech, recalling the benefits and highlights of the training we experienced together. I gave Casey his pendant, and we all prayed together for him. The men hoisted Casey above their shoulders and marched around the fire.

We capped off the night with a wild hog hunt on the ranch. Until that night, Casey and I had never had the thrill of chasing a 175-pound animal that smelled like an unwashed tennis shoe and looked like a roto-tiller with fur. We bagged one, or I should say our hosts bagged one, and let us share in the glory. It was a great night!

The stage of young manhood is the first of four key passages in a boy's journey toward becoming an adult. The other three are high school graduation, college graduation, and marriage. If he does not have a smooth transition through the first stage, the others will be far more difficult.

Believe it or not, the completion of this stage marks the end of your role as a trainer in your son's life. Certainly there will be other opportunities to teach during his teen years and beyond, but your role transitions from trainer to coach in the later teen and young adult years. In other words, after the early teen years, parents primarily coach and encourage those principles and skills that they have already taught their children.

To a great extent the CHAMPION Training is like a delayed fuse. It is essential to communicate the importance of developing courage, mental toughness, and purity during the early teen years. Realistically, depending upon his age and situation, your son may not have had the opportunity to apply many of these principles in his life yet. He may not even understand the reason for covering some of the CHAMPION topics. Ideally, the training helps your son to develop godly character and set his convictions before he encounters problems. For example, your son may not have been tempted yet to view pornography, but he will understand the danger of doing so after you and he complete session 6. Then later, when one of his peers encourages him to visit a pornographic Web site, the delayed fuse of your previous discussion will ignite.

Stay involved with your son after the CHAMPION Training is complete by:

▲ Framing his Summary of Success with a photo of the celebration as a reminder

▲ Encouraging him to execute the action points on his Sheet of Deeds

▲ Keeping your eyes open for materials to pass on to your son (articles, books, tapes, etc.)

▲ Continuing informal coaching and discussions

▲ Creating opportunities for further training

▲ Continuing to seek out and involve mentors in your son's life

▲ Initiating Bible devotionals with him (at least occasionally)

> *As I grow older, I pay less attention to what men say. I just watch what they do.*
>
> Andrew Carnegie

Brent and Casey's Story

My son Casey is not a man yet. Even though he's now a strapping 6' 1" 16-year-old, convinced he's one step away from bench-pressing more than his old man, I've still got a lot of coaching to do before my arrow is finally released from the bow. But, on October 16, 1996, I formally acknowledged him before family and friends as a young man moving ahead toward mature manhood. I am convinced that the investment I have made in Casey's life will continue to produce long-term returns, which in the years to come will dwarf any compensation I could ever receive from my career or other pursuits.

THINK TANK

The CHAMPION Training program is not intended to be a one-time event, but a way to integrate the CHAMPION characteristics into your son's and your family's everyday life. There are two practical ways to accomplish this: the CHAMPION Sheet of Deeds and the Critical Maneuvers.

CHAMPION Sheet of Deeds (Part 1 of the Think Tank)

At the end of each session, you will be pointed to page 9 in your son's *Mission Guide* where your son will record one action point that he will begin to apply before you tackle the next session. Recommended deeds are summarized in each CHAMPION Session and then outlined in more detail in part 1 of this Think Tank. Choose one of these options or design your own. These deeds are designed to help develop character-enhancing habit patterns that he can apply for the rest of his life.

Critical Maneuvers (Part 1 of the Think Tank)

After you choose a deed and your son logs it on his Sheet of Deeds, you will be asked to accomplish a critical maneuver. Critical maneuvers are hands-on, fun projects that you and your son can do together to practically reinforce what he has learned. These include books to read, suggestions for interviews to conduct, motion pictures to watch, and other activities to provide a springboard for conversation between you and your son. Suggested critical maneuvers for each session are identified in part 1 of this Think Tank. You may also create your own maneuver using a resource listed in part 2.

Please be aware that the deeds and the critical maneuvers have two unique purposes. Try to do one deed and one maneuver for each session.

CHAMPION Choices (Part 2 of the Think Tank)

An index of books, audio cassettes, motion pictures, and activities is provided in part 2 of this Think Tank. Good books, movies, and other forms of media can be helpful in developing character and addressing issues we face in life. As you choose which media resources you will use in your son's CHAMPION Training, I encourage you and your son to apply Philippians 4:8 to every part of your media diet: " ... whatever is true, whatever is honorable, whatever is right, whatever is pure, whatever is lovely, whatever is of good repute, if there is anything is worthy of praise, dwell on these things."

PART 1:
SHEET OF DEEDS AND CRITICAL MANEUVERS BY SESSION

You should ask your son to write a brief report about what he learns for each critical maneuver as indicated below. A report will help him to think through the subject matter and what he has learned. In addition, he will have a record of important lessons to refer back to. However, you may want to give your son some variety in the reporting approach or even work with a medium that better fits his interests and learning style. Following are some suggested ways for your son to report on his maneuvers:

▲ Brief written report

▲ Personal discussion with you

▲ Creative writing such as a poem, song, or rap

▲ Multi-media presentation or Web site design

▲ Creative expressions such as painting, photography, sculpting, drama, or oral presentation

▲ Feel free to be creative and tailor the approach to meet your son's bent

SESSION 1

Sheet of Deeds Options:

1. Suggest that your son do his part to grow in his relationship with God by taking time to read one psalm and one chapter of Proverbs at least five days for the next two weeks. Get him a journal and have him write what he learns from these passages in the journal. Encourage this as an ongoing discipline.

2. Help your son to start developing a list of his fears and worries to discuss at your next CHAMPION Session. It might also help him if you made a list of your fears or worries. At your next session, help him pray through these fears and reinforce the truth of Philippians 4:6-7. It will help to review the concept of the Rings of Responsibility with him, highlighting areas where he can take responsibility and where he must release to God.

3. Encourage your son to read one new chapter of the Bible at least three days each week. Some type of regular Bible reading and prayer time is vitally

important to his spiritual growth. If he is not accustomed to reading the Bible, provide him with a translation that is both reliable and easy to understand. You might suggest that he begins by reading the Gospel of John. Try to read with him at least once or twice each week. Pray together about what you read. Have your son ask these questions as he reads:

■ What's happening in this chapter?

■ Who are the people involved (if any)?

■ What lesson can I learn from this chapter?

■ How can I apply what I have learned to my life today?

Ask your son to keep a journal to write down the biblical reference (book and chapter number) and any key thoughts from the passages he is reading.

Critical Maneuver Options:

1. If your son has never invited Jesus Christ into his life, go over the exercise in Appendix A of your son's *Mission Guide*, entitled "Just Do It!" Review the material yourself first, and then walk him through the steps involved in beginning a personal relationship with God through faith in Jesus Christ. Be careful not to force your son toward a decision. Offer the opportunity when you think he is ready to hear it. There will be other opportunities during his CHAMPION Training.

2. Watch the movie "Iron Will" together. This fine movie portrays a young man facing fears and taking personal responsibility to complete a great task and contribute to his family's triumph. Ask your son to use the Media Report Form (in chapter 6 of your *Mentor Guide*) to write a brief report or utilize one of the other reporting approaches listed at the beginning of this section. You will discuss this at your next session.

Session 2A

Sheet of Deeds Options:

Both of these options are designed to help your son gain insight into his enemy's evil tactics in this world and to develop an ongoing, healthy awareness of spiritual warfare and the power of prayer and dependence on God.

1. Begin to listen together to the audio version of C.S. Lewis' classic book *The Screwtape Letters* for an eye-opening and entertaining fictional account of Satan's scheming strategies. This is the classic fiction book on the topic of spiritual warfare and an excellent resource for understanding how Satan and his demons work to ruin the life of a Christian. The audio version narrated by comedian John Cleese offers an excellent performance of this audio

version. Discuss some of Satan's strategies and schemes, as well as our defense. NOTE: This resource is recommended for mature teens only.

2. Ask you son to begin to read the book *This Present Darkness*. You should read the book as well so you can discuss it with him. Frank Peretti provides an interesting perspective on the power of prayer, teamwork, and spiritual warfare in this well-written fictional account of a raging spiritual battle. Ask your son to use the Media Report Form (in chapter 6 of your *Mentor Guide*) to write a brief report or utilize one of the other reporting approaches listed at the beginning of this section. NOTE: An abridged version of this book is available on audio cassette (audio book).

Critical Maneuver Options:

1. Watch the movie "Dr. Jekyl and Mr. Hyde" (1943 version starring Spencer Tracey) together. Ask your son to use the Media Report Form (in chapter 6 of your *Mentor Guide*) to write a brief report or utilize one of the other reporting approaches listed at the beginning of this section. This movie relates well to session 2A. Like Magos, Dr. Jekyl was a brilliant scientist intent on doing good. Due to Dr. Jekyl's pride, however, he made a terrible decision that left him a creature of evil. Point out to your son that even when Dr. Jekyl eventually wanted to stop transforming himself into Edward Hyde, he could not because the serum had permanently altered his chemical makeup. Jekyl had become, in fact, more Hyde than Jekyl. Discuss the lure of evil and the potential risk of becoming evil ourselves when we deliberately partake of evil for a period of time.

Additional questions about the movie:

■ Question: Why did Dr. Jekyl take the serum in the first place?

Answer: He was not willing to wait for the appropriate time to test his invention. Overcome with pride and impatience, he tried it on himself.

■ Question: At the end of the movie, why couldn't Dr. Jekyl just stop taking the serum and go back to his normal life?

Answer: Because he had taken so much of the serum over a period of time that his blood chemistry had changed. He was no longer the Dr. Jekyl that his friends and family admired. He was now someone different, changed and distorted by the serum he had consumed.

2. Ask you son to look through the newspaper or watch the evening news on television in the coming week to identify events or activities that could be the result of Satan's strategies, temptations, or deceptions in the world. Have him write down each one he finds and briefly explain why he thinks Satan could be involved. Discuss some of those strategies and schemes with him so that he begins to see Satan for who he is—the father of lies and an enemy of Almighty God and His plans.

Sheet of Deeds Options:

1. If your son receives an allowance or earns spending money, help him to set up a simple budget system using envelopes. This exercise will give him a start in developing habits of effective *Ownership* by tithing, spending wisely, saving, and giving. This will also help him to develop a lifelong habit of stewardship. Give him five envelopes labeled with the following titles:

   A. Tithe—Help him to get into the habit of giving a portion of his money to the Lord's work. Start with 10 percent, a tithe, and help him build over time from that level.

   B. Clothing and expenses—Agree on what "need" expenses will be his responsibility.

   C. Savings—A set percentage should be set aside every time he receives money.

   D. Gifts—Help him develop the mindset of setting aside money to purchase gifts for others.

   E. Miscellaneous—This money will be used for fun, "wants," or unexpected expenses.

2. Ask your son to commit to avoiding impulse purchases. Set specific guidelines with him, for example, to commit to pray about every decision, "sleep on" or delay any purchase until he has had time to think it through, and seek advice for any purchase over $5, $15 ... or some other limit you set with him.

Critical Maneuver Options:

1. Ask your son to create a list of all the purchases made during the week by close friends and family. Have him categorize each purchase as a "want" or "need." When you meet again, ask him how he decided what was a "need" and how the purchases in the "want" category might have been handled differently.

2. Ask your son to look through the newspaper ads and/or watch the television commercials in the coming week with a tally sheet in hand. Have him track whether the advertisements are attempting to meet a "want" or a "need." Ask your son to write a brief report or utilize one of the other reporting approaches listed at the beginning of this section. You should also ask him to describe his view of the purpose of advertising and to identify what each of the ads is really selling. When you meet again, discuss conclusions that he draws about advertising and spending habits in our culture.

Sheet of Deeds Options:

1. Ask your son to determine how far he is willing to go physically in any relationship before marriage. Ask him to consider committing the Wedding Kiss or another high standard of purity. It may seem early for him to make such a decision, but most young people know the answer to this question by age 12. Don't let him answer immediately. Instead, ask him to pray and give serious consideration to his decision. Have him share his decision with you when he is ready. You should discuss his thinking, gently persuade him toward a high standard, and then offer to lovingly hold him accountable to his decision. Of course, his convictions could migrate over time, so stay connected.

2. Ask your son to become more aware of controlling his thoughts. Have him begin to practice capturing stray or sinful thoughts and redirecting them to be in obedience to Christ (2 Corinthians 10:3-5). Encourage him to ask himself, "What does God want me to do in this situation?" Continue to ask him how he's doing in this area and reaffirm that winning this battle for his mind is critical and worth the struggle.

Critical Maneuver Options:

1. Set up a meeting for you and your son with one or more of the following people:

   ■ A young, married man who remained a virgin until marriage

   ■ An older teen who has set high standards for himself and is committed to remaining sexually pure until marriage

   Ask these people to share their convictions about sexual and emotional purity. Help your son prepare some questions in advance and discuss guidelines for conducting an interview (see the Activities section part 2 of this Think Tank). Have your son ask questions about why these people chose to remain pure. Your son should ask questions concerning the struggles of remaining pure, as well as the benefits of doing so. He might also ask them to share the precautions they have taken to protect their purity. Discuss the interview with your son at your next CHAMPION Session.

2. Have your son read the first chapter of the book *I Kissed Dating Goodbye* by Joshua Harris, (Sisters Oregon: Multnomah Publishers, 1997). This chapter will help him to gain a new perspective on guy-girl relationships. Ask your son to use the Media Report Form (in chapter 6 of your *Mentor Guide*) to write a brief report about Josh's perspective on relationships or utilize one of the other reporting approaches listed at the beginning of this section.

Session 4

Sheet of Deeds Options:

1. Have your son make a list of all his friends and then mark down whether they are a good influence, a neutral influence, or a bad influence. Ask him put an asterisk by the ones he spends the most time with. At your next session, discuss the list and encourage him to identify which of his friends he should spend *less time* with and which he should spend *more time* with. Then ask him why he made these decisions. Help him make a habit of regularly assessing his friendships.

2. Have your son assess whether or not he is a good friend by reviewing the characteristics of a good friend from this session and the critical maneuver for session 4. At your next session, discuss his areas of strength and his opportunities to improve as a friend. Help him to determine what he should do to become a better friend to others.

Critical Maneuver Options:

1. Watch the movie "Star Trek II, the Wrath of Kahn" together. Notice the respectful and sacrificial nature of Kirk and Spock's relationship. Ask your son to use the Media Report Form (in chapter 6 of your *Mentor Guide*) to write a brief report on their relationship or utilize one of the other reporting approaches listed at the beginning of this section.

2. Ask one of your closest friends, perhaps one of your son's mentors, to meet with you and your son. Have your friend describe what you have meant to him, as a companion and Christian brother, and why. If you share an accountability relationship with this friend, ask him to describe how you hold each other accountable. You should share similar comments for your friend. Ask your son to write a summary on this conversation or utilize one of the other reporting approaches listed at the beginning of this section.

3. Have your son read 1 Samuel 20, which describes Jonathan and David's famous friendship. Their commitment and loyalty provide an excellent example for your son to imitate. These two companions embody the statement made by Lieutenant Worf in the television series "Star Trek": "A warrior never lets a friend face danger alone." Ask your son to write a brief report about what he learned from this passage describing the characteristics of friendship it reveals. As always, you may utilize one of the other reporting approaches listed at the beginning of this section.

Sheet of Deeds Options:

1. Ask your son to identify one area where he needs to become more teachable. For example:

   - Home

   - School

   - Relationships in the family

   - Relationships outside of the family

   - Chores, etc.

   Once he identifies an area, suggest that he listen to your counsel or your wife's counsel with a calm and teachable attitude. Gently help him make adjustments and praise him for making the effort.

2. Ask your son to commit to a daily time of Bible reading and prayer, if he has not already done so. Have him start with just ten minutes a day. Encourage him to keep a journal to capture the reference to passages read, new insights, prayer requests, and answers. Don't be legalistic, but encourage him to be consistent. It would be a great motivator for most sons if you asked them to join you during your "quiet time" with God for a few days. Continue having quiet times together periodically.

Critical Maneuver Options:

1. Read the story of Samson (Judges 13-16) together or have your son read it on his own. Then ask him to write a one-page report on how the world's strongest man destroyed himself and hurt the nation of Israel with his prideful attitude. As always, feel free to utilize one of the other reporting approaches listed at the beginning of this section.

2. Watch the movie "The Empire Strikes Back" together and ask your son to write a brief report or talk with you about Luke Skywalker's pride. Have him use the Media Report Form (in chapter 6 of your *Mentor Guide*). In addition, ask him to share his views on how Luke's decision to prematurely leave his training endangered his friends as well as the entire mission. Ask him to discuss what happened and what potentially could have happened if Luke had finished his training.

3. Watch the video "The Picture of Dorian Gray" (1945 version) together or check out the audio version from the library. This classic story describes the eerie descent of one man into self-absorption. Although somewhat involved,

this film vividly portrays the result of hidden sin. Ask your son to use the Media Report Form (in chapter 6 of your *Mentor Guide*) to write a brief report or utilize one of the other reporting approaches listed at the beginning of this section. Have him concentrate his brief report on the results of Dorian Gray's prideful attitude. CAUTION: Use this option only if your son is at least thirteen and mature.

SESSION 6

Sheet of Deeds Options:

1. Ask your son to open all possible doors for your wife during the next two weeks. In addition, ask him to pull out her chair whenever she sits down. Your wife can help by waiting at the chair or car door until your son responds. During this exercise, encourage him to also open doors and pull out chairs for any women or girls that he's around. The goal is for these actions to become a habit over time. And remember, our children learn best from our example.

2. If he has brothers or sisters, ask your son to pay at least one genuine compliment (no empty flattery) each week to each of them. If he has no siblings, ask him to apply this same idea with his close friends. Encourage him to make a habit of complimenting and encouraging others. There are enough people passing out insults and discouragement already!

Critical Maneuver Options:

1. Help your son to identify a man that effectively models the trait of valuing and honoring people. Choose one of your friends, a man in full-time ministry, or even a public official. If possible, arrange an interview between this person and your son. Before the interview, help your son to develop questions that will clarify both why this man values people and what he does to encourage and honor others. Remember to review with him the guidelines for an interview in the Activities section of part 2 in this Think Tank. If you can't arrange the interview, ask your son to observe the man in order to create a list of behaviors. This maneuver will provide a great model and some practical guidelines for honoring people to your son. Ask your son to write a brief report summarizing what he learned or utilize one of the other reporting approaches listed at the beginning of this section.

2. Ask your son to read the story of Joseph in Genesis 37-45. Ask him to write a brief report based on the question: Why did Joseph show honor to his brother, after they had treated him so badly?

   NOTE: Joseph saw God's purposes revealed through his trials. Ultimately, he became Pharaoh's second in command. This position allowed Joseph to save his family from starvation. This family was the root of the Israelite people and the line through which Jesus, the Savior of the world, would be born. God protected this family and used them to ultimately bring salvation to the whole world!

SESSION 7

Sheet of Deeds Options:

1. Develop a proactive media plan with your son. Based on this session, work together to devise a set of parameters that both you and your son will commit to use for the various entertainment mediums. Include parameters for *what* to consume AND *how much*. It is important that you, as his father, get involved and help guide your son through the media minefield. Your plan should include what you watch, what you read, and what you listen to:

   - ■ Movies (videos)

   - ■ Reading material (books, magazines, etc.)

   - ■ Music (lyrics)

   - ■ Internet

   - ■ Television (regular network, as well as cable)

   - ■ Video games

   - ■ Billboards, posters, and artwork

2. Have your son get a separate sheet of paper for each piece of the armor of God found in Ephesians 6 (this is nine sheets) and write the name of the piece of spiritual armor at the top of each page. Ask him to evaluate and write down whether each piece of his own spiritual armor is strong or weak. You should rate him as well. Work with your son to list some specifics things he can do over time to develop those weak areas. Also list some things you can do to help him strengthen weak pieces of armor and maintain pieces that are strong. Pull out these sheets periodically and review his progress with him.

Critical Maneuver Options:

1. Ask your son to keep two tally sheets for all of his TV viewing for the next week. The first one is for commercials. This sheet will have two columns: one for ads that use sex to sell the product and one for ads that don't. Your son should put a check in the appropriate column for each commercial he sees. The second tally sheet is for TV programs and videos. This sheet will also have two columns: one for programs that portray a loose attitude toward

sex or show lustful passion and one for programs that portray the biblical view of sex within the context of marriage and nobody else in the bedroom (including us viewers). At the end of the week, discuss what he found and expose the exploitation of sex and the pervasiveness of ungodly, non-biblical portrayals of sex in the media.

2. Ask your son to refrain from watching television and/or accessing the Internet for one week. At the end of the week, ask him to describe what he felt he missed and what he didn't miss. Were there any benefits he gained, such as more time for productive pursuits, more time for relationships, or less distraction in his life?

Session 7 Actions for Dads Only:

A. Review the book *Human Sexuality: A Christian Perspective* (from the *Learning About Sex Series*), by Roger Sonnenberg.

B. If you use the Internet, go to www.crosswalk.com, www.screenit.com, or www.movieguide.org before you watch a movie. All relevant categories, including sexual content, violence, language, and so on are covered in detail.

C. Subscribe to a reliable movie-review magazine. Several excellent periodicals offer a detailed description in each review of the language, violence, and sexual content involved.

- ■ "Preview" can be obtained from Family Movie and TV Review by calling 1-800-807-8071.

- ■ "MovieGuide" is available from the Christian Film and Television Commission by calling 1-800-889-6684 or by accessing www.movieguide.org on the Web.

- ■ For further ideas, guidelines, and suggestions regarding media, contact FamilyLife (1-800-FL-TODAY or www.familylife.com) or The Christian Film and Television Commission (1-800-889-6684 or www.movieguide.org).

SESSION 8

Sheet of Deeds Options:

1. Ask your son to identify one of his fears that you would like to help him overcome. Then help him to set up an activity where he can face that fear. For example, public speaking offers a great setting for facing and overcoming fear. Whatever you decide, it would probably be a real encouragement to your son if you also participate in the activity you set up for him. Encourage your son to make a habit of facing and overcoming fears, one at a time.

2. Ask your son to make a list of all his sins, failures, and shortcomings. Then review 1 John 1:9 with him, highlighting confession, repentance, and God's promise of forgiveness and cleansing. Ask him to get alone with God to pray for forgiveness for each specific item, asking God to help him turn away from these thoughts and behaviors. Then, *without looking at his list*, help him to burn the list to symbolize God's complete forgiveness and removal of the penalty of those sins. God promises to remember our sins no more after we confess and repent. CAUTION: Burn the list in a protected area to avoid accidental fires, or have your son tear the paper into small bits as a safer alternative. The goal is to make confession, repentance, and recovery a lifetime habit over time.

Critical Maneuver Options:

1. Rent and watch the movie "The Four Feathers" together. This classic film about courage and honor deals with the story of four soldiers, one of whom initially declines his duty to fight for his country during a war. But through a change of heart, he recovers from his unsuccessful failure and heroically saves his fellow countrymen. Ask your son to use the Media Report Form (in chapter 6 of your *Mentor Guide*) to write a brief report concentrating on how the lead character recovered from his unsuccessful failure or utilize one of the other reporting approaches listed at the beginning of this section.

2. Rent and watch the movie "Apollo 13" together. Ask your son to use the Media Report Form (in chapter 6 of your *Mentor Guide*) to write a brief report about why the Apollo 13 mission was a successful failure or utilize one of the other reporting approaches listed at the beginning of this section. Be sure to discuss the movie with your son.

3. Read the book of Jonah together in *The Living Bible* or *The Message* (available late 2000). This is a classic example of a man who denied God's call but recovered in time to lead one of the most successful evangelistic campaigns in history.

Session 9

Sheet of Deeds Options:

1. Help your son to list some of his comfort zones. Then ask him to identify some key areas where he needs to challenge his fears and step out of his comfort zones so he can grow to be the man that God wants him to be. Help your son list three activities that would take him out of each of his comfort zones. Finally, ask him how you can come alongside him to help him begin accomplishing these activities.

2. Help your son choose one significant activity that will help him face a

different fear than he chose in session 8. Then, create an opportunity for your son to face that fear. Each week, with God's help, one man in Texas tries to accomplish at least one thing that scares him just to stay in the habit of overcoming his fears. "When we do the thing we fear," a wise man once said, "the fear will die."

Critical Maneuver Options:

1. Rent and watch the movie "The Spirit of St. Louis." Jimmy Stewart plays the heroic Charles Lindberg to perfection. This film displays a young man pushing himself out of the comfort zone in order to accomplish one of the major milestones of the 20th century. Ask your son to use the Media Report Form (in chapter 6 of your *Mentor Guide*) to write a brief report about his feelings after watching this movie or utilize one of the other reporting approaches listed at the beginning of this section.

2. Read the story of Elijah and "the contest" in 1 Kings 18 together with your son. This passage describes Elijah's departure from his comfort zone as he obeys God and humiliates the prophets of Baal. Then, discuss together what enabled Elijah to take those risks.

Session 9 Action for Dads Only:

Read chapter 6 in the book *Telling Yourself the Truth* by Will Backus and Marie Chapman. This chapter, entitled "Misbelief in Anxiety," gives an excellent description of how your son can begin to manage his need to be accepted by others. The desire to be liked and accepted is overwhelming during adolescence. Discuss this topic with your son, especially if he struggles in this area.

--- SESSION 10 ---

Sheet of Deeds Options:

1. Ask your son, "What does 'good enough' mean to you?" Help him identify one key area where he is just getting by. Help him to understand why he should be "raising the bar" in this area (mental, physical, spiritual, or social). Ask him to discuss what he thinks he could do to pursue excellence in this area. Have him write this on his CHAMPION Sheet of Deeds. Encourage him to start with pursuing excellence in this area and then systematically tackle other areas in his life.

2. Encourage your son to identify one situation or person that makes him angry. Discuss the formula for anger management with him so that he understands how to apply it when he senses his temper rising. Have him write this formula along with the situation or person he needs to apply the formula with on his CHAMPION Sheet of Deeds.

Critical Maneuver Options:

1. Watch the movie "Rudy" together. This film depicts the true story of a young man who rose above his mediocre ability and environment to accomplish a lifelong objective to play football for Notre Dame. Ask your son to write a brief report about the benefits of striving for excellence and the effort required. If your son is more of an auditory learner or you want to give him a break from writing, you may discuss these topics with him instead or utilize one of the other reporting approaches listed at the beginning of this section.

2. Watch the movie "The Searchers" together. In this famous Western, John Wayne plays the lead character who must overcome a history of anger, bigotry, and bitterness in order to save a member of his family. Ask your son to use the Media Report Form (in chapter 6 of your *Mentor Guide*) to write a brief report about how anger was managed in the movie or utilize one of the other reporting approaches listed at the beginning of this section.

Session 11

Sheet of Deeds Options:

1. If your son has invited Jesus Christ into his life, help him to write out his personal testimony of how he came to faith in Christ. If he was a Christian at a young age, encourage him to focus more on his commitment to the Lordship of Christ. His story should include three segments:

   ■ What life was like before he became a Christian

   ■ Specifically how and when he came to know and commit his life to Jesus Christ

   ■ What changes have occurred in his life since he trusted Christ as Savior and Lord in his life

2. If your son has an unhealthy romantic relationship with a young woman, discuss the struggles and potential pitfalls ahead. You should also discuss the benefits of waiting for the right person and God's timing to begin romance (when he is ready for marriage). Encourage him to make the tough phone call to end the relationship.

Critical Maneuver Options:

1. If your son did not use this maneuver in an earlier session, have him read chapter one of Joshua Harris' book, *I Kissed Dating Goodbye* by Joshua Harris, (Sisters Oregon: Multnomah Publishers, 1997). Even though you may think the topic is a bit premature, it just isn't premature to discuss dating with preteens and young teens, given our culture. Ask your son to write a brief

report on what Josh has to say about dating and romantic relationships. He provides a fresh perspective on the practices of dating and courtship. In addition, be sure to discuss this with your son after you have both read the chapter. Ask your son to use the Media Report Form (in chapter 6 of your *Mentor Guide*) to write a brief report about Josh's perspective on relationships or utilize one of the other reporting approaches listed at the beginning of this section.

2. Have your son interview a young man who is either a senior in high school or in his first two years of college. The person you choose should be someone you and your son respect for his healthy perspective on dating. Have your son ask questions focusing on the purpose of dating and relationships. Ask your son to write a brief report about the interview or utilize one of the other reporting approaches listed at the beginning of this section.

Session 12

Sheet of Deeds Options:

1. Ask your son to identify which of the three categories in the "downhills of discouragement" affects him the most. Then help him develop ways to improve his situation or his response in that area. For example, if he needs to change his diet, help him to set up a healthy eating regimen.

2. Explain to your son how to apply the truths of 1 John 1:9 (confession) and John 10:10 (abundant living) using an exercise called "spiritual breathing," a term used often by Bill Bright, founder and president of Campus Crusade for Christ. In spiritual breathing, figuratively exhale by confessing our sins to God. Then, we inhale by taking in His forgiveness and appropriating His strength to overcome the sin in our lives. This should be as natural as breathing ... and almost as frequent. We need to keep very short accounts with God so that we always stay in close relationship with Him. Remind your son often about spiritual breathing.

Critical Maneuver Options:

1. Watch the movie "Mr. Smith Goes to Washington" together. Ask your son to use the Media Report Form (in chapter 6 of your *Mentor Guide*) to write a brief report about how Mr. Smith overcomes discouragement in the face of overwhelming obstacles or utilize one of the other reporting approaches listed at the beginning of this section.

2. Have your son read through the book of Job, and write a report on Job's life and attitude. Have him concentrate on Job chapters 1 and 2 for the disasters and chapters 38 through 42 for the outcome of Job's story and then answer these questions:

- What happened to Job?

- How did Job respond to God initially and then ultimately?

- How did God bless Job for his faithfulness?

Session 13

Sheet of Deeds Options:

1. Ask your son to identify one important objective or task that he has continued to put off. Help him to work through the principles for completing a task based upon Davis's example and the six T's of how to focus in order to accomplish that objective. Help him to begin to incorporate these six T's as a life pattern for completing tasks.

2. Encourage your son to keep a journal to capture specific instances where God has delivered him through difficult times. Encourage him to document instances when God has provided for him in the good times, too. This is a great way to give honor to God and to build his confidence in God's faithfulness. Suggest that he start by making a list of key areas where God's hand has been evident in his life in the past.

Critical Maneuver Options:

1. Read Luke 22-24. There is no more amazing example of focus than the life of Jesus Christ as He faced mockery, torture, crucifixion, and death for our sake. Jesus completed the ultimate act of love and sacrifice through focused dependence on His Heavenly Father during the three darkest days of human history before His glorious resurrection.

2. Watch the film "October Sky" together. This movie is based on the true story of Homer Hickam and his quest to win the national science fair. Hickam's focus in the face of numerous obstacles is inspiring and convicting. Ask your son to use the Media Report Form (in chapter 6 of your *Mentor Guide*) to write a brief report or utilize one of the other reporting approaches listed at the beginning of this section.

3. Watch the movie "Chariots of Fire" with your family. This is a true story of two Olympic athletes who focus, for different reasons, on completing worthwhile objectives. One of them, Eric Liddel, demonstrates in a powerful way what it means to do what's right when right isn't the easy thing to do. Ask your son to use the Media Report Form (in chapter 6 of your *Mentor Guide*) to write a brief report or utilize one of the other reporting approaches listed at the beginning of this section.

Sheet of Deeds Options:

1. Ask your son to brainstorm with you on specific ways that he can use the strengths that he highlighted in his T-E-A-M assessment to help his family, friends, or church. Then, help him put some of these activities into action.

2. Work with your son to identify weak temperament traits that he needs to strengthen. Help him develop and implement a plan for strengthening these traits.

Critical Maneuver Options:

1. Watch the movie "Hoosiers" together. This film provides an excellent example of how different people with different personalities and skills can come together and accomplish a larger objective than could have been achieved by individuals pursuing their own agendas.

2. Ask your son to survey several family members and friends regarding his strengths and how he brings value to the family of group. Have him document the results of his survey. This will be a great source of encouragement to him.

3. Ask your son to read the Gospel of John. Ask him to provide a report as to the different vocations and personalities of the twelve disciples. Jesus chose a wide variety of individuals—including a doctor, a tax collector, and a fisherman—to complete His team. Ask your son to evaluate why he thinks that Jesus chose such a diversified team to carry on the Great Commission after His death and resurrection.

SESSION 15

Sheet of Deeds Options:

1. Ask your son to write a brief essay that describes the key principles that he learned during his CHAMPION Training. Ask him to read this at his celebration ceremony.

2. Ask your son to develop a set of goals for the next year based on what he has learned from his CHAMPION Training. Work with him to strengthen his plan and ask how you can support him.

Critical Maneuver Options:

1. Watch the movie "Ten Commandments" together. Ask your son focus on how Moses, superbly portrayed by Charlton Heston, used his gifts from God to impact an entire nation of people and, in turn, the world. Ask your son to use the Media Report Form (in chapter 6 of your *Mentor Guide*) to write a brief report or utilize one of the other reporting approaches listed at the beginning of this section.

2. Watch the movie "Prince of Egypt" together. This excellent animated feature also focuses on how Moses used his gifts from God to impact an entire nation of people and, in turn, the world. Ask your son to use the Media Report Form (in chapter 6 of your *Mentor Guide*) to write a brief report or utilize one of the other reporting approaches listed at the beginning of this section.

PART 2:
CHAMPION CHOICES

This index provides helpful tools to use for your son's critical maneuvers during his CHAMPION Training. Each of these books, audio series, songs, and motion pictures was chosen with the CHAMPION characteristics in mind.

Many of these resources are not written from a Christ-centered, biblically based perspective, but you can see God in every one of them. These resources teach strong lessons that reinforce God's truths from the Bible—whether from a positive or negative viewpoint.

The CHAMPION Choices should be used to stimulate discussion. They are divided into three categories:

▲ Books and Audio Presentations

▲ Motion Pictures

▲ Activities

I encourage you to use all of these mediums, as well as new technologies such as educational compact discs, to bring a varied and creative element to your son's critical maneuvers. You can rent books and tapes at no charge from your local library.

Some of these resources would be great for you and your son to read, listen to, or watch together. They would also be good for your son to read or watch on his own. Each of these resources is marked with a check mark. ✔

BOOKS AND AUDIO PRESENTATIONS

We are living in a headline news and sound bite sermon age. God chose the written word—the Bible—to record His story for us. Time and time again, the men that are the strongest leaders are the ones that are well read. They understand current events and trends, they have knowledge of classic literature, and understand modern dialog.

The average adult living in the United States reads only about one book a year. Let me challenge you to read one more book per year than you're reading now. Vary what you read between non-fiction and fiction. Many of you travel like me. I've found it easier at times to listen to audio books or messages in the car. That's another good way to digest these lessons.

Resources for Spiritual Growth

Experiencing God by Henry Blackaby and Claude King

Knowing God does not come through a program, a study, or a method. Knowing God comes through a relationship with a Person. This is an intimate love relationship with God. Through this relationship, God reveals Himself, His purposes, and His ways; and He invites you to join Him where He is already at work. There is a teen version available as well.

The Disciplines of a Godly Man by R. Kent Hughes

Beginning with a stirring challenge from 1 Timothy 4:7b, "train yourselves to be godly," Hughes calls Christian men to the task of equipping themselves spiritually. Chapters address such issues as integrity, leadership, prayer, friendship, and work.

"Ecclesiastes," audio series by Tommy Nelson

(To order, contact Hudson Productions at hudsonproductions.com or 1-800-729-0815.)

In the book of Ecclesiastes, Solomon has the courage to be honest about life. Where can a person find true meaning and purpose? How does he live in a world that seems so out of control? Why does life always seem to disappoint? Solomon not only asks these questions, he gives us answers that truly satisfy. God has given us a road map to help us navigate the deep questions of life. A companion study guide is available for this audio series.

A Godward Life by John Piper

This book is made up of 120 daily meditations that are solid meat and sweet milk from God's Word. They will brace the mind with truth and nourish the heart with God's sovereign grace. Their aim is to spread a passion for the supremacy of God in all things for the joy of all peoples. Readers will discover not only why, but how to more fully delight in the Lord in John Piper's life-changing devotional.

A Godward Life Book Two by John Piper

This follow-up to the popular *A Godward Life* is another life-changing devotional with 120 daily meditations that are solid meat and sweet milk from God's Word.

How to Read the Bible for All It's Worth by Gordon D. Fee and Douglas Stuart ✔

This book is a guide to understanding the Bible in its literary dimensions with techniques for interpreting Scripture while being faithful to the literary types. It's an easy-to-follow book written for the layman.

The Screwtape Letters by C.S. Lewis ✔

(available on audio book—excellent)

This classic satiric work consists of a series of letters from Screwtape, an elderly devil, advising his nephew, Wormwood, an apprentice devil, how to corrupt his earthly "patient." Lewis delves into questions about good and evil, temptation, repentance, and grace, offering knowledge and guidance to all who are trying to live strong Christian lives. (For mature teens.)

Living Above the Level of Mediocrity by Charles Swindoll

Charles Swindoll has written a book for those who have settled for less than their best and have convinced themselves that quality, integrity, and authenticity are negotiable. He calls for men and women to reach their full potential.

For more resources on spiritual growth, visit www.familylife.com and browse the online store.

Resources to Make You a Better Leader

As Iron Sharpens Iron by Howard Hendricks and William Hendricks

Howard and Bill Hendricks have written a primer on the process of mentoring, hoping to encourage men to enter into mentoring relationships with a view toward sharing what is best in themselves with one another.

Basic Training for a Few Good Men by Tim Kimmel

(A "FamilyLife Today" audio series is also available.)

Basic Training is a crash course in character; a no-holds-barred study of things that turn men of faith into men of God. "If you are serious about being a soldier for Jesus Christ, then you have to be absolutely committed to personal character," says author Tim Kimmel. "Character trickles down. Men of character create marriages with character. Men of character have a lot easier time expecting and receiving high standards of character from their kids."

Ordering Your Private World by Gordon MacDonald (available on audio book)

In today's busy world, it is increasingly difficult to discover the inner peace and order that bring an outward sense of stability and joy. By working through five specific areas, MacDonald gives helpful advice for fighting the disorder within, finding personal growth and spiritual development.

The Seven Habits of Highly Effective People by Stephen Covey (available on audio book)

"Knowledge is the quickest and safest path to success in any area of life. Stephen Covey has encapsulated the strategies used by all those who are highly effective. Success can be learned and this book is a highly effective way to learn it." –Charles Given, President, Charles J. Givens Organization, Inc., author of *Wealth Without Risk*.

"Courage When Facing Great Challenges" Audio Cassette by Joel Hunter

(To order, contact Northland Community Church, Orlando, Florida at 407-830-7146.)

This tape explains how to appropriate God's resources when facing a great challenge. Dr. Hunter describes how to join God when He leads us into opportunities. He elaborates on how God will provide what we need to accomplish the great tasks He has given us.

For more resources on leadership, visit www.familylife.com and browse the online store.

Resources for Your Manhood Journey

The Christian Husband by Bob Lepine

(A "FamilyLife Today" audio series is also available.)

Almost 20 years of marriage have taught Bob Lepine one thing about being a husband—follow God's Word! With his unique blend of humor and biblical insight, Lepine helps men understand what being godly means, the three roles of husbands, and how to really love their wives. This is must reading whether you've been married 50 years or are getting married in 50 days.

A Father for All Seasons by Bob Welch ✔

A Father for All Seasons celebrates the wonder of the father/son relationship and shows how everything in life changes when the two connect.

Four Pillars of a Man's Heart by Stu Weber

(A "FamilyLife Today" audio series is also available.)

Building upon the "Four Pillars of Manhood" model set forth in his popular bestseller *Tender Warrior*, Stu Weber leads readers upon an expanded, in-depth biblical exploration of what it means to be a King, Warrior, Mentor, and Friend. Short, practical chapters focus on areas of struggle and opportunity faced by men of all ages and backgrounds.

Halftime by Bob Buford

(Available on audio book. A "FamilyLife Today" audio series is also available)

In *Halftime*, a book about mid-life, Buford focuses on the possibilities at this stage for revitalization, for catching new vision, and for living the second, most-rewarding half of life. He promises that the second half of life can be better than the first.

The Man in the Mirror by Patrick Morley ✔

(abridged version available on audio book)

This powerful book invites men to take a probing look at their identities, relationships, finances, time, temperament, and most importantly, the means to bring about lasting change. It offers a life-changing look at how to trade the rat race for the rewards of godly manhood.

"Men's Fraternity: A Journey into Authentic Manhood" audio series by Robert Lewis ✔

(To order, contact Fellowship Bible Church at www.fbclr.org or 501-224-7171.)

This series of 26 messages on 12 audio cassettes is an eye-opening exploration of the cultural and biblical definitions of manhood. Lewis has designed this series to help men in the exciting process of discovering authentic biblical masculinity; it is full of practical, time-tested teaching.

Point Man by Steve Farrar

Leading your family through the moral chaos of our times is like leading a small patrol through enemy territory. If your family is going to make it through the jungle intact, they will need a trained, God-appointed leader at the point.

Temptations Men Face by Tom L. Eisenman

In this personal and practical book, Tom L. Eisenman discusses the temptations men face (being macho, having an affair, misusing power, loving money, trying to be perfect) and shows how they can be resisted.

Tender Warrior by Stu Weber (available on audio book)

(A "FamilyLife Today" audio series is also available.)

Leader. Protector. Friend. Lover. Men are expected to fill a wide variety of roles, and it can be extremely difficult to achieve a healthy balance. But God has provided a powerful blueprint for balanced manhood, and Stu Weber takes an in-depth, life-changing look at that plan in Tender Warrior.

For more resources on manhood, visit
www.familylife.com and browse the online store.

Resources to Strengthen Your Marriage

Moments Together for Couples by Dennis and Barbara Rainey

This timely collection of devotional thoughts offers practical words for couples who want to keep their trust in the Lord a daily focus, and their commitment to each other a lifelong reality. Each day, spend a few minutes with each other ... and the Savior.

The Mystery of Marriage by Mike Mason

Celebrate your God-ordained union with this beautifully written book. Your marriage can grow deeper and totally alter the way you relate to each other and to God. Elisabeth Elliot says, "I don't need to read any other books on the subject."

The New Building Your Mate's Self-Esteem by Dennis and Barbara Rainey

Bring out the best in the one you love! Learn how to accept, appreciate, honor, and encourage your mate and experience new levels of love and fulfillment—individually and as a couple. (Hardback book with free pocket card.)

Sexual Intimacy in Marriage by William Cutrer and Sandra Glahn

In a humorous and caring manner, Dr. Bill Cutrer provides medically and spiritually competent advice to the most common questions that couples would like to ask but often don't. This is not just another "technical manual" that leaves out the personal dimensions of sexuality.

"The Song of Solomon" audio series by Tommy Nelson

(To order, contact Hudson Productions at hudsonproductions.com or 1-800-729-0815.)

This excellent audio series comes on six cassettes and is comprised of twelve 30-minute sessions covering the entire message. It is great for singles or marrieds, and includes a study guide.

Loving Your Marriage Enough to Protect It by Jerry Jenkins

In our culture the temptation toward marital infidelity is almost overwhelming. Jerry Jenkins provides ways to practice preventative medicine. Study questions have been added for you to make the lessons personal. Talk them over with your spouse or a small group.

For more resources on marriage, visit
www.familylife.com and browse the online store.

Resources to Make You a Better Father

Different Children, Different Needs by Charles F. Boyd

Pastor Boyd teaches parents how to parent more effectively by understanding the personality God has given each child. He shows how to respond to the God-given design of each of their kids, introducing a personality assessment system to help them better understand, accept, and appreciate their children's temperaments.

Parenting Today's Adolescent by Dennis and Barbara Rainey

FamilyLife's executive director Dennis Rainey and his wife, Barbara, offer parents a proven plan for connecting with their adolescents and preparing them for the teen years. You will be encouraged by their biblically based insight on peer pressure, music, grades, dating, sex, discipline, and more. Includes special single-parent sections.

Passport to Purity by Dennis and Barbara Rainey

Passport to Purity gives parents a workable plan and effective tools to successfully prepare a preteen for the adolescent years. This guided weekend retreat for a father and son or a mother and daughter will prepare your preteen to make wise, biblical choices. As a parent of a preteen you need Passport to Purity ... because your preteen needs you. Visit www.familylife.com for more information about this exciting resource!

Raising a Modern Day Knight by Robert Lewis

In this dynamic book for fathers with sons, Lewis provides practical help to show a dad how to equip his son for the "higher things" of manhood. Features include helpful guidelines for the use of creative manhood ceremonies to commemorate key passages in a boy's life, from puberty to marriage.

For more resources on parenting, visit
www.familylife.com and browse the online store.

Resources for Your Son to Read

I Kissed Dating Goodbye by Joshua Harris ✔

If you or someone you know is looking for real answers to guy-girl relationships, you must read this runaway national best-seller. Discover how you can live a lifestyle of sincere love, true purity, and purposeful singleness in the light of God's Word.

Right from Wrong by Josh McDowell ✔

Major research shows that our young people don't know what truth is. According to Josh McDowell, there is hope. He explains why certain truths are universal and shows how to teach youth to determine between right and wrong. There are several other books available to support Josh's Right from Wrong campaign.

For more resources for teens, visit
www.familylife.com and browse the online store.

Resources to Make You Think

In the Shadow of the Almighty by Elisabeth Elliot

This is the best-selling account of the martyrdom of Jim Elliot and four other missionaries at the hands of the Auca Indians in Ecuador. "Elisabeth Elliot's account is more than inspirational reading; it belongs to the very heartbeat of evangelic witness"– *Christianity Today*.

Through Gates of Splendor by Elisabeth Elliot

After several preliminary overtures of friendship, five young missionary men set out on a crucial January day in 1956 for a meeting with the Auca tribesmen who had reacted with apparent tolerance to earlier gifts and messages. This is the poignant story of their martyrdom told by the widow of one of the slain members of the group.

The Book of Virtues **edited by William Bennett (available on audio book)**
This remarkable collection of stories will help children develop that most important quality–character. Former secretary of education Bennett includes stories from the Bible, and from sources as diverse as well-known fairy tales, the philosophy of Plato, the poetry of Robert Frost and Maya Angelou, and Aesop's fables.

The Picture of Dorian Gray **(cassette tape version recommended)**
The story describes the terrible effects of vanity and the eerie descent of a man into self-absorption. (CAUTION: This resource is only for more mature young men.)

The Lion, the Witch, and The Wardrobe **by C.S. Lewis (available on audio book)**
(CD version via Focus on the Family at www.family.org or 1-800-A-FAMILY)
This fantasy story creatively depicts story of Christ's sacrifice, death, and resurrection. Paul Scofield narrates the Focus on the Family CD version. *The New York Times* called this popular fantasy "deeply moving and hauntingly lovely." First in a seven-part series, *The Lion, the Witch and the Wardrobe* is the tale of three children who wander into the Land of Narnia through an enchanted closet.

The Moral Compass **edited by William Bennett (available on audio book)**
The perfect companion to Bennett's #1 national bestseller, *The Book of Virtues*, this compendium of instructional and engaging writings will help the entire family meet the challenges they face in each of life's different stages. This inspiring and instructive volume offers many more examples of good and bad, right and wrong, in great works from literature and in exemplary stories from history.

Quality Modern Fiction

Dominion **by Randy Alcorn**
When a murder drags him into the disorienting world of inner-city conflict, journalist Clarence Abernathy seeks answers to the violence and to his own struggles with race and faith in the newest mystery novel from the best-selling author of *Deadline*.

Left Behind **by Tim LaHaye and Jerry Jenkins (available on audio book)**
This book and the series it spawned has been on the top of the charts for a couple of years. In one cataclysmic moment, millions from around the globe disappear. Join the story of those left behind when the rapture occurs—a gripping story of one potential scenario of the end times.

This Present Darkness **and** *Piercing the Darkness* **by Frank E. Peretti (available on audio book)**
These two blockbuster spiritual thrillers that changed Christian fiction

forever have individually sold over 3.5 million copies—and now both are finally available together in one complete hardcover volume. Frank E. Peretti has been called "America's hottest Christian novelist" and is the author of several best-selling action-packed works.

The Testament by John Grisham (available on audio book)

Troy Phelan hates his greedy, spoiled children. The aging multibillionaire knows that they're circling like vultures as he waits to die. Phelan's surprising last will and testament names a heretofore unknown beneficiary—a missionary living deep in the wilds of Brazil. Nate O'Riley, a lawyer fresh from his fourth stay in rehab, is sent to find her. Along the way, he learns about God and himself, and he discovers that the dangers of alcohol pale in comparison with the perils of the jungle. (CAUTION: This resource is only for more mature young men.)

Motion Pictures

Movies are an excellent tool to illustrate a principle. The film "Iron Will," for example, depicts courage, endurance, self-motivation, and overcoming fear. The 1943 version of "Dr. Jekyl and Mr. Hyde" vividly paints a picture of the classic internal struggle between good and evil. Movies also add another benefit by providing an opportunity to spend time with your son, as you watch and study the film together.

The Classics

"Ben Hur" (1959) G

CHAMPION characteristics: Navigation, Courage, Attitude, and Honor

Value of film: This movie shows how one man (played by Charlton Heston), through trials and adventures, finally finds freedom from anger and bitterness in Jesus Christ. Winner of eleven academy awards, including Best Picture, and Best Actor for Heston. Bring your dinner to this one; it's three hours long.

"Dr. Jekyl and Mr. Hyde" (1943 version starring Spencer Tracey) not rated

CHAMPION characteristics: Purity and Integrity

Value of film: The story provides an excellent example of good vs. evil, where evil triumphs as the result of an addiction that eventually overtakes and controls Dr. Jekyl.

"The Four Feathers" (1939) not rated

CHAMPION characteristics: Mental Toughness, Integrity, Courage, and Honor

Value of film: This classic movie is about a soldier, once accused of cowardice, who eventually risks his life to rescue his accusers. This movie provides a great illustration of recovering from unsuccessful failure.

"High Noon" (1952) not rated

CHAMPION characteristics: Courage, Mental Toughness, and Integrity

Value of film: One courageous man stands against a mob. Gary Cooper, in his famous role as a sheriff in the old West, stands his ground against crime when everyone deserts him.

"The Robe" (1953) not rated

CHAMPION characteristics: Courage and Navigation

Value of film: Victor Mature portrays of a Roman soldier that witnesses the death of Jesus Christ. His life is changed forever as   he leaves his post in the Roman army to become a faithful follower of Christ. This is a classic film depicting the world-changing faith of the early Christian martyrs.

"Mr. Smith Goes to Washington" (1939) not rated

CHAMPION characteristics: Courage, Mental Toughness, and Integrity

Value of film: James Stewart's portrays of a young congressman who must stand on his principles, even when the entire Senate is against him.

"The Searchers" (1956) not rated

CHAMPION characteristics: Attitude and Navigation

Value of film: John Wayne stars as a resentful man, with a tortured past. He must overcome anger and bitterness to save a member of his family captured years before by Indians.

"Support Your Local Sheriff" (1969) G

CHAMPION characteristics: Courage and Integrity

Value of film: James Garner stars in this comedy version of "High Noon." If you need a light-hearted break in your son's application points, this movie will fill the bill.

"Ten Commandments" (1956) G

CHAMPION characteristics: Courage, Ownership and Navigation

Value of film: This biblical epic remains a favorite, with masterful filmmaking by Cecil B. DeMille. It provides a powerful examination of Moses, superbly portrayed by Charlton Heston.

The Modern

"Deep Impact" (1998) PG-13

CHAMPION characteristics: Courage and Mental Toughness

Value of film: This movie highlights the characteristics of heroism and self-sacrifice in the face of calamity. There is some profanity in this film, however. Go to www.screenit.com to get a full description of the language.

"Hoosiers" (1986) PG

CHAMPION characteristics: Attitude and Mental Toughness

Value of film: This show highlights how dedication and teamwork can overcome the most difficult of obstacles.

"Man from Snowy River" (1982) PG

CHAMPION characteristics: Mental Toughness and Attitude

Value of film: This movie demonstrates how persistence and hard work, combined with strong values learned from his father, help a young man to transition into the responsibilities of manhood.

"Star Trek II: The Wrath of Kahn" (1982) PG

CHAMPION characteristics: Attitude, Honor, and Courage

Value of film: This movie provides an example of dedication, sacrifice, and teamwork, in the context of a strong friendship between Captain Kirk and Mr. Spock. There is some profanity.

The True Stories

While Hollywood has tried to maintain the integrity of these stories, to make these films work, they've had to eliminate characters and events and invent dialogue at places. Books about these people and events can fill in the gaps that Hollywood left.

"Apollo 13" (1995) PG-13

CHAMPION characteristics: Courage, Attitude, and Mental Toughness

Value of film: This true story portrays the dedication and creativity of a team (NASA and the Apollo 13 astronauts) as they work through a "successful failure." Unfortunately, there is strong language in this movie.

"Chariots of Fire" (1981) PG

CHAMPION characteristics: Courage, Integrity, Attitude, and Navigation

Value of film: This is the true story of Olympic gold medal winner, Eric Liddel, who chose to stand firm in his beliefs and shocked the world by refusing to run an Olympic race because it was held on Sunday. It is a great portrayal of how one man, dedicated to the Lord, can make a difference. "Chariots of Fire" won an Oscar for Best Picture.

"The Hiding Place" (1975)

CHAMPION characteristics: All

Value of film: The Jewish Holocaust carried out by Adolf Hitler during World War II is one of the greatest examples of evil in all history. Corrie ten Boom's family walked through these dark days. The best movie Billy Graham's Worldwide Pictures ever made.

"Iron Will" (1994) PG

CHAMPION characteristics: Courage, Honor, Attitude, Mental Toughness, and Integrity

Value of film: This true story shows the courage and persistence of a young man, as he assumes responsibility and major risk to save his family's farm.

"October Sky" (1999) PG

CHAMPION characteristics: Courage and Navigation

Value of film: Based on a true story, this movie shows a young man who maintains focus against incredible odds to achieve his dream. Some profanity is included. Look to www.screenit.com for details.

"Rudy" (1993) PG

CHAMPION characteristics: Courage, Honor, and Attitude

Value of film: Watch this true story of a young man who persisted against the odds to accomplish his goal of playing football for Notre Dame. It provides an excellent example of how one man's dedication and enthusiasm can affect an entire team.

"Sergeant York" (1941) not rated

CHAMPION characteristics: Integrity, Courage, Honor, and Attitude

Value of film: Gary Cooper's academy award winning portrayal of Alvin York, winner of the Congressional Medal of Honor in World War I is the subject of this movie. It offers an excellent example of a man's courage and integrity when he is under fire.

"The Spirit of St. Louis" (1957) PG

CHAMPION characteristics: Courage and Mental Toughness

Value of film: James Stewart offers superb performance as Charles Lindberg, the first man to fly across the Atlantic. Ingenuity, focus, and determination are all depicted in this movie.

"Stanley and Livingston" (1939) not rated

CHAMPION characteristics: Courage and Navigation

Value of film: This is a true story starring Spencer Tracey that shows the incredible persistence and courage of two men.

ACTIVITIES

▲ **Interview people, for example:**

    ■ A couple married over 50 years

    ■ A missionary

    ■ A politician

    ■ A person who has exhibited strong character in his decision making

    Guidelines for conducting an interview:

    1. Dress appropriately. When in doubt, wear your best clothes.

    2. Try to interview the person on the job where they can demonstrate as well as answer questions. It makes for a much better interview.

    3. Ask open-ended questions, and then listen carefully. Don't interrupt.

    4. Take good notes or use an audio or video recorder.

    5. At the end of the interview as the person if there is anything else he/she wanted to say.

    6. Make sure to send a thank you note to the person for taking time for your interview.

    7. Take a photograph of the two of you together. They make incredible memories.

▲ **Visit a challenging new environment, and write a report (visit an Emergency Room, for example).**

▲ **Participate in public speaking; it offers a great setting for overcoming fear.**

▲ **Take a white water rafting trip.**

▲ **Go on a short-term mission trip.**

▲ **Visit men you respect at their work (different than your career).**

▲ **Take a CHAMPION Training trip to Washington, D.C.** Visit the Smithsonian, the Capitol, the Holocaust Museum, and many other exhibits. Washington, D.C., is the Hall of Fame for American heroes.

CHAPTER SIX

FATHER'S ARSENAL

This section includes:

CHAMPION Training Commitment Form

Understanding Your Son's Bent

Media Evaluation Report Form

Fiction Glossary

Greek Terms in the Story

Guiding Insights Request Letter (Sample)

Summary of Success (Sample Presentation)

CHAMPION Symbol and Gift Ideas

CHAMPION
Training Commitment

I, _____ agree to participate in CHAMPION Training.
(Son's name)

I understand what is expected of me, and I accept this responsibility with enthusiasm and expectation. I will attempt at all times to approach challenges and successes with a positive attitude and dependence on God. I recognize that my father's role is to encourage, help, and mentor me.

I am committed to completing my assigned tasks and to regularly interacting with my father during our CHAMPION Sessions. I look forward to what God will teach me in the coming year. I am excited about our adventure together and the celebration of my young manhood that awaits me at the end of my training. When I receive the symbol of my young manhood, I will wear it with honor.

I, _____, agree to lead _____,
(Father's name)   *(Son's name)*

in his CHAMPION Training. I understand what is expected of me, and I accept this responsibility with enthusiasm and expectation. I will attempt at all times to approach my son's challenges and successes with a positive attitude and dependence on God. While my son must take responsibility to gain the most from his training, I realize that I need to help him succeed and to be available to support him in any way that I can.

I am committed to prayer, preparation, and personal involvement in guiding the CHAMPION Training. I look forward to regularly interacting with my son and to what God will teach both him and me in the coming year. At the end of my son's training, I will celebrate his transition into young manhood with pride and joy.

_____   _____
(Son's signature)   *(Father's signature)*

Date: _____   Mentor/Witness: _____

He will restore the hearts of the fathers to their children and the hearts of the children to their fathers. Malachi 4:6a

Understanding Your Son's Bent

Have you ever felt as if you and your son are like a couple of magnets? Maybe you're two peas in a pod, understanding each other completely and having little or no conflict. Or perhaps your personalities are different, but you naturally appreciate each other's strengths in such a way that mutual projects are easily handled. You may even interact like the wrong ends of a magnet trying to come together: an invisible wall between you pushes the two of you apart before you can ever get close.

Proverbs 22:6 instructs you to raise or train up your son in the way he should go. Some have translated this phrase, "according to his bent." We are all born with God-given bents (or temperaments) that affect our motivation, our reactions to various circumstances, and our relationships with others. Understanding your son's bent or temperament could greatly affect how you guide his CHAMPION Training. What motivates him?

- Does he like to talk or to listen?

- Is he decisive or indecisive?

- Does he want to lead or to follow others?

- Will he take risks or avoid them?

- Does he like things done "by the book" or does he look for creative solutions?

- Does he prefer variety or predictability?

There are few needs more important to your son than his need to be understood. Using the results of this temperament assessment, you will have a better understanding of your son's strengths, limitations, and motivators. You should utilize this assessment to plan activities and choose projects for your CHAMPION Sessions based on your son's motivational bents. During the training, you might also consider choosing a project specifically designed to help your son step out of his comfort zone and challenge his weaknesses.

Take time to determine your own bent as well. This can help you anticipate how your temperament type meshes with your son's.

Assess Your Son's Bent

Step 1: Under each letter category of the T-E-A-M Chart, circle every word or phrase that describes a consistent character trait or behavior that your son exhibits as he interacts *within your family*.

Step 2: Total the number of items circled in each quadrant and write the total in the box at the end of each category.

Step 3: Plot the totals from each box on the next page entitled "Plot Your Son's Bent." Put an "X" on each arrow scale to indicate the score for each category.

Step 4: Review the descriptions of the four temperament types (T, E, A, and M).

IMPORTANT: DO NOT share the results of this assessment with your son until you both complete session 14 in the *Mission Guide*, where he will have the opportunity to explore his temperament and his role on God's "T-E-A-M."

T

demanding
adventurous
dominant
strong-willed
decisive
task-oriented
authoritative
wants the bottom line
fearless
likes challenge
insensitive
risk taker
wants choices
competitive
problem solver
likes direct answers
confident
controlling
firm
likes freedom from control

"T" TOTAL

E

tolerant
friendships are very important
good listener
peacemaker
wants to be liked
pleasant or likeable
passive
careful
sensitive
likes security
nurturing
avoids confrontation
likes established work patterns
patient
indecisive
thoughtful
wants to please
adaptable
calm
people-oriented

"E" TOTAL

A

precise
correct
scheduled
calculating
consistent
likes "to do" lists
accurate
competent
analytical
cautious
likes Daytimers™ or electronic organizers
perfectionist
organized
likes support from others
detailed
predictable
likes defined tasks
discerning
practical
factual

"A" TOTAL

M

comes up with ideas
impressive
likes to look good
very verbal
enthusiastic
comic
inspiring
influencer
optimistic
prideful
motivator
promoter/ marketer
enjoys change
fun
good mixer in crowds
spontaneous
energetic
likes variety
enjoys popularity
visionary (sees the big picture)

"M" TOTAL

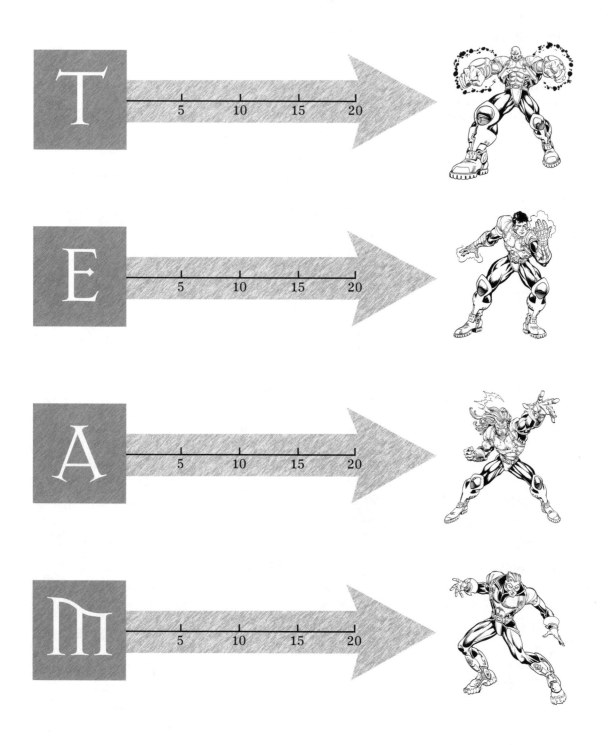

Review Your Son's Bent

Look at the letter category in which your son had the highest score. Although he is likely to have one predominant bent, most people have a mix of several. The following four temperament types are based on the behaviors and actions of four key characters from *Teknon and the CHAMPION Warriors.*

Tharreo
(Tor)

Motto	Description	Motivators
Don't worry, I've got everything under control!	In Greek, *tharreo* means "having courage, confidence, and boldness." This is a potential future leader. Usually the captain of a team, he likes to be in charge. He needs challenges and choices and he usually likes to get involved in a variety of activities. He tends to guard his feelings. Although leadership ability is his strength, this type of person needs to learn to involve others in decision-making.	Challenges, leadership opportunity, choices, adventure

Epios
(Epps)

Motto	Description	Motivators
You can depend on me!	In Greek, *epios* refers to one who shows patience and gentleness to others. Gentleness and loyalty describe this individual. His friendliness and good humor make him very likeable, but he can often allow others to take advantage of him. Because he is a great listener, others gravitate toward him to share their problems. Dependable and often shy, he makes a great friend because he is often very forgiving. This type of person needs to learn to be more assertive and to take more risks in relationships.	Friendships, acceptance, opportunities to be part of a team (especially as an assistant to a leader)

Artios
(Arti)

Motto	Description	Motivators
Let's do it right the first time!	*Artios*, in the Greek, refers to something that is fitted perfectly or complete. If your son is one who likes to complete his tasks thoroughly and to the letter of the law, this may be his bent. Typically, he is competent, analytical, and likes to do one thing at a time until it is finished. He loves information that helps him to make decisions. Seldom does he take risks and try new things. He is motivated by opportunities to serve others. He actually reads instruction manuals. He needs a happy and positive atmosphere and can become frustrated when his friends are less enthusiastic about accuracy. He needs to learn and accept that it is all right to make a mistake and call for assistance to solve a problem. Be careful of using critical speech with him during instruction and discipline.	Security, order, opportunities to serve, reviewing data, completing tasks

Mataios
(Matty)

Motto	Description	Motivators
Let's party!!!	The Greek *mataios* describes vanity and seeking attention. This guy likes to be recognized and tends to talk a lot to get attention. Pleasing others is essential to him, and entertainment can be his focus. If there's fun to be had, he's leading the way or he's not far behind. He is likely to be motivating, enthusiastic, and creative. If you need an idea for a project, don't hesitate to call him. He is great at networking among friends. He doesn't like pressure or deadlines. Usually, guys like this need to learn to concentrate on the needs of others and on making others look good, too.	Fun, influencing others, looking good

Summary

All people and their temperaments are designed and crafted by God, and we can learn to appreciate them all. Enjoy your son's bent, and try to motivate him with the understanding and encouragement that God created him a valuable part of the "T-E-A-M." It takes a variety of people with their unique bents to make an effective team.

CAUTION: While assessments like these can be helpful in understanding our differences, it is important not to place too much focus on temperament types. Be careful about locking your son into a stereotype as an excuse for a negative trait or a reason to avoid developing a positive trait. As he grows and matures, his temperament will shift and take on traits from the other temperament categories. Regardless of your son's bent, his real model must be Jesus Christ.

Media Evaluation Report

When using movies, audio cassettes, and books for action points, consider asking your son to write a one-page report that answers the following questions.

1. How would you summarize the movie, audio cassette, or book?

2. What is the main point of the story?

3. Who is the hero? Who is the villain?

4. What skills or gifts did the hero rely on to succeed?

5. Do you agree with the hero's behavior and the methods he used? If not, what would you have done in his place?

6. What CHAMPION characteristics did the hero exhibit?

7. As you think of this story, name one story or passage from the Bible that it reminds you of.

8. How do the messages in this apply to me?

9. List other special questions identified in the *Mentor Guide* for each session:

   ●

   ●

   ●

Fiction Glossary

Admiral Ago (ăd´mər-əl ä´go) – Chancellor of the planet Basileia and good friend to the CHAMPION movement

amacho (ə-mä´chō) – Fierce beast that roams Kairos, often hunting in packs. Large claws, powerful legs, and a   poisonous barbed tail allow it to prey on other animals.

Ameleo (ä-mē´lē-o) – Overindulgent father of Pikros and Parakoe, who meets the CHAMPION Warriors on the *Ergonaut*

amuno (ə-moo´nō) – Fighting style of the CHAMPION Warriors taught to Kratos and then to Teknon by Tor, Epps, Arti, and Matty. Primarily focused on defense, it resembles several martial arts disciplines.

android (ăn´droid) – Mechanical robotic creature

Apoplonao (ä-pŏp´lŏn-ā´ō) – Perasmian maiden, nicknamed Lana, whom Teknon meets at a spring-fed pool near Bia. Lana is actually Scandalon disguised as a beautiful young lady.

Artios (är´tē-ōs) – Nicknamed Arti, he is a mentor to Teknon and member of the CHAMPION movement. An amuno master from the Mache Region, Arti created a face band that enables him to shoot a paralyzing ray or a beam that identifies individuals or objects cloaked by a holographic image.

Basileia (băs-ĭ´lē-ə) – Home planet of Kratos, Teknon, the mentors, and Magos

Basileia Technology Institute (BTI) – Famous university on Basileia that produces many of the engineers and inventors for the planet. This is also the school where Kratos and Phil met.

Bia (bē´ə) – Small, rugged town on the planet Kairos where Kratos and Teknon meet the Harpax gang

bionic (bī-ŏn´ĭk) – Having physical characteristics enhanced by electrical or mechanical components

biosynthetic matrix (bī´ō-sĭn-thət´ĭk mā´trĭks) – Technology designed by Magos and Kratos that allows a human to merge his mind and body with computer circuitry. Magos further develops this technology to provide what he believed to be mechanized immortality.

CHAMPION (chăm´pē-ən) – One who exhibits Courage, Honor, Attitude, Mental Toughness, Purity, Integrity, Ownership, and Navigation as he battles evil and changes his world for Pneuma's glory

cyborg (sī´bôrg) – A being that is partly human and partly machine

Daimons (dā´mənz) – An evil army of aggressors that threatened to overthrow Basileia in the days of the ancient League of CHAMPION Warriors

Didasko (dī–dăs´ kō) – One of the CHAMPION instructors who can be accessed through the Logos

digmite (dĭg´ mīt) – Small, carnivorous insect, capable of inflicting a painful, fever-inducing bite

dinar (dĭ–när´) – Basic currency used on the planet Basileia

domicat (dŏm´ ə–kăt) – Tame and calm domestic house pet

Dolios (dō´ lē–ōs) – An extremely powerful kako android created by Magos that guards the Logos. Dolios has the ability to appear in the form of his opponent's greatest fear.

Epios (ĕp´ ē–ōs) – Nicknamed Epps, he is a mentor to Teknon and a member of the CHAMPION movement. He comes from the Mache Region and is an amuno master. Epps created special gloves that allow him to heal injuries and illnesses, as well as cause the people he touches to become completely honest and friendly for a brief period of time.

Ergo (ûr´ gō) – Resort town on the planet Kairos, where Kratos and Matty battle the amachos

Ergonaut (ûr´ gō–nôt) – Cruise ship that shuttles between Ergo and Sarkinos on the planet Kairos

Eros (ĕr´ ōs) – Host of one of the holographic imaging salons in the Sarkinos Underground

fibronic (fī–brän´ ĭk) – Consisting of a special technology that enables digital transmissions between androids

footsoldier (foot´ sōl–jər) – Mindless android created by Magos primarily for the purpose of maintaining security for Sheol and destroying his enemies

florne (flôrn) – White, sweet-smelling, delicious, and soothing drink

gleukos (gloo´ kōs) – Intoxicating drink that produces a mind-altering effect similar to alcohol or marijuana

gorgon (gôr´ gŏn) – Dangerous reptilian creature that ranges from five to 10 meters in length

hammerhoop (hăm´ ər–hoop´) – A popular Basileian sport where opposing teams of three players each attempt to send a spherical "pulsar" into statically energized nets called chambers, as they avoid being swatted by mechanized arms used to guard the chamber area. The game is played in an anti-gravity environment and requires tremendous physical conditioning.

Harpax (här´ păks) – Attractive but vicious race of people, who use their strength and intelligence to hurt, rather than help, others. Harpax usually travel in para-military gangs.

Hedon Bay (hē′dən bā) – Body of water on the planet Kairos that lies south of the Northron Peninsula and empties into the sea north of the Thumos Mountain range

Hilarotes (hĭ-lâr′ə-tēz′) – Teknon's sister, nicknamed Hilly, and daughter of Kratos and Paideia

hodgebeast (hŏj′bēst) – Large, aggressive mammal with long tusks that spike upward from its lower jaw. Its fur is short and coarse, and it emits a strong, unpleasant odor.

holographic image (hŏ-lə-grăf′ĭk ĭm′ĭj) – Artificial, three-dimensional (3D) representation of a real-life object or environment produced by sophisticated laser technology

holographic image salon – Establishment where people go to view and interact with sexually oriented holographic images for entertainment

Hoplon (hŏp′lŏn) – The highly technical, multi-dimensional shield created by Kratos and Phileo

hoverboard (hŭv′er-bôrd) – Aerodynamic piece of sporting equipment used on Basileia to ride snow-covered slopes or the crest of large waves on the coastline

Hudor Sea (hoo′dôr sē) – Body of water on the planet Kairos that Teknon, Kratos, Matty, and Tor cross on the *Ergonaut*

hydronic engine (hī-drŏn′ĭk ĕn′jĭn) – Powerful machine that produces its own energy through an ingenious protonic regenerating process developed by Kratos. Because if its capabilities, only three engines are required to maintain the elevated status of the suspended mansion.

hydrovessel (hī′drō-vĕs-əl) – Aquatic transport ship propelled by engines that force water through the hull of the ship and out the back

infra-illuminator (ĭn′frə-ĭ-loo′ mə-nā-tər) – Infrared light device that allows sub-light vision capabilities without revealing its location to surveillance systems

interactive non-woven alloy – Man-made fiber constructed by Matty to create his suit. The filament is interactive at a molecular level, performing when desired as a chemical catalyst in the body to produce great speed.

Kairos (kī′ros) – Planet where Kratos, Teknon, and their team battle Magos and attempt to retrieve the Logos

kako (kā′kō) – Type of powerful android created by Magos and programmed to carry out his instructions. Kakos have the ability to process information and make decisions. Several, such as Scandalon and Dolios, have special abilities.

keline (kē´ līn) – Domesticated animal on Kairos, which provides delicious meat for consumption

kilometer (kĭl´ ə-mē´ tər) – Unit of measurement to determine longer distances on Basileia, equal to one thousand meters or 0.62 miles

Kopto (kŏp´ tō) – Commercial town where Kratos, Teknon, and the rest of their team first arrive on Kairos

Kopto Commercial Market – Large, outdoor shopping market located in the city of Kopto

Kratos (krā´ tōs) – Father of Teknon and leader of the new CHAMPION movement

Lacerlazer (lā´ sər-lā´ zər) – Powerful tool used by the Phaskos to penetrate the hard surface of Kairos for the purpose of mining

Lady Trophos (trō´ fōs) – Owner of the tavern in the Thumos Mountains and an undercover operative working against Magos

leviathan (lə-vī´ ə-thən) – Large, aggressive sea creature that hunts off the Northron coast and is a threat to swimmers

locator beacon – Small transmitting device that allows Paideia to track Kratos and his team via satellite, wherever they might be

Logos (lö´ gös) – Small, spherical object that holds all of the teachings of the CHAMPION Warriors

Maches (mä´ shāz) – Warriors from the Mache Region of Basileia, known as the only remaining tribe on the planet that practices amuno, the fighting style of the ancient CHAMPION Warriors

Mache Region (mä´ shā rē´ jən) – An isolated and rugged area of Basileia that is home to Tor, Epps, Arti, and Matty

Magos (mä´ gōs) – Old friend of Kratos, turned evil cyborg (part human, part android) and enemy to the CHAMPION movement. The fixture on the side of Magos' head enables him to control all of the creatures and computer equipment in his empire.

mamonas (mä-mō´ näs) – Valuable mineral used to produce memory chips for highly advanced computer equipment

Mataios (mä-tā´ ōs) – Nicknamed Matty, he is a mentor to Teknon. Matty comes from the Mache Region and is a member of the CHAMPION movement. Matty created a suit that enables him to attain incredible speed, protective eyewear that gives him 360-degree vision, and boots that allow him to easily scale walls and other vertical surfaces.

mentor (měn´ tôr) – One who helps, teaches, and cares for another person. Teknon's mentors are all committed to helping and training him to become a CHAMPION Warrior.

meter (mē´ tər) – Fundamental unit of measurement to determine length; equivalent to 3.28 feet

molecular matrix (mə-lĕk´ yə-lər mā´ trĭks) – Cell level structure of a person or object that can be restructured and transmitted via particle assimilator to other locations

Mount Purgos (mount pûr´ gōs) – Magnificent mountain on the planet of Basileia, near the home of Kratos, Padeia, Teknon, and Hilly

nela (nē´ lə) – Soothing beverage that can be served either hot or cold, made from the ground leaves of the nela plant grown on Basileia

neurosynaptic (nŏŏ´ rō-sĭ-năp´ tĭk) – Pertaining to the process that occurs when transmissions are sent from the brain across the nervous system of the human body and into the devices developed by the various CHAMPION Warriors. For example, the Hoplon responds to Kratos' brain waves.

Northros (nôrth´ rös) – Small, primitive town located on the Northron Peninsula of Kairos, and a temporary stopping place for the CHAMPION Warriors before they entered the Thumos Mountains

Paideia (pā-dē´ ə) – Wife of Kratos, mother to Teknon, and a member of the CHAMPION team

Parakoe (pâr´ ə-kō) and Pikros (pĭk´ rōs) – Immature teenage brothers and sons of Ameleo who meet Teknon on the *Ergonaut***Paranomia** (pâr-ə-nō´ mē-ə) – Nicknamed Pary, she is the beautiful girl from Northros whom Teknon finds attractive and spends time with

particle assimilator – Common device designed to transport individuals and objects instantly from one place to another through transformation of their molecular matrix

Perasmos (pâr-ăs´ mōs) – Thick forest on Kairos that Kratos and Teknon travel through on their way to Bia

phago (fä´ gō) – Very large reptilian creature with long claws and fangs. It can grow to 25 meters in height and is a natural predator of the amachos.

Phasko (făs´ kō) – Group of mining people located on Kairos. Short and powerful, they have the ability to drill through the ground with incredible speed and accuracy.

Phileo (fĭl-ā´ ō) – Also called Phil, he is a Phasko and long-time friend to Kratos

Plutos Region – Tropical territory on the coast of the Hudor Sea where Kratos and Teknon enter the lavish resort of Ergo

Poroo (pō-rōo´) – Distinguished but arrogant manager of the resort town of Ergo

Poneros (pə-när´əs) – Inherently sinister, powerful, and brilliant evil master of Magos

Pneuma (nōo´mə) – The eternal Warrior King whom the CHAMPION Warriors follow and serve. He is the all-powerful Spirit who desires that all people choose to come into a personal relationship with Him.

Pseudes (sōods) – Informant for Magos in the Sarkinos Underground who reveals all he knows to the CHAMPION team after Epps touches him with his special gloves

Rhaima (rā´mə) – Small planet inhabited by prison colonies

Rhegma (rĕg´mə) – Leader of the Harpax gang whom Kratos and Teknon encounter in the town of Bia

sabercamel (sā´bər-kăm´əl) – Tri-hump, foul-smelling, shaggy beast used primarily for transporting cargo across desert terrain

sandsnipe (sănd´snīp) – Small, foul-smelling Basileian rodent, which can produce a noxious liquid spray from its nose if provoked

Sarkinos Underground (sär´kə-nōs ŭn´dər-ground) – Also know as Lower Sarkinos, a popular adult entertainment community on Kairos that offers gambling, luxurious lodging, holographic imaging salons and other forms of illicit entertainment

Scandalon (skăn´dl-ŏn) – Kako android and one of Magos' most dangerous creations. Scandalon has the ability to change his appearance to whatever form will cause the most harm to Kratos, Teknon, or whomever else he targets as an enemy. He works primarily through the methods of deception and seduction.

scratchbacks (scrăch´băks) – Thieves and murderers who form nomadic gangs of that roam the dark alleys in urban areas on the planet Basileia

seismos (sīz´mōs) – Large, thick-skinned carnivore that roams the Thumos Mountains

Sensatron (sĕn´sĭ-trŏn) – Small diagnostic device that Arti carries on his belt. The Sensatron can take many different kinds of readings, including weather, enemy advancement, and material composition.

sheepalopes (shēp´ə-lōps) – Mindless domestic animals that are used for food and clothing

Sheol (shē´ōl) – Fortress and headquarters of Magos located deep in the Thumos Mountains. Sheol can be readily recognized by its three large, sinister towers.

Shocktech (shŏk′ tĕk) – Hand-held weapon purchased by Teknon at the Kopto Commercial Market

speca (spĕ′ kə) – Basic unit of currency used in the Kopto Commercial Market on the planet of Kairos

spike rat (spīk′ răt) – Small, barely edible rodent found along the trails of Kairos

swampcrusher (swŏmp′ krŭsh-r) – Carnivorous, multi-tentacled creature that lurks in the rivers of the Basileian rain forests

tantronic energy (tăn-trŏn′ ĭk ĕn′ ər-jē) – Highly volatile and dangerous power source that can vaporize human flesh if the energy intensity is high enough

Tarasso (tär-ăs′ ō) – Region on planet Karios west of the Hudor Sea where the city of Sarkinos is located

Teknon (tĕk′ nŏn) – Son of Kratos and Paideia and primary character in the story

ten high – Card game usually associated with gambling and played frequently in the Sarkinos Underground casinos

Tharreo (thär-rā′ ō) – Nicknamed Tor, this mentor to Teknon is from the Mache Region. He is second in command on the CHAMPION Warrior team and an amuno master. Tor created arm braces that enable him to fire energy beams that can lift and hold tremendous weight. The beams increase Tor's already enormous strength.

Thumos Mountains (thoo′ mōs) – Treacherous mountain range on Kairos known for violent weather changes and dangerous terrain

transfer station – Place where travelers can start and end trips using a particle assimilator

transtron racer (trăns′ trŏn) – Sleek, fast vehicle that can hover several meters above the ground

transparent carbonic alloy – Clear, impenetrable man-made substance constructed in a patented process that uses several rare elements found on both Basileia and Kairos

vealplant (vēl′ plănt) – Delicious vegetable that is large enough to be cut into servings that resemble steaks

wartmouse (wôrt′ mous) – Small, sharp-toothed rodent capable of eating five times its body weight each day

GREEK TERMS IN THE STORY

Following is a translation of Greek terms used in the story *Teknon and the Champion Warriors*. The names for each of the characters and many of the places were selected because of the meaning of those names in the Greek language that was used in the original writing of the New Testament books of the Bible.

- amacho—brawler
- Ameleo—neglectful, careless
- amuno—defend
- Apoplanao—seducer
- Artios—perfect, complete
- Basileia—kingdom
- Bia—violence
- Didasko—teacher
- Dolios—demon
- Epios—gentle, patient
- Harpax—extortioner
- Hilarotes—cheerfulness
- Hoplon—armor, weapons of warfare
- Hudor—water
- Gleukos—wine
- Kairos—God-given opportunity
- kakos—evil, wicked
- Kopto—wail
- Kratos—power, strength (leader)
- Logos—the word (used as a name for God's verbal and written Word)
- Magos—sorcerer
- Mataios—vanity
- Northros—slothful, lazy

- Paideia—instruction
- Parakoe—disobedience
- Paranomia—transgression, iniquity
- Perasmos (spelled pierasmos)—temptation
- phago—gluttonous
- Phasko—affirm
- Phileo—love
- Pikros—bitter
- Pneuma—spirit
- Poneros—evil, malicious
- Poroo—harden
- Pseudes—false, liar
- Rhegma—ruin
- Sarkinos—carnal
- Scandalon (spelled skandalon)—falling, temptation
- seismos—earthquake, tempest
- Sheol (Hebrew word)—world of the dead, grave, pit
- Teknon—child
- Tharreo—boldness, courage, confidence
- Thumos—fierceness, anger
- Trophos—nurse

Guiding Insights Request Letter

(Sample)

Dear _____,

    It is with great pride and anticipation that I write this letter to you. My son, _____, will soon celebrate his transition to young manhood. Since (date/month/year) my son has worked through what we call CHAMPION Training. The purpose of _____'s training has been to provide a systematic process to help him transition into young manhood. We have done this by applying biblical principles to help him develop godly character and convictions in his life.

    On (month/day) we will have a ceremony to celebrate his accomplishments and to recognize _____ as a young adult. You can be a part of this important event in my son's life.

    Enclosed is a blank (video/audio) tape.   Would you please take a few minutes to record yourself answering the following three questions?

1. If you were _____'s age again, what would you do differently?

2. What skills would you recommend that _____ develop?

3. What is the most important thing for_____ to remember as a young man?

    This tape will be played at _____'s celebration ceremony and then packaged as a gift to him. After you finish the recording, please put the tape in the enclosed addressed envelope and drop it in the mail to me by (deadline date).

    Your participation in _____'s CHAMPION Training would be greatly appreciated by both of us. Thank you in advance.

Sincerely,

Summary of Success

(Sample Presentation)

The Summary of Success is a presentation or speech that you should write and deliver to your son at his CHAMPION Celebration Ceremony. The Summary of Success should encourage your son by recapping the highlights of his CHAMPION Training, while reminding him of important issues you want him to remember. Your son will cherish this presentation for years to come if you make the extra effort to have it nicely typed up and printed on high quality paper for framing. Include a place for a photo of you and your son at the celebration on the Summary of Success document.

Following is a portion of what I (Brent) read to my son at his celebration ceremony. This statement now hangs on my son's wall in a frame with a picture of my son and me from his ceremony.

Casey, tonight is a special night for both of us. The little bruised bundle that was delivered more than 12 years ago is now standing before me, almost my own height, ready to enter the most adventurous years of his life. We have had a great year together in your training, and we will have many memories ahead.

Tonight, you have been encouraged not only by the men here, all of whom I trust and admire, but also by those who have had an impact in my life from all corners of the nation. Sam Bartlett, Don Jacobs, Rex Roffler, Chester Kennedy, Martin Shipman, Roger Berry, Bert Chandler, Nick Repak, Jack McGill, Uncle Paul, Uncle Bill, Don Garrison, and finally my own father have all contributed to your celebration. They have given you their pearls, the benefit of their hindsight that can only come from years of experience. Cherish their advice and refer to it often in the years to come.

I also encourage you to remember and apply the lessons we learned together over the past year. I say 'we,' because as you know, my life has changed almost as much as yours.

Remember:

- *The lessons we learned from the* Experiencing God *series. The most important thing you can ever do is to develop your personal love relationship with Jesus Christ.*

- *The books you read, including* Tender Warrior, Developing the Leader Within You, *and* This Present Darkness.

- *The audiocassettes you heard from Joel Hunter, Dennis Rainey, and Howard Hendricks. Remember especially the example of those men who gave the messages.*

- *The movies you watched and reported on. Keep in mind that the director of a movie is always trying to communicate a message, whether it is encouraging or destructive.*

- *The biographies you read. Remember the character and courage of such godly men as David Livingstone and Jim Elliot.*

- *The value of controlling your temper. Always present a demeanor of confidence with eye contact, a smile, and a firm shake to the people you meet.*

- *The value of thanking people, and how a short note of thanks communicates volumes.*

- *The importance of respecting authority, because God will never make you a leader unless you are a faithful follower.*

- *To constantly challenge yourself. Continue to identify and face the dragons that stand in your path. You have seen time and again that towering dragons reduce to sniveling lizards when they are faced bravely in battle.*

- *In addition to success, there will be times of failure in your life. Three words: recover, recover, and recover.*

- *To continue writing in your journal and keep learning how to express your deepest emotions. Realize that if you can't write it, you don't understand it.*

- *To present yourself always as a faithful steward of the resources God has entrusted to you. Your time, talents, intelligence, and financial possessions should always be used to His glory.*

- *To revere God as part of loving Him.*

- *To keep a high standard of purity, remembering that purity is not only a commandment from God, but also includes tremendous benefits both now and in the future. Keep yourself accountable and honest with me, your mentors, and one or two other Christian friends that you trust.*

- *Casey, in your own words, that "It's right, to do right, because it's right!" You can never lose by keeping your integrity in check, and doing what you know God wants you to do. Serve Him and others faithfully.*

There is an old saying that a man is not a man until his father says that he is. As I give you your pendant, representing your training and maturity, I say with love and confidence that you are indeed a young man. Along with these men around you, I am committed to your success and look forward to your progression to full manhood. I love you, Casey.

To paraphrase Psalm 19:13, may God continue to refine your life mission as He keeps you from willful sins as His servant; may they not rule over you.

CHAMPION
Symbol and Gift Ideas

CHAMPION Symbol

A fighter pilot shows off the wings pinned on his chest. An Olympic athlete sports his medal. A Green Beret proudly wears a ring on his hand with the Latin phrase De Oppresso Libre (Free the Oppressed) engraved on it. A CHAMPION Symbol is a great way to honor your son's accomplishment in completing the CHAMPION Training. Present it during his celebration ceremony to recognize and commemorate his transition from boyhood into young manhood. This will be a significant and lasting reminder of this milestone in his life, as well as the lessons he has learned with you.

The most meaningful CHAMPION Symbol will be something that your son can wear—a piece of jewelry such as a ring or a pendant. You may locate your own meaningful piece of jewelry or order the specially engraved CHAMPION ring or pendant by going online at www.familylife.com/teknon.

Gift Ideas

Mentors, family members, or friends may want to give your son a special gift in celebration of his accomplishment in completing the CHAMPION Training. Here are some ideas to stimulate your thinking:

- Leather study Bible (engraved)
- Engraved pocketknife
- A compass to remind him to keep his focus on the "true north" of God's Word
- Unique piece of clothing
- Fine writing instrument
- Piece of a collection (coin, stamp, figurine, sports card, etc.)
- Signed and numbered art print
- Key chain
- Specialty coin
- Personalized stationary
- Christian music CD or video
- Mug with a special saying on it
- Binoculars
- A family heirloom with meaning
- Begin a toolbox (with hammer, screwdriver set, wrench set, etc.)
- Telescope
- Leather luggage
- Camera
- Pictures and frames (a frame for snapshots taken during CHAMPION Training or at the celebration ceremony)

Teknon
AND THE
Champion
Warriors

Mission Guide

**AN INTERACTIVE
ADVENTURE TO
EXPLORE COURAGEOUS
MANHOOD**

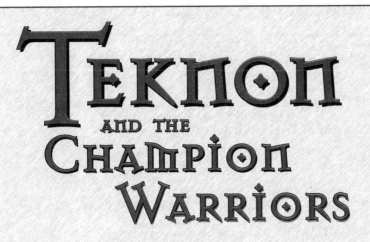

TEKNON
AND THE
CHAMPION
WARRIORS

Mission Guide

An Interactive Adventure to Explore Courageous Manhood

TABLE OF CONTENTS

Vital Documents

What Is a CHAMPION Warrior? 3

CHAMPION Warrior Creed 5

CHAMPION Code 6

The Map of the Mission 8

CHAMPION Sheet of Deeds 9

CHAMPION Sessions

Discussion topics

Session 1   Destination: Kairos . . . . *Fear of the unknown* 11

Session 2A   My Enemy, Your Enemy . . . . *Spiritual warfare* 21
           Part 1

Session 2B   My Enemy, Your Enemy . . . . *Effective stewardship* 31
           Part 2

Session 3   The Second Look . . . . *Boundaries for physical* 41
                                                  intimacy

Session 4   The Company I Keep . . . . *Discernment with friends* . . .53
                                                  Failure recovery–1

Session 5   Ergonian Pride . . . . *Pride; Teachability* 63

Session 6   A Storm of Dishonor . . . . *Honoring family and others* .73

Session 7   An Excellent Choice . . . . *Sexual temptation* 83
                                                  Pornography

Session 8   Faced With Fear . . . . *Fear of rejection and failure* .99

Session 9   Recover, Recover, Recover . . . . . *Comfort zones* 111
                                                  Failure recovery–2

Session 10   Good Enough . . . . *Mediocrity; Anger* 123

Session 11   The Element of Doubt . . . . *Personal integrity* 137
                                                  Romantic relationships

Session 12   Nothing More, Nothing Less, . . *Discouragement* 149
             Nothing Else

Session 13   A Job to Finish . . . . *Perseverance; God's power* .161

Session 14   Back to Back . . . . *Power of the team* 173
                                                  Unique bents

Session 15   Celebration . . . . *Charting your course* 187
                                                  Giving glory to God

Appendix A: Just Do It! . . . . . *How to invite Christ into your life* 198

Appendix B: The CHAMPION Training Program 202

Acknowledgements and Notes 203

About the Author and Illustrator 204

WHAT IS A CHAMPION WARRIOR?

What comes to mind when you hear the word *warrior*? Today, that word refers to many things, like the road warrior who just invested his entire savings into an overpriced motorcycle and dominates the road. Or the weekend warrior, an overstuffed couch potato who sits in an overstuffed chair, watching whatever stuff ESPN is showing all weekend long. And what comes to mind when you hear the word *champion*? Do you think of the guy who won several gold medals in the Olympics? Or the winner of the Indy 500? Those definitions may be true, but they bear little resemblance to the real warriors and champions of years past.

Many years ago, Native Americans living on the Western plains rode on horseback into battle when they reached their 14th birthday. A boy trained with his father early in life so that he could assume responsibility, take care of others, and, if necessary, fight to protect the safety of the tribe. These sons were more than teenagers; they were young men, each with the *soul of a warrior*.

In July 1776, General George Washington led his 5,000 troops, many under the age of 15, into battle against 25,000 of the finest soldiers Great Britain had to offer. Washington's outnumbered armed forces courageously held their position and played a vital role in gaining the freedom Americans enjoy today. These brave soldiers were more than teenagers; they were young men, each with the *heart of a champion*.

Since those days, many in our society have lost the vision for developing courageous young men. As a result, young men have not been given the responsibility they are capable of taking on. Many have not been challenged to think big thoughts and dream big dreams. How about you? Are you infected with the venom of low expectations or are you setting high standards for yourself? What are your values? What are your goals? Are you living a life full of challenge, adventure, and fulfillment?

How would you like to become a young man with the soul of a warrior and the heart of a champion? You can! Are you ready to begin the quest toward courageous manhood? Are you willing to invest the time and energy? If so, the CHAMPION Training adventure is for you!

Your *Mission Guide* includes 16 CHAMPION Sessions that you will complete and then discuss with your dad or leader over the course of several months. You will probably meet together every other week.

Elements of a CHAMPION Session

▲ **CHAMPION Characteristics**—One or two key character traits are highlighted for each session.

▲ **Discussion Topics**—Key subjects you will address in the session are summarized.

▲ **Mission Debrief**—Debriefing is a military practice where a soldier recaps his previous mission activities. This section provides you an opportunity to review with your dad the mission that was assigned at your previous session. You will debrief on your critical maneuver, your action point from the Sheet of Deeds, and the new power verse you memorized.

▲ **Reconnaissance**—Reconnaissance (or "recon") is also a military activity in which a soldier explores an area to gather important information for the mission ahead. In this section you and your dad will discuss an episode from *Teknon and the CHAMPION Warriors*.

▲ **Strategy and Tactics**—Strategy refers to the overall planning of a mission. Tactics refers to the methods used to secure the objectives planned out in the strategy. In this section you and your dad will discuss specific CHAMPION characteristics, investigate strategies and tactics from the Bible, and discover how to apply them in your life.

▲ **Your Mission**—At the end of each CHAMPION Session, your dad will assign a mission to you to be completed before the next session. Each mission includes:

■ **Power Verse:** A new Bible verse related to the session for you to memorize.

■ **Critical Maneuver:** A fun, hands-on project or activity for you and your dad to do together to reinforce what you discussed during your session (movies, interviews, tally surveys, Bible discovery, books, and more movies!).

■ **CHAMPION Sheet of Deeds:** You and your dad will agree on an action point that you will begin to apply before the next session and that you will carry on as you develop these deeds for a lifetime as a CHAMPION.

Get ready for a challenging experience that will change your life!

Courage · Honor · Attitude · Mental toughness · Purity · Integrity · Ownership · Navigation

THE
CHAMPION
WARRIOR CREED

"If I have the Courage to face my fears; Honor, which I show to God[+] and my fellow man; the proper Attitude concerning myself and my circumstances; the Mental Toughness required to make hard decisions; Purity of heart, mind, and body; the Integrity to stand for what I believe, even in the most difficult situations; effective Ownership of all that is entrusted to me; and focused Navigation in order to successfully chart my course in life; I will live as a true CHAMPION Warrior, committed to battling evil, and changing my world for God's glory."

* Note: In the fiction book, *Teknon and the CHAMPION Warriors*, the Warrior King called Pneuma is a fictional character intended to represent God (Father, Son, and Holy Spirit). For this study, the name Pneuma is only used when referring to the fictional story character.

The CHAMPION Code

C OURAGE
H ONOR
A TTITUDE
M ENTAL TOUGHNESS
P URITY
I NTEGRITY
O WNERSHIP
N AVIGATION

Character is the moral strength that grows out of our relationship with God.* Personal growth is expressed through the physical, emotional, social, mental, and especially spiritual areas of our lives.

Characteristics of a CHAMPION Warrior

COURAGE

I will cultivate bravery and trust in God. I will break out of my comfort zone by seeking to conquer my fears. I will learn to recover, recover, and recover again.

HONOR

I will honor God by obeying Him and acknowledging Him as the complete source of my life, both now and through eternity. I will treat my parents, siblings, friends, and acquaintances with respect. I will appreciate the strengths and accept the weaknesses of all my "team members."

ATTITUDE

I will cultivate a disposition of humility. I will assume a correct and hopeful view of myself as a member of God's family. I will improve my ability to manage anger and discouragement. I will develop and enjoy an appropriate sense of humor.

Mental Toughness

I will allow God to direct my thinking toward gaining common sense and wisdom. I will use discernment when making hard decisions. I will desire respect from others rather than compromise my convictions for acceptance or approval.

Purity

I will train myself to keep the temple of my body and mind uncorrupted mentally, emotionally, and physically. I commit to avoid and flee sexual temptation.

Integrity

I will seek to acquire a clear understanding of who I am in Christ so that I may have a deeper comprehension of what I believe, what I stand for, and how I can live out those convictions in the most difficult circumstances, whether I am alone or with others. I will allow other people to hold me accountable to standards of excellence.

Ownership

I will apply effective stewardship by using my life and the resources God entrusts to me—including my possessions, time, and talents—for His glory. I will seek contentment in God's provision for my needs. I will learn to practice delayed gratification.

Navigation

I will allow God to chart my course by accepting my mission from Him, and I will complete that mission by trusting in Him. I will study the Bible, God's Word, so I can know Him better and gain His strength and direction for my life. I will become goal-oriented by learning to focus my attention on completing worthwhile short-term and long-term objectives.

*Note: In the fiction book, *Teknon and the CHAMPION Warriors*, the Warrior King called Pneuma is a fictional character intended to represent God (Father, Son, and Holy Spirit). For this study, the name Pneuma is only used when referring to the fictional story character.

The Map of the Mission

1
15

2
Kopto

Northros

12 13

10 11

3
Forest
of
Perasmos

Hedon
Bay

9

14

4
Bia

8

6

7

5   Ergo

Hudor
Sea

SARKINOS
underground

The CHAMPION Sheet of Deeds

Following are my personal action points for each session of my CHAMPION Training. I will strive to apply these action points during my training adventure and also will make an effort to continue applying them as I seek to grow in godly character for a lifetime of living as a CHAMPION.

SESSION 1: _____

SESSION 2A: _____

SESSION 2B: _____

SESSION 3: _____

SESSION 4: _____

SESSION 5: _____

SESSION 6: _____

SESSION 7: _____

SESSION 8: _____

SESSION 9: _____

SESSION 10: _____

SESSION 11: _____

SESSION 12: _____

SESSION 13: _____

SESSION 14: _____

SESSION 15: _____

SESSION 1:
DESTINATION:
KAIROS

CHAMPION Characteristics

Courage and Navigation

POWER VERSE: PHILIPPIANS 4:6-7

Be anxious for nothing, but in everything by prayer and supplication with thanksgiving let your requests be made known to God. And the peace of God, which surpasses all comprehension, will guard your hearts and your minds in Christ Jesus.

STORY SUMMARY

This initial episode introduces most of the primary characters in *Teknon and the CHAMPION Warriors*. As the story begins, we learn that Kratos and his son, Teknon, are journeying to the planet Kairos, accompanied by Teknon's mentors—Tharreo (nicknamed Tor), Epios (Epps), Artios (Arti), and Mataios (Matty). Although we don't know the exact reason for their mission, it appears that the team is preparing to battle an evil threat to their home planet, Basileia. Teknon is somewhat anxious about what awaits them.

In this session, you will have the opportunity to discuss with your son the importance of taking responsibility for his actions and attitudes, as well as how to trust God for what is rightly God's responsi-bility. You'll also be able to explore the process of overcoming fear of the unknown when preparing for a specific challenge.

Question #2 Tip:

In order for your son to see the value in memorizing the creed, you need to join with him in reading and memorizing it. He will take his cues from you.

Do the thing you fear, and fear will die.

Anonymous

Discussion Topics

Preparing for a challenging task

Overcoming fear of the unknown

Accepting my responsibility and trusting God with the rest

Mission Debrief

1. Normally, this section will be used to debrief together about how your mission assignment from the previous session went.

2. Read the CHAMPION Warrior Creed out loud together (see page 5).

Reconnaissance

1. Carefully review the Map of the Mission on page 8 before beginning this section. Identify where the team is located in episode 1.

2a. What is the CHAMPION definition of **Courage**? Of **Navigation**? (Refer to the CHAMPION Code on page 6.)

Answer: "I will cultivate bravery and trust in God. I will break out of my comfort zone by seeking to conquer my fears. I will learn to recover, recover, and recover again."

Answer: "I will allow God to chart my course by accepting my mission from Him, and I will complete that mission by trusting in Him. I will study the Bible, God's Word, so I can know Him better and gain His strength and direction for my life. I will become goal-oriented by learning to focus my attention on completing worthwhile short-term and long-term objectives."

3. **What opportunity do you think the team has before them on the planet Kairos?**

   Answer: Judging from Kratos' response to his wife, Paideia, (" ... too much is at stake ... ") the team is pursuing a mission to protect and defend something of great value. They are clearly embarking on a mission that has great risks.

4. **Why do you think Teknon was nervous about this mission?**

   Answer: Teknon feared the unknown. He was facing challenges that were out of his comfort zone. It also appears that Teknon's spiritual foundation is not developed at this point.

Optional Questions

5. **What kind of training do you think Teknon undertook to prepare for this journey?**

   Answer: Even though you don't yet know the nature of the team's trip, you can brainstorm with your son that Teknon needed to prepare himself physically, mentally, and spiritually for the challenges ahead.

6. **What do you think Teknon's responsibilities were as he prepared physically, mentally, and spiritually for this mission?**

   Answer: To train diligently without grumbling and to learn all he could from his father and mentors.

---

7. **As the team members stood on the assimilator platform, Kratos said, "... no man is worthy who is not ready at all times to risk body, status, and life itself for a great cause." What do you think Kratos meant? What kind of cause do you think he was talking about?**

   Answer: A great cause, such as the team's upcoming mission, often requires great risk and effort. Such a cause, if given to us by God, is worth whatever sacrifice He requires of us to accomplish it.

At the end of episode 1, the team is leaving for the planet Kairos. *Kairos* is a Greek word that refers to a God-given opportunity at a specific point in time. Tell your son about the meaning of Kairos and then discuss question 3.

You may also want to explain that many Greek names appear in this story because the Bible's New Testament was first written in Greek, the key trade and cultural language during the first century A.D.

QUESTION #5 TIP:
Emphasize to your son the importance of preparation when faced with a formidable challenge or task.

There lives in each of us a hero, awaiting a call to action.

H. Jackson Brown, Jr.

8. How would you apply Kratos' advice to Teknon: "It's all right to be nervous. The trick is learning to channel that nervous energy into something productive"?

Answer: Nervousness can alert us to dangers. It is not a problem if we learn to control our fear and focus our nervous energy toward completing the task at hand. Worrying, in and of itself, is unproductive at best.

STRATEGY AND TACTICS

1. Review Philippians 4:6-7. What do these verses say about fear or anxiety? How can we face our fears and be at peace?

Answer: God does not want His people to be fearful or anxious about anything. If we give over our fears and concerns to God in prayer, then He will give us a peace that cannot be explained.

TAKING RESPONSIBILITY

In 1917, Will Stoneman gathered all of his courage as he stepped out of the train and into the frigid Canadian air of Winnipeg, Manitoba. He gazed for a moment at the bright lights and endless activity. At age 17, this rugged farm boy from the hills of South Dakota was about to undertake the greatest challenge of his life. In a few short hours, he would begin a 500-mile dog sled race in hopes of winning the $10,000 first prize.

Will needed the money to save his family's farm and pay for his college education. His father had died in a sledding accident only a few weeks earlier, leaving the family without the income from their cabinet-making trade. Now Will was alone in a big city, about to race against the finest sled teams in the world over some of the roughest territory in North America.

What would most teenagers have said if they were faced with Will's challenge?

What can I do? I'm just a teenager.

It's too late for me to make a difference now.

Even if I tried, I'd probably drop out the first day, so I won't bother.

I don't have the experience. Why can't somebody else race for our family?

Will Stoneman didn't choose to make excuses. He saw an opportunity to help his family, and he jumped at it. He courageously took responsibility to compete in a difficult race, even though he had only a month to prepare for it. During that month, he worked as hard as he could, training himself to race on little food and even less sleep than any of his competitors. He did everything within his ability to contribute to his family's success.

His determination shocked the entire country when, against incredible odds, he won the race! His unwillingness to give up, regardless of the circumstances, earned him the nickname "Iron Will."

2. Read James 1:22-26. What happens if we only listen to the Word and do nothing? (See verse 22.)

    Answer: We cannot merely listen to the Word of God; we must take responsibility to obey it. Otherwise, we delude or fool ourselves.

3. What will happen to the person who takes responsibility to do what the Word says? (See verse 25.)

    Answer: An effectual doer of the Word will be blessed in all he does.

The Rings of
Responsibility are pro-
vided to help your son
identify the areas in
which he can assume
responsibility. Help
him to start thinking
through this process.
He will have opportun-
ities throughout the
CHAMPION Training
to understand what he
can and cannot assume
responsibility for in his
life.

Read the following
quote to your son to
further explain the con-
cept of the
CHAMPION's Ring.
In *The Book of Virtues*,
William Bennett wrote,
"To be responsible is to
be answerable; to be
accountable.
Irresponsible behavior is
immature behavior.
Taking responsibility,
being responsible is a
sign of maturity. When
we strive to help our
children become
responsible persons, we
are helping them toward
maturity."

THE RINGS OF RESPONSIBILITY

GOD'S RING

CHAMPION's RING

THE CHAMPION's RING

Notice that the Hoplon shield has two rings on it. These circles represent the CHAMPION Warrior's Rings of Responsibility
in life. The inner ring is the CHAMPION's Ring, which symbol-
izes the behaviors and activities in which the CHAMPION can
make a difference by obeying God. Inside this ring, a CHAMPI-
ON completes his responsibilities without grumbling and without blaming other people for the choices he makes.

A CHAMPION regularly reads the Bible and prays for direction so that he can know how God wants him to think and act.
He trusts God to give him the power to make the best choices,
while at the same time taking responsibility to do everything he
can to live like a CHAMPION.

When we obey God and courageously take responsibility for
our choices and actions, we move a step closer toward becoming
CHAMPIONs.

4. What are some behaviors and activities that should go into
    the CHAMPION's Ring?

    Answers: Help your son identify some activities that you know he has
    control over:

    * Studying   * Proper physical exercise   * Bible reading
    * The words he speaks   * Praying, time with God   * His attitude
    * Family chores   * Eating nutritiously

5. In what areas do you need to assume more responsibility in your life? Be specific!

GOD'S RING

There are also times when a CHAMPION should not attempt to assume responsibility. Look at the outer ring of the Hoplon. This section of the shield represents God's Ring.

6. Read Psalm 28:7-8. Where does the strength of a CHAMPION come from?

Answer: These verses say it is the Lord who is our strength and our shield.

7. Read John 15:4-5. What do you think it means to abide (some Bible translations say "remain") in Christ?

Answer: A branch cannot survive unless it is completely bound to the vine. We must continually seek to be in close relationship to Jesus Christ to experience both His continuing forgiveness and His power.

8. What can we accomplish if we don't abide in Christ?

Answer: Nothing that has any eternal value to God.

QUESTION #5 TIPS:
Help your son think through his options, and come up with one area of responsibility. You can use his choice as the action point (Deed) for this session, or choose another.

Earlier, you mentioned to your son that *kairos* is Greek word that refers to a God-given opportunity at a specific point in time. Remind him that God gives us opportunities, big and small, to join Him to make a difference and help others.

Let me assert my firm belief, that the only thing to fear is fear itself.

Franklin D. Roosevelt

QUOTE NOTE:
In what *Time* magazine called one of the three most significant speeches of the 20th century, President Roosevelt inspired Americans to look beyond the fear caused by the Great Depression. He knew that if fear were not controlled, it would paralyze the people's efforts to recover as a nation. This may be a good time to ask your son, "Why do we need to control our fear?"

"Have I not
commanded you?
Be strong and
courageous. Do
not be tremble or be
dismayed, for the
Lord your God is
with you wherever
you go."

Joshua 1:9

A CHAMPION takes responsibility for his actions, but everything else in life is God's responsibility and remains in God's Ring. If we obey God and seek Him daily, He will take care of us in every way.

9. Read Joshua 1:9. Why should we be strong and courageous?

> Answer: Because God has promised that He will be with us wherever we go. With God as our protector, we have no one and nothing to fear.

10. Name one thing that you worry about, something you currently keep in the CHAMPION's Ring that really should be placed into God's Ring.

> Answers:
>
> · What other people think about me
>
> · How others respond to me
>
> · My parents' relationship with me
>
> · My friends' choices

IMPORTANT NOTE:
If your son has not invited Christ into his life, walk him through the exercise entitled "Just Do It!" Read it several times before you share it with your son. If you, personally, haven't invited Christ to live in you, to forgive you, and to make you a new creation, now would be a good time so that you can grow in your spiritual relationship along with your son as you proceed through the remainder of the CHAMPION Training.

God's Ring encircles the CHAMPION's Ring because God is constantly with us, and His love surrounds us wherever we are. It is God's responsibility to watch over us and protect us. In fact, the Bible tells us that God is our shield (Psalm 28:7).

God is even responsible for paying for our failures and sins. Only He can give us eternal life through His Son, Jesus Christ. When we receive Jesus into our lives, we are given a special relationship as a son in God's family and covered by the protection of His all-powerful love.

If you don't yet have this kind of personal relationship with God, but would like to be under His love and protection, turn to the section entitled Just Do It! in the Appendix.

The Main Things I Learned

in this Champion Session are:

_____

_____

_____

_____

_____

CHAMPION Sheet of Deeds

Go to the **CHAMPION** Sheet of Deeds on page 9 and write down **one thing you will do** in the upcoming days (and beyond) to apply the main things you learned in session 1.

Check one of the suggestions below for your son to write down as his action point on his CHAMPION Sheet of Deeds for session 1. Descriptions and explanations of these action points are provided in the Think Tank (chapter 5) of this *Mentor Guide*.

❏ Ask you son to read Psalms and Proverbs according to a regular schedule and to keep a journal for capturing what he learns.

❏ Help your son develop a list of his fears and worries. Then pray with him and reinforce Philippians 4:6-7 and the concept of the Rings of Responsibility.

❏ Help your son begin reading his Bible regularly, using a basic set of study and application questions and a journal for recording what he is reading.

❏ Create your own unique action point.

MAIN THINGS:
Help your son by suggesting some key truths that he should have learned during this session, such as what things are his responsibility (CHAMPION's Ring) and what things are God's responsibility (God's Ring), ways to overcome fears and preparation for a challenge.

There are times when obedient acts of self-sacrifice and courage merit both admiration and profound gratitude.

William Bennett

SHEET OF DEEDS:
Only a *brief* description of each action point is provided here. Go to the Think Tank (chapter 5) for complete instructions.

Your Mission

Complete your mission and CHAMPION Session prep before you meet for session 2A.

POWER VERSE: PHILIPPIANS 4:6-7

Date memorized: _____

CRITICAL MANEUVER

This will reinforce what you learned today. Obtain your manuever instructions from your father.

CHAMPION SHEET OF DEEDS

Begin to apply your action point from your Sheet of Deeds.

CHAMPION SESSION PREP

Reread episode 2 of *Teknon and the CHAMPION Warriors*, and then complete the questions in session 2A of your *Mission Guide* on your own. **Our next CHAMPION Session will be:**

DATE: _____

TIME: _____

PLACE: _____

CRITICAL MANEUVER:
Go to the Think Tank (chapter 5 of this guide) and select one of the critical maneuvers listed under session 1 to accomplish with your son.

SESSION PREP:
Ask your son to invest the time to complete his mission and CHAMPION Session prep on his own before your next session. Explain that if he does this, your CHAMPION Session will be smoother, shorter, and much more effective for him.
.

SCHEDULE TIP:
First, check both your calendar and your son's calendar. Each of you should record the date, time, and place for your next session in the space provided.

CHAMPION circular emblem with surrounding text: Courage · Honor · Attitude · Mental toughness · Purity · Integrity · Ownership · Navigation

SESSION 2A:
MY ENEMY,
YOUR ENEMY

CHAMPION Characteristics

Mental Toughness and Navigation

POWER VERSE: JAMES 4:7–8A

Submit therefore to God. Resist the devil and he will flee from you. Draw near to God and He will draw near to you.

STORY SUMMARY

In this episode, Kratos, Teknon, and the mentors arrive on the diverse planet Kairos, where they will carry out their mission. In the commercial market of the village of Kopto, Teknon makes an impulse purchase he later regrets. A skirmish occurs in which the team members use their unique weapons for the first time. Tor, Epps, Arti, and Matty are separated from Kratos and Teknon. Teknon and his father set up camp in the wooded outskirts of Kopto. Teknon learns from his father about the team's weapons and about Magos, the powerful enemy who is bent on destroying the societal values of Basileia. While building an army on Kairos, Magos is setting a plan into motion that will lead to his domination of Basileia unless he is stopped. Kratos then tells Teknon the origin of the CHAMPION Warriors and invites him to become a CHAMPION Warrior. He also challenges Teknon to join him in the quest to defeat Magos and recover the Logos. Teknon accepts on all counts. At the close of the episode, Kratos coaches Teknon on the pitfalls of impulse spending.

You will have the opportunity during this session to discuss the topic of spiritual warfare with your son. It's vital, as episode 2 brings out, to accurately assess the enemy's capabilities. Satan, our brilliant enemy, is plotting to ruin as many people as he can. We must not underestimate Satan and his desire to cause our demise. We live in a sinful world, and it's important for us to understand Satan's strategies in deception and temptation.

However, you will be able to encourage your son with the knowledge that our all-powerful God has defeated Satan through Christ's death on the cross. Even though we will face daily spiritual battles concerning issues of right and wrong, we can remember that God has already won the war (Romans 8:1-2), and He will eventually establish His kingdom and seal Satan's defeat.

QUESTION #3 TIP:

If your son successfully memorized the verse, have him date the verse in session 1 of his *Mission Guide*.

DISCUSSION TOPICS

Assessing the enemy
Embracing the mission you have been given
Learning to defeat the enemy

MISSION DEBRIEF

1. Discuss your mission from session 1. Did you complete your maneuver? If so, what did you learn? If not, why not?

2. Did you start applying your first action point from your Sheet of Deeds? If so, what did you learn? Have you had any struggles in trying to apply it?

3. Recite your memory verse (Philippians 4:6-7) from session 1.

4. Read the CHAMPION Warrior Creed out loud together again (see page 5).

RECONNAISSANCE

1. Carefully review the Map of the Mission on page 8 before beginning this section. Identify where the team is located in episode 2.

2. What is the CHAMPION definition of **Mental Toughness**? Of **Navigation**? (Refer to the CHAMPION Code on page 6.)

Answer for Mental Toughness: "I will allow God to direct my thinking toward gaining common sense and wisdom. I will use discernment when making hard decisions. I will desire respect from others rather than compromise my convictions for acceptance or approval."

Answer for Navigation: "I will allow God to chart my course by accepting my mission from Him, and I will complete that mission by trusting in Him. I will study the Bible, God's Word, so I can know Him better and gain His strength and direction for my life. I will become goal-oriented by learning to focus my attention on completing worthwhile short-term and long-term objectives."

Nearly all men can stand adversity, but if you want to test a man's character, give him power.

Abraham Lincoln

3. In this episode, Kratos describes the team's primary enemy. Who is he and why is he so dangerous? What is he trying to do?

Answer: Magos is dangerous because he's brilliant and his objective is to destroy the moral and spiritual foundation of the people of Basileia. If he succeeds, the people will lose their ability to distinguish right from wrong and will forget their spiritual heritage. They will thus become more susceptible to tyrannical rule. Then, with the help of his android army, Magos plans to control and rule the planet.

4. Who is the team's secondary enemy created by Magos? What is his function?

Answer: Scandalon's function is to obey Magos by deceiving, tempting, and injuring the team.

5. **Why does Magos want to defeat Kratos?**

   Answer: Years before, Kratos made the right choice and refused Magos' offer to become a cyborg. Magos has long resented Kratos' refusal, but he also knows that his old business partner would still be a great ally in conquering Basileia. Regardless, Magos knows that Kratos is now committed to stopping his evil plan.

6. **What did Magos steal? Why did he steal it? Why did Kratos want to get it back?**

   Answer: He stole the Logos to remove the only remaining archive of the CHAMPION Warriors and Pneuna's teachings from the people of Basileia. Kratos knew the importance of the Logos and its purpose as a beacon to point his people toward a relationship with Pneuma, as well as providing direction to live according to Pneuma's principles.

7. **Why did Kratos refuse to be recreated and join Magos?**

   Answer: Because he knew becoming a cyborg was a prideful and dangerous act. Kratos believed in the principles taught by the ancient CHAMPION Warriors. He would not risk violating his convictions and his relationship with Pneuma by taking Magos' offer.

8. **What did Kratos mean when he said, "Where there is no character, there is no threat to Magos."**

   Answer: Without people of character who are opposed to the moral and spiritual decay of their society, Magos would have little trouble in dominating the planet Basileia.

9. **The Greek word *artios*, refers to something that is complete and fitted perfectly. What does Artios (Arti) do to live up to his name?**

   Answer: In episode 1 Epps says, "You know Arti doesn't understand plus or minus, Matty. He's always on target." Arti is the team member who is responsible for accurate and detailed analysis of the environment through the use of his Sensatron (his own invention). Arti, who disables the lynch mob in this episode, has an analytical temperament. Organized and controlled, Arti likes things done right the first time.

STRATEGY AND TACTICS

ENEMY ASSESSMENT

A hunter in the wilderness aimed at a bear with his gun. Suddenly the bear shouted, "Why do you want to shoot me?"

The hunter replied, "I need a fur coat for the winter."

The bear responded, "Well, all I want is a good breakfast. Why don't we sit down and discuss our needs?"

The hunter thought for a minute, then sat down and discussed the issue with the bear. After a short time, the only one left was the bear, who did indeed enjoy a good breakfast. The hunter ended up with a fur coat, but not at all in the way he had planned. In other words, the hunter let his guard down at the wrong time.

In the same way, Kratos knew he could not join Magos, or even discuss joining him. Kratos hated everything that his former partner wanted to accomplish. To join Magos, Kratos would have had to become like the cyborg, almost a part of the enemy he sought to defeat. Kratos realized he could not let his guard down for a minute with his enemy.

WHO IS YOUR ENEMY?

Did you know that the Bible says you have an enemy? And did you realize that you should hate this enemy and everything that he stands for? Your enemy is Satan, also known as the devil. At one time, Satan was an angel, part of God's heavenly host (Isaiah 14:12-15, Luke 11:14-23).

But Satan became prideful and actually challenged God's authority. Like Magos, who chose to transform himself, Satan took matters into his own hands and allowed his pride to direct his actions. He wanted to become something he was not. He wanted to become God. As a result, God kicked him out of heaven forever.

When Satan was cast out, many of the other angels joined him in his rebellion. These angels now serve him around the

IMPORTANT NOTE: Throughout *Teknon and the CHAMPION Warriors*, your son will see four distinctly different temperaments illustrated through Teknon's mentors. In session 14 he will have an opportunity to identify the strengths of his own temperament as a result of reading about Tharreo, Epios, Artios, and Mataios.

world, which is currently in his control (1 John 5:19), by tempting, seducing, and enticing us to disobey God. Just like Scandalon is serving Magos, these angels serve Satan in his evil schemes.

Satan hates you and everything about you because he hates God. If you have invited Christ into your life, you are going to spend eternity with Christ in heaven. That is something Satan will never be able to do. Satan's mission is to ruin as many people as he can. He wants to accomplish his mission before Christ comes back again to rule forever.

1. Read 1 Peter 5:8. What does the Bible say that Satan wants to do to us?

   Answer: He wants to devour (ruin, destroy) us. We must realize that Satan is always at battle with us.

2. How should we respond to Satan's plan for us?

   Answer: Be self-controlled, sober in spirit, and alert. We need to make sure we are spending adequate time with the Lord to gain His direction, wisdom, and protection. We cannot let our guard down in any area where Satan could introduce temptation.

Satan wants to infect our thoughts, our desires, and our actions so that we will be ineffective for God. If you are a Christian, Satan can't prevent you from going to heaven, but he can make your life ineffective and miserable if you allow him to do so. What's worse, he will use your poor choices, ineffectiveness, and disobedience to display you as a poor example of God's sons to the world.

3. What do you think Satan would like for us to think about?

Answer: Any desire or thought that would hinder our relationship with God and others (anxiety, lust, bitterness, envy, etc.).

Remember, Satan is a brilliant enemy (see Ephesians 6:10-18). Never underestimate him. He knows what tempts you and then plots to bring those temptations into your path. Every time you make a decision in obedience to God, Satan loses. Every time you make a wrong decision, like telling a lie or cheating on a test, he leaves you to deal with the consequences and brings a more serious temptation into your path, hoping you will make the wrong decision again.

But there's good news! God knows that Satan is your enemy. Your Heavenly Father wants to provide all of the strength you need to defeat Satan every day. Through Jesus' death, burial, and resurrection, He has defeated the devil (Genesis 3:15) and has overcome the world (John 16:33). All you have to do is put your trust in Christ and obey His instructions to be victorious.

IMPORTANT NOTE: Throughout the CHAMPION Training, your son will be faced with two key realities. The first is to trust God, letting Him control God's Ring. The second is to work diligently to obey God in thought and deed, taking responsibility for the CHAMPION'S Ring.

DEFEATING THE ENEMY

4. Read James 4:7-8. What does the Bible say to do to the devil to make him flee from you?

Answer: First, submit to God. Then resist Satan and his temptations. You must cleanse your hands (actions) and purify your heart (thoughts, attitudes, willful desires). He will help you if you draw near to Him.

My message to you is: Be courageous! ... Be as brave as your fathers before you. Have faith! Go forward.

Thomas A. Edison

IMPORTANT NOTE:
Encourage your son to continue facing his fears. During this and future CHAMPION Sessions, encourage him to identify his fears one by one, and help him devise ways to overcome them on a regular basis. In effect, you will be teaching him to be a "Dolios Slayer." Teknon, at the end of his journey, will face Dolios, a creature who has the ability to transform himself into that which his opponent fears the most.

IMPORTANT NOTE:
Another key element in spiritual warfare is putting on the "full armor of God" (Ephesians 6). You will discuss this topic with your son in session 7.

"Have I not commanded you? Be strong and courageous! Do not tremble or be dismayed, for the Lord your God is with you wherever you go."

Joshua 1:9

---

5. **Why is it important for us to admit that Satan has influence in this world?**

   Answer: We need to recognize that we have an enemy and become aware of his schemes and tactics.

6. **Should we fear Satan? Why or why not?**

   Answer: No, but we must learn his strategies and always be on the alert.

The Bible also says, "Greater is He [Christ] who is in you than he who is in the world [Satan]." You must realize that Satan is a formidable enemy, but you do not need to fear him. If you are a Christian, you belong to Almighty God, so He will give you guidance and protection. God also assigns His angels to us; they are charged with guarding those who fear and follow Him (Psalm 34:7, 91:11).

7. **What can you do to protect yourself according to God's instructions in Psalm 119:9-11?**

   Answer:

   (1) Stay pure by living according to God's Word.

   (2) Seek God with all your heart. According to Jesus in Mark 12:30, the greatest commandment is to "... love the Lord your God with all your heart, and with all your soul, and with all your mind, and with all your strength."

   (3) Continue pursuing a strong relationship with the Lord.

   (4) Treasure and store up His Word in your heart—read, study, and memorize it.

MAIN THING:

Help your son by suggesting some key truths that he should have learned during this session, such as submitting to God, overcoming temptation, and understanding and resisting Satan's schemes.

THE Main Things I learned in this Champion Session are:

_____

_____

_____

_____

_____

CHAMPION Sheet of Deeds

SHEET OF DEEDS:

Only a *brief* description of each action point is provided here. Go to the Think Tank (chapter 5) for complete instructions.

Go to the CHAMPION Sheet of Deeds on page 9 and write down **one thing you will begin to do** before the next session (and beyond) to apply the main things you learned in session 2A.

Check one of the suggestions below for your son to write down as his action point on his CHAMPION Sheet of Deeds for session 2A. Descriptions and explanations of these action points are provided in the Think Tank (chapter 5) of this guide.

❏ Listen together to the audio version of C.S. Lewis' classic book *The Screwtape Letters* for an eye-opening and entertaining fictional account of evil scheming (for mature teens).

❏ Ask your son to read the fiction book *This Present Darkness* on the topic of spiritual warfare and the power of prayer. You should read it as well so you two can discuss it.

❏ Create your own unique action point.

YOUR MISSION

Complete your mission and CHAMPION Session Prep before you meet for session 2B.

POWER VERSE: JAMES 4:7–8A

Date memorized: _____

CRITICAL MANEUVER

This will reinforce what you learned today. Obtain your maneuver instructions from your father.

CHAMPION SHEET OF DEEDS

Begin to apply your action point from your Sheet of Deeds.

CHAMPION SESSION PREP

Reread episode 2 of *Teknon and the CHAMPION Warriors*, and then complete the questions in session 2B in your *Mission Guide* on your own. **Our next CHAMPION Session will be:**

DATE:
_____

TIME:
_____

PLACE:
_____

Courage • Honor • Attitude • Mental toughness • Purity • Integrity • Ownership • Navigation

Session 2B: My Enemy, Your Enemy

CHAMPION Characteristic

Ownership

Power Verse: Luke 16:10 (NIV)

Whoever can be trusted with very little can also be trusted with much, and whoever is dishonest with very little will also be dishonest with much.

Story Summary

In this episode, Kratos, Teknon, and the mentors arrive on the diverse planet Kairos, where they will carry out their mission. In the commercial market of the village of Kopto, Teknon makes an impulse purchase he later regrets. A skirmish occurs in which the team members use their unique weapons for the first time. Tor, Epps, Arti, and Matty are separated from Kratos and Teknon. Teknon and his father set up camp in the wooded outskirts of Kopto. Teknon learns from his father about the team's weapons and about Magos, the powerful enemy who is bent on destroying the societal values of Basileia. While building an army on Kairos, Magos is setting a plan into motion that will lead to his domination of Basileia unless he is stopped. Kratos then tells Teknon the origin of the CHAMPION Warriors and invites him to become a CHAMPION Warrior. He also challenges Teknon to join him in the quest to defeat Magos and recover the Logos. Teknon accepts on both counts. At the close of the episode, Kratos coaches Teknon on the pitfalls of impulse spending.

In this session, you will
have the opportunity to
discuss with your son
the importance of effec-
tive financial steward-
ship. Learning how to
spend money wisely is
an important lesson that
will help your son as he
gains greater financial
responsibility in the
future. The hazards of
impulse spending will
also be discussed.

Discussion Topics

Learning that God owns all things
Becoming an effective steward of our resources

Mission Debrief

1. Discuss your mission from session 2A. Did you complete your maneuver? If so, what did you learn? If not, why not?

QUESTION #3 TIP:

If your son successfully
memorized the verse,
have him date the verse
in session 2A of his
Mission Guide.

2. Did you start applying your new action point from your Sheet of Deeds? How are these action points affecting your mind-set?

3. Recite your power verse (James 4:7-8a) from session 2B.

4. Read the CHAMPION Warrior Creed out loud together again (see page 5).

Reconnaissance

1. Carefully review the Map of the Mission on page 8 before beginning this section. Identify where the team is located in episode 2.

2. What is the CHAMPION definition of **Ownership**? (Refer to the CHAMPION Code on page 6.)

Answer: "I will apply effective stewardship by using my life and the resources God entrusts to me—including my possessions, time, and talents—for His glory. I will seek contentment in God's provision for my needs. I will learn to practice delayed gratification."

3. Why did Teknon buy the Shocktech?

Answer: Because it looked sharp and felt good in his hand. He spent impulsively on emotion and then tried to justify his decision.

4. Did Teknon need the Shocktech? Why or why not?

Answer: Teknon did not need it because his father and the mentors had already provided for his needs for protection and defense.

5a. Was Teknon free to spend his money the way he chose to spend it?

Answer: Yes, it was Teknon's money and his father did not scold him for spending it.

5b. Was Teknon wise in the spending choice he made? Why?

Answer: No, he made an impulsive purchase and did not take time to consider the implications of his purchase. One example of the lack of wisdom was that he used the majority of his money right at the beginning when it was set aside to cover expenses for his entire journey.

6. What did Kratos recommend to Teknon about spending money?

Answer: In order for him to spend wisely, not impulsively, Kratos gave three specific guidelines:

Ask yourself if you really need it.

Take time to think before making a purchase.

Consider how much you have to spend and what it is best spent on.

QUESTION #7 TIP:
Discuss specific examples of needs and wants in your life and in your son's life.

7. What do you think is the difference between a need and a want?

QUESTION #8 TIP:
Ask your son to identify some specific examples for this question. Give him an example of a time when you practiced delayed gratification with regard to your finances. Try to suggest a purchase he wants to make or one he has made recently where he should give (or should have given) his decision greater consideration.

8. Kratos said, "You can splurge once in a while, but give yourself enough time to think about it before you make the purchase." What items are you tempted to buy impulsively?

STRATEGY AND TACTICS

EFFECTIVE STEWARDSHIP

1. Is it wrong to spend money? Absolutely not, but God wants us to spend it wisely. Did you know there are more verses in the Bible concerning money than on almost any other subject? Why do you think there are so many verses about money?

    Answer: Because money is such an integral, and visible part of our lives. How we handle money is an outward reflection of our inner beliefs and convictions. It has been said that if you want to see what's important to a man, look at his calendar and his checkbook.

    Money is a tool God has given each of us to use and to manage. The way you manage money often reflects what you think about Who provided it to you. Managing money is a visible expression of your relationship with God—your values and your trust in Him.

2. What can happen when a family gets into the habit of spending money on the spur of the moment like Teknon did?

    QUESTION #2 TIP: This is an opportunity to discuss how easily impulsive spending can lead to unnecessary and/or extravagant purchases that create harmful personal debt. Accumulating debt can develop into a dangerous habit that is hard to break and will hurt you and your family later.

3. Ecclesiastes was written by King Solomon, one of the richest people who ever lived. Solomon had more money than he could spend, although the Bible says he spent quite a bit. What does Ecclesiastes 2:10-11 say about spending money?

    Answer: Even if we have all that we can spend, and deny ourselves nothing, as Solomon did, we still will not find true happiness in the experience. He said the pursuit of pleasure, wealth, and even accomplishment is like chasing the wind—a total waste of time and energy. Possessions and wealth are only tools to help us serve God; they will not provide us with long-term contentment and satisfaction.

Solomon realized that he shouldn't have been so frivolous and irresponsible in his spending. Likewise, whether you have a lot of money or a little money, God expects you to use it wisely. When you do that, you are considered a good steward or manager.

4. According to Matthew 25:14-30, how much money did the owner give each servant? How did he decide what to give each one?

Answer: The amount varied for each servant. The owner gave to each of his servants according to his particular ability.

5. What did the owner want the servants to do with the money?

Answer: The passage says the owner entrusted the money to his servants, meaning that they should be good stewards of the money and invest it wisely.

6. Which servants were good stewards?

Answer: All of the servants, except for the one who buried his money and did not accomplish anything with the amount entrusted to him.

7. What do you think is the difference between an owner and a steward?

Answer: An owner has legal possession and rights to something. A steward is one who is entrusted with the possessions of the owner, but he has no rights to those possessions.

God is the owner of all good and perfect things on this earth. We are His stewards. What a privilege we have to be entrusted by God with His resources! God doesn't mind if you spend money. He may not even mind if you occasionally spend money on something you really want that you really don't need. But that should be the exception, not the rule.

Remember, God owns it all—our time, our talent, our possessions, and our money. He entrusts them to us. Think about what you buy before you buy it. Don't buy on the spur of the moment. Think and pray for wisdom before you make a big purchase. Seek wise counsel from others who are good stewards.

8. How can you become a good steward of your money and possessions?

QUESTION #8 TIP: Even at this age, your son can begin to be a good steward. He can begin the process of tithing, saving, and spending wisely.

Be a good steward of everything that God entrusts to you. And remember, never spend more than 100 specas for a Shocktech!

MAIN THINGS:

If needed, help your son by suggesting some key truths that he should have learned during this session, such as the importance of effective stewardship and avoiding impulse spending.

THE Main Things I learned in this Champion Session are:

_____

_____

_____

_____

_____

SHEET OF DEEDS:

Only a *brief* description of each action point is provided here. Go to the Think Tank (chapter 5) for complete instructions.

So often we spend money we don't have, on things we don't need, to impress other people we don't even like.

Sam Bartlett

CHAMPION Sheet of Deeds

Go to the CHAMPION Sheet of Deeds on page 9 and write down **one thing you will begin to do** before the next session (and beyond) to apply the main things you learned in session 2B.

Check one of the suggestions below for your son to write down as his action point on his CHAMPION Sheet of Deeds for session 2B. Descriptions and explanations of these action points are provided in the Think Tank (chapter 5) of this guide.

❑ Help your son set up a simple budget system using envelopes. This exercise will help him begin the process of effective ownership and will develop a lifelong habit.

❑ Ask your son to commit to avoiding impulse purchases. Set specific guidelines with him.

❑ Create your own unique action point.

YOUR MISSION

Complete your mission and CHAMPION Session Prep before you meet for session 3.

POWER VERSE: LUKE 16:10

Date memorized: _____

CRITICAL MANEUVER

This will reinforce what you learned today. Obtain your maneuver instructions from your father.

CHAMPION SHEET OF DEEDS

Begin to apply your action point from your Sheet of Deeds.

─── CHAMPION SESSION PREP ───

Reread episode 3 of *Teknon and the CHAMPION Warriors*, and then complete the questions in session 3 in your *Mission Guide* on your own. **Our next CHAMPION Session will be:**

DATE:

_____

TIME:

_____

PLACE:

_____

CRITICAL MANEUVER: Go to the Think Tank (chapter 5 of this guide) and select one of the critical maneuvers listed under session 2B to accomplish with your son.

Session 3:
The
Second Look

Champion Characteristic

Purity

Power Verse: 1 Corinthians 6:18

Flee immorality. Every other sin that a man commits is outside the body, but the immoral man sins against his own body.

Story Summary

In this episode, Magos sends Scandalon, an android, to assume the form of an attractive young woman in order to tempt Teknon. Her name, Apoplanao (Lana), in the Greek language means "seducer." Teknon is both confused and enticed by the temptation and begins to make wrong choices based on his physical attraction to Lana. Later, he realizes he has been deceived. Kratos discusses the importance of sexual purity and offers guidelines to prepare against failure in this area. Kratos also proposes a somewhat radical approach toward setting boundaries in physical intimacy known as the Wedding Kiss.

Establishing physical boundaries within relationships with the opposite sex and maintaining sexual purity before marriage are important topics, yet they can be difficult for a father and son to discuss. Teknon's temptation and decisions by the spring-fed pool, plus the wisdom shared by Kratos, will give both of you a natural opportunity to explore these important aspects of life. Consider using this opportunity to tell your son about sexual seduction and why it's important to avoid the temptations of an aggressive young woman. Also, challenge him to avoid being physically aggressive with young ladies and to respect and protect their purity as well.

QUESTION #3 TIP:
If your son successfully memorized the verse, have him date the verse in session 2B of his *Mission Guide*.

Discussion Topics

Understanding the right context for sex
Establishing boundaries in physical intimacy
Setting high standards to guard your purity

Mission Debrief

1. Discuss your mission from session 2B. What did you learn from your maneuver? How is what you've learned affecting your thinking or behavior?

2. Did you start applying your new action point from your Sheet of Deeds? Any progress to report? Any struggles?

3. Recite your power verse (Luke 16:10) from session 2B.

4. What are a few things that God has entrusted to you (for example: money, talents, time) that require good stewardship? How will you be a faithful steward?

5. Recite as much as you can of the CHAMPION Warrior Creed from memory (see page 5).

RECONNAISSANCE

1. Review the Map of the Mission on page 8 and determine the team's location in episode 3.

2. What is the CHAMPION definition of **Purity**? (Refer to the CHAMPION Code on page 6.)

   Answer: "I will train myself to keep the temple of my body and mind uncorrupted mentally, emotionally, and physically. I will commit to avoid and flee sexual temptation."

3. Why do you think Scandalon tempted Teknon?

   Answer: In order to cause Teknon to suffer failure, experience guilt, and ultimately to destroy his character so that he would cause grief to Kratos and to Pneuma.

4. When should Teknon have returned to camp? Why?

   Answer: He should have returned to camp as soon as he realized there was a scantily clad woman in the pool. This would have prevented the possibility that he could be tempted to sin in his mind or body. Whether a girl has good intentions or is trying to ensnare you, lust is always a trap.

Scandalon changes into an attractive young woman in episode 3 in order to tempt Teknon. "Her" name is Apoplanao, which in Greek means "to seduce" or "seducer." Warn your son about sexual seduction, and reinforce why he should avoid the seductive temptations of an aggressive young woman, either in person or in pornographic materials. The Bible refers to temptations as "bait" that will hook you like a hungry fish. Pornography is another form of sexual bait; you will discuss this specifically in session 7.

5. What did Teknon mean when he said, "I guess I shouldn't have taken the second look"?

Answer: Instead of turning away from the young woman in the pool after he first saw her, Teknon hesitated and allowed himself to become more visually involved. By taking the second look, he became tempted to sin in his mind.

6a. What did Kratos mean when he said, "Error increases with distance"?

Answer: Most failures in the sexual arena begin with a series of bad choices. Bad decisions, however small, will set us off from God's course and can lead to bigger mistakes and ultimately to serious failure.

6b. How does that insight relate to physical and sexual intimacy?

Answer: Physical closeness, even holding hands and kissing, can and will naturally lead to deeper levels of intimacy. This natural progression will only be stopped by making a proactive effort to stay on the course to purity.

7. What point did Kratos want to make by mentioning the story of the transtron racer and the cliff?

Answer: He wanted to illustrate the importance of preparing ahead of time to avoid sexual temptation. It is vital to decide how far you will go physically before the opportunity presents itself.

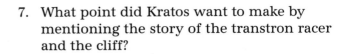

8. **Why do you think Kratos suggested that Teknon wait until marriage to kiss a woman?**

   Answer: Kratos was trying to communicate that physical involvement naturally increases emotional involvement and commitment. He was encouraging Teknon to avoid unnecessary hurt or premature commitment with a young woman. Most important, he was challenging Teknon to set a high standard in the area of purity.

9. **How did Teknon react to the idea of the Wedding Kiss?**

   Answer: He was interested, but uncertain as to whether he was willing to make such an extreme commitment.

Optional Questions

10. **Kratos said, "If a couple will wait to experience sex in the correct setting of marriage, they will receive incredible benefits of trust, bonding, and sheer enjoyment. However, if sex is misused, many long-term problems can occur." What kind of problems is he talking about?**

    Answer: Some of the problems from misuse of sex (sex before marriage or outside of marriage) are emotional scars, guilt now and throughout life, broken relationships, unwanted pregnancy, diseases, disappointment of loved ones, altered plans for your future, and a ruined Christian witness. In addition to a young man's own problems, he could ruin the life or reputation of a young lady.

11. **What do you think Kratos meant when he said, "Once you take a step closer to the edge [physical intimacy], it's very difficult to take a step back"?**

    Answer: Take this opportunity to help your son understand that engaging in any kind of physical activity (even holding hands) is a step in the direction of increasing sexual temptation. Once a step is taken in the direction of closeness, the next step will be easier. For example, it's difficult to stop at holding hands once kissing takes place; it's difficult stop at kissing once touching below the neck occurs, etc.

STRATEGY AND TACTICS

RIGHT TIME, RIGHT PLACE, RIGHT PERSON

I have been
crucified with
Christ; and it is no
longer I who live,
but Christ lives in
me; and the life
which I now live in
the flesh I live by
faith in the Son of
God, who loved me
and gave Himself
up for me.

Galatians 2:20

While leading a discussion on the topic of sexual purity with a class of engaged couples, the teacher explored the importance of waiting until marriage to have sexual intimacy. He brought out a small, bright, delicate metal object and asked, "What do you think this is?"

"A small pair of pliers," someone replied.

"Actually," the teacher said, "this is a $500 pair of fishhook removers." He held the tool in the air and pretended that he was removing a hook from a fish's mouth. "If you reach way down into the fish's mouth, you can remove the hook without damaging the fish."

The couples were quite impressed, but then another person asked, "Why in the world would anyone pay that much money for a fishhook remover?"

"My point exactly. Why would anyone pay that much to remove a hook from a fish's mouth?" the teacher responded. "Actually, this isn't really a fishhook remover. It's a delicate 'needle holder' used in brain surgery to hold a suture. This tool holds a suture so fine that it's hardly visible to the human eye. The neurosurgeon uses this surgical instrument under a powerful microscope during surgery. This instrument is so carefully balanced that it doesn't make the surgeon's hand tired when he sews brain tissue for long periods of time. And because of its special design and its $500 price tag, the instrument is handled carefully throughout the hospital. When used in the proper environment—the operating room—it's a wonderful tool.

"Now," the teacher continued, "can this valuable surgical instrument be used as a fishhook remover?"

"Yes," the couples answered.

"Is a tackle box the environment for which this finely crafted instrument was made?" the teacher asked.

"No!" the couples exclaimed.

"Likewise," the teacher went on, "God created sex for a

◆ TEKNON AND THE CHAMPION WARRIORS ◆

special environment—marriage. Whenever we take sex out of the environment for which it was created, it becomes tainted and corroded, just like this fine surgical instrument would be if it were tossed into a tackle box."

As this story illustrates, sex is wonderful. God designed it that way. The book in the Bible called the Song of Solomon reveals the physical love between a husband and wife and the beauty of their sexual relationship. God designed sex to be the ultimate physical closeness that a man and his wife can experience. No wonder it's difficult to keep our minds from becoming consumed with the subject of sex! It is something to look forward to, but to experience all of the blessings God has for you in a marriage relationship, you must wait for His perfect timing. God's plan for some men is that they do not marry so that they can be set apart in a special way as a single man in His service. But for most of us, God already has a special woman picked out to be our bride and partner for life.

Dear brothers, you are only visitors here. Since your real home is in heaven I beg you to keep away from the evil pleasures of this world; they are not for you, for they wage war against your very soul.

1 Peter 2:11 (TLB)

1. Read 2 Corinthians 10:3-5. How can we win the battle for purity in our minds and hearts?

    Answer: By taking every thought captive to the obedience of Christ. To do this, you need to (1) know His commands by reading and studying the Bible, (2) ask Him on a daily basis to control your thoughts, and (3) pay attention to every thought, grab it, and make sure it is acceptable to God.

2a. Read Romans 6:12-13. What does God say we should not do with our bodies?

    Answer: Do not present or offer parts of your body to sin, as instruments of wickedness (unrighteousness).

2b. What does He say we should do with our bodies?

    Answer: Offer ourselves totally to God as an instrument of righteousness.

Just as Scandalon tempted Teknon, your enemy—Satan—wants to tempt you to fail in the area of sexual purity. If he can destroy your character, you are no longer a threat to him. Satan often uses sex to tempt us to sin. He sets traps for us and, if we don't allow God to control our desires, we'll walk right into them.

3. What does the Bible say about temptation in 1 Corinthians 10:13? How much can we depend on God when we are tempted?

    Answer: No temptation we experience is unique to us. Other men struggle in the same areas. God understands you personally and will not allow you to be tempted beyond what you are able to endure if you depend on Him. He is always faithful to provide a way to escape so that you can endure the testing of your character.

God promises to provide a way out during any temptation we face. It may mean that we shouldn't take the second look. It will probably mean getting out of the tempting situation as quickly as possible. Remember, God promises to provide the power for you to live a pure life.

THE WEDDING KISS

Now, think about the Wedding Kiss. It's a pretty radical idea, right? But why not take every precaution possible to make sure that you will have the most fulfilling and intimate life possible with the wife God may eventually bring into your life? The world's approach to sex is not about creating more exciting and satisfying relationships, although the movie and music industry would try to tell us otherwise. Sure the Wedding Kiss challenge sounds weird in today's society, but it's worth waiting for the benefits you'll receive in the long run. Besides, God is the one who designed sex; let's try it His way! Kratos said that he wished someone had challenged him to meet such a goal. There are probably many men today who wish they had received a challenge like this when they were your age.

4a. Read 1 Thessalonians 4:1-5. How do the Gentiles (non-Christians) behave regarding sexual activity?

    Answer: They follow their lustful passions and engage in sexual activity whenever they want to, thinking only of themselves.

QUESTION #5 TIP: It will help you to understand your son's view on peer pressure. What his friends think will greatly affect your son's perspective at this age. If he has difficulty discussing this, you might ask what things other guys have discussed with him about different levels of physical intimacy, such as holding hands, kissing, passionate hugging and kissing, fondling, and intercourse.

◆ TEKNON AND THE CHAMPION WARRIORS ◆

4b. How does God say He wants you to behave in this area?

Answer: You should do everything to please God. You must be set apart (different) from the world.

The idea of the Wedding Kiss is not just a trendy fad to consider for a while and then move on to something else. It is a brave and bold commitment to purity. It's holding on to the precious gift of your body and emotions until you can give that gift to one special person. People who choose to refrain from sexual intimacy before marriage will be blessed by God in powerful ways.

5. What do you think your friends would think about the idea of the Wedding Kiss? How far do you think most teens will go physically with a girl?

6. Whether you go for the Wedding Kiss or not, you need to decide in advance how far you will go emotionally and physically with a girl before you are married. Have you ever really thought about how far you plan to go?

You may have already taken a few steps toward the cliff that Kratos talked about. You may have kissed a girl, or maybe become even more physically and emotionally involved with her. If you have, now is the time to confess this to God and seek His forgiveness. Then, recommit yourself to a higher standard. Claim God's promise of forgiveness and cleansing (1 John 1:9), and start fresh today in this area of purity.

Optional Question

7. What would you have said and done if you were Teknon when Lana surprised him behind the bushes?

QUESTION #6 TIP:
After teaching sixth graders for many years, Dennis Rainey, executive director of FamilyLife, says he found that by age 12, most of the boys in his class had already made the decision about how far they would go physically. You don't need to press your son on this point or try to force your views. But take the time to share your values and boundaries, and then invite him to accept these as his own. At the end of the session, one suggested action point (Deed) for your son is to pray and think about where his boundaries will be.

QUESTION #7 TIP:
There will probably come a time when your son is confronted with an aggressive young woman. How will he handle it? To begin a discussion on how to handle an uncomfortable situation with a girl, use question 7. Be sure you also challenge him to avoid being physically aggressive with young ladies and to respect and protect their purity as well.

If needed, help your son by suggesting some key truths that he should have learned during this session, such as establishing boundaries, fleeing temptation, setting high moral standards, and the Wedding Kiss.

Walk by the Spirit, and you will not carry out the desire of the flesh.

Galatians 5:16b

SHEET OF DEEDS:
Only a *brief* description of each action point is provided here. Go to the Think Tank (chapter 5) for complete instructions.

IMPORTANT NOTE:
Let your son know that you will be giving him a CHAMPION Symbol when he completes his training. This symbol of young manhood and purity will be a reminder to him of his commitment to remain sexually pure until he marries the woman whom God has chosen to be his mate.

THE Main Things I learned in this Champion Session are:

_____

_____

_____

_____

_____

CHAMPION SHEET OF DEEDS

Go to the CHAMPION Sheet of Deeds on page 9 and write down **one thing you will begin to do** before the next session (and beyond) to apply the main things you learned in session 3.

Check one of the suggestions below for your son to write down as his action point on his CHAMPION Sheet of Deeds for session 3. Descriptions and explanations of these action points are provided in the Think Tank (chapter 5) of this guide.

❏ Ask your son to determine how far he is willing to go physically in any relationship before marriage. Ask him to consider the Wedding Kiss or another high standard.

❏ Ask your son to begin to practice capturing stray or sinful thoughts and redirecting them to be in obedience to Christ.

❏ Create your own unique action point.

Your Mission

Complete your mission and CHAMPION Session prep before you meet for session 4.

Power Verse: 1 Corinthians 6:18

Date memorized: _____

Critical Maneuver

This will reinforce what you learned in this session. Obtain your maneuver instructions from your father.

CHAMPION Sheet of Deeds

Begin to apply your action point from your Sheet of Deeds.

CHAMPION Session Prep

Reread episode 4 of *Teknon and the CHAMPION Warriors*, and then complete the questions in session 4 in your *Mission Guide* on your own. **Our next CHAMPION Session will be:**

DATE:

_____

TIME:

_____

PLACE:

_____

CRITICAL MANEUVER:
Go to the Think Tank
(chapter 5 of this guide)
and select one of the
critical maneuvers
listed under session 3
to accomplish with
your son.

Session 4:
The Company
I Keep

CHAMPION Characteristics
Mental Toughness and Integrity

Power Verse: 1 Corinthians 15:33

Do not be misled: "Bad company corrupts good character." (NIV)

Story Summary

    This episode finds Kratos and Teknon at the end of a week-long trek through a desolate forest. They are tired, hungry for "real" food, and ready for a change of pace. As they reach the city of Bia, which is known for its raucous nightlife and chaotic society, Kratos is hesitant to stop there to eat and spend the night. Teknon, on the other hand, sees the bright lights, hears the diverse sounds, and pictures the dinner delights awaiting them. Realizing that this is an opportune time for his son to learn more about discernment in decision-making, Kratos agrees to enter Bia. The Harpax, a local gang, provide the "classroom" for Teknon to learn this lesson the hard way.

Recognizing the importance of discernment in choosing friends
Realizing that there are always consequences to our choices
Recovering from failures—part 1

Mission Debrief

You'll be able to discuss with your son the importance of using good judgment when choosing friends—and having the integrity to stand for what's right. Today, peer pressure plays an important role in young people's lives. In addition to discussing Teknon's choices—and their consequences—you and your son will explore the wisdom that God gives to people who have placed their personal faith in Jesus Christ and seek to know Him better through Bible reading and prayer.

Question #3 Tip:

If your son successfully memorized the verse, have him date the verse in session 3 of his *Mission Guide*.

Question #4 Tip:

Remind your son that most men struggle with their thought life and desires. Encourage him that he can confide in you concerning his mental struggles and that they can be overcome with God's help (see 1 Corinthians 10:13).

1. Discuss your mission from session 3. Are you taking the responsibility to complete and learn from your critical maneuvers?

2. Are you continuing to apply your action points from the Sheet of Deeds? If so, how is it going? If not, what would help you to start applying your action points?

3. Recite your power verse (1 Corinthians 6:18) from session 3.

4. Are you struggling with any sexual desires that could lead to temptation? If so, what can you do to deal with those desires (the CHAMPION's Ring)? What strength and protection do you need to gain from the Lord (God's Ring)?

5. Try to recite at least half of the CHAMPION Warrior Creed from memory (see page 5).

Reconnaissance

1. Review the Map of the Mission on page 8 and determine the team's location in episode 4.

2. What is the CHAMPION definition of **Mental Toughness**? Of **Integrity**? (Refer to the CHAMPION Code on page 6.)

Answer for Mental Toughness: "I will allow God to direct my thinking toward gaining common sense and wisdom. I will use discernment when making hard decisions. I will desire respect from others rather than compromise my convictions for acceptance or approval."

Answer for Integrity: "I will seek to acquire a clear understanding of who I am in Christ so that I may have a deeper comprehension of what I believe, what I stand for, and how I can live out those convictions in the most difficult circumstances, whether I am alone or with others. I will allow other people to hold me accountable to standards of excellence."

3a. Do you believe Teknon used good judgment in Bia? Why or why not?

Answer: No. He became overly impressed with appearance rather than character. He did not choose his companions wisely.

3b. If not, at which moments in this episode did he show a lack of discernment?

Answer: The first time was when he was willing to risk entering an unfavorable environment (Bia) to get a good night's sleep and a hot meal. He also decided to start a conversation with the Harpax instead of following his father's advice to get some rest. Later on, he did not pull away from the Harpax when he heard their vulgar speech and rebellious attitudes.

It's not whether you get knocked down, it's whether you get up.

Vince Lombardi

4. When should Teknon have realized that he should avoid the Harpax?

Answer: When his dad encouraged him to get a good night's sleep instead of staying up late.

5. The leader of the Harpax is named Rhegma. The Greek word *rhegma* means "ruin." In what ways could a person like Rhegma ruin the life of a young man who would join the Harpax group

Answer: Rhegma is charismatic and attractive, but he is also evil. Teens can be drawn in by the physical appearance and popularity of people like Rhegma if they are not grounded in a relationship with Christ.

There's a story about a zoo that had a lion pavilion. One day, a visitor to the zoo was astonished as he looked in the lion cage and saw a lamb and a lion lying down together. The man couldn't believe that the natural enemies lived so peacefully together. He grabbed the zookeeper by the arm and asked him how such a wonderful relationship could occur. The zookeeper replied, "It's easy, Mister, we just add fresh lambs now and then."

When you make friends with the wrong people, like Teknon did with the Harpax, you can end up in trouble. Bottom line: be careful whom you trust and to whom you offer friendship.

Optional Question

6. Why do you think Kratos allowed Teknon to meet with the Harpax?

Answer: Because he knew he could learn a valuable lesson. A wise man once said, "A good scare is worth more than good advice."

7. **What did Kratos mean when he said, "It's better to be trusted and respected than it is to be liked"?**

   Answer: Kratos wanted to encourage Teknon that, although it's great to be liked, he can get into trouble by trying to please others in order to be accepted. If acceptance is the goal, compromise soon follows. In the end, people who live by their convictions are respected and trusted by others.

8. **Kratos also told Teknon that he must learn from his mistake and to recover. What does it mean to recover? How would you recover if you made a mistake like Teknon made?**

   Answer: Kratos wanted Teknon to admit his mistakes, learn from them, and move ahead with his mission.

QUESTION #8 TIP:
Your son will learn more about the principle of "recovering" later in the CHAMPION Training.

OPTIONAL QUESTIONS

9. **Kratos cautioned, "Observe all of the characteristics of a person." What characteristics should you watch for?**
   Answer:

   GOOD Characteristics:
   ▲ Honesty
   ▲ Self-control (especially in speech and temper)
   ▲ Willingness to help others
   ▲ Respect of family members and others
   ▲ Desire to know God and obey Him

   BAD Characteristics:
   ● Dishonesty
   ● Bad temper
   ● Vulgar speech
   ● Disrespect of parents and others
   ● Lack of desire to develop his relationship with Christ or to obey God

10. **What do you think Kratos meant when he said, "Bad humor is a sign of bad morals"?**

    Answer: Vulgar language and humor is rampant among teenagers today. Your son needs to understand that friends who use profanity and bad humor may have deeper spiritual problems.

Hold yourself responsible for a higher standard than anybody else expects of you. Never excuse yourself.

Henry Ward Beecher

STRATEGY AND TACTICS

We need friends that not only make us feel good, but also cause us to do good things. Because of this, it is important to seek God's wisdom as you develop friendships.

Most of the book of Proverbs in the Old Testament was written by one of the wisest men who ever lived, King Solomon. In this book, Solomon instructed his sons and the young men of his kingdom about the difference between knowledge (having the facts) and wisdom (applying those facts to life). Like Teknon, young men can choose to reject the wisdom of their parents and the Word of God. As they grow older, however, they will increase their knowledge, but not their wisdom and discernment. In Proverbs 1, Solomon described the danger of being a young man who lacks discernment.

1a. Read Proverbs 1. What can a person do to begin obtaining wisdom? (See verses 7-9.)

Answer: First, he must revere (fear) God and study His teaching. Second, he must respect his parents' authority and guidance.

1b. What advice did Solomon give in verses 15 and 16 concerning the importance of choosing the right friends?

Answer: Do not go along with bad companions because they will drag you along into evil. Their way may seem attractive, but it leads to destruction.

1c. According to verses 23-27, why should we listen to sound advice and wisdom?

Answer: Because it will save us from bad choices that lead to ruin.

1d. What will happen if we don't obey God and use discernment? (See verses 28-32.)

Answer: If we ignore God's wisdom, He will allow us to suffer the negative consequences that we have brought on ourselves.

1e. What will happen if we use good judgment and listen to wisdom? (See verse 33.)

Answer: We will benefit (live securely) as a result of wise choices and decisions.

Always remember two things about your Heavenly Father: God loves you and He is trustworthy.

GOD LOVES YOU

Just as Kratos loved Teknon despite his bad decisions, so your Father in heaven loves you no matter what you do. He understands that you are growing and learning how to follow Him. Sometimes you will succeed, and sometimes you will fail. As you grow to know Him better and seek to obey His Word, you will increase in discernment and find it easier to make better choices.

But no matter how hard we try, we will still sin and disobey God. Romans 3:23 tells us that we have all sinned. God understands us and loves us so much that He sent Jesus to die on the cross and then raised Him again from the dead to pay for our sins (or failures). After we sin, we recover by confessing our failure to God and then claiming His promise of forgiveness. Then, we turn from our own way and go God's way. We should also apologize to anyone we have offended.

2. **What does 1 John 1:9 say about God and confessing our sins to Him? How does this make you feel?**

Answer: "If we confess our sins, He [God] is faithful and righteous to forgive us our sins and to cleanse us from all unrighteousness." If we confess, He promises to forgive us and totally cleanse us.

GOD IS TRUSTWORTHY

God is trustworthy and all-knowing. If you need wisdom, you can trust Him to provide it for you. All you have to do is ask.

"If you want to know what God wants you to do, ask Him, and He will gladly tell you, for He is always ready to give a bountiful supply of wisdom to all who ask Him; He will not resent it." (James 1:5 TLB)

Associate yourself with men of good quality if you esteem your own reputation; for it is better to be alone than in bad company.

George Washington

3. **In what ways can God give you answers about choosing friends and other issues?**

Answer: Help your son to understand that God willingly provides wisdom and discernment if we ask Him. The most reliable source for God's direction is from His Word, the Bible. Other ways God can communicate His wisdom and guidance to us are by speaking directly to our hearts through parents and other authorities in our lives, through godly friends, and even through circumstances or events.

4. **Why is belief in who God is so important?**

Answer: If God is NOT all-powerful, all-knowing, and ever-present, then He is not fully trustworthy.

As a future CHAMPION, you must remember to ask for wisdom before you enter situations like those Teknon faced in the city of Bia. In other words, use good judgment ahead of time and study how God wants you to respond before you enter a tempting situation.

QUESTION #5 TIP:

This question relates to integrity as well as to discernment. If we were invisible, we could go wherever we wished, unnoticed. But even if we were invisible to the world, God, being omniscient (all-seeing) and omnipotent (all-powerful), could still see us.

QUESTION #6 TIP:

Help your son understand the characteristics of a good friend who will build him up and challenge him to love and obey God. Point to the CHAMPION characteristics as a good starting point. The critical maneuver for this week will give him more insight in this area.

QUESTION #7 TIP:

It's difficult to be lonely because of commitments you have made to high standards. Your son may have to make a decision to be alone at times because of his commitment to stay clear of bad company.

OPTIONAL QUESTIONS

5. **Kratos used the Hoplon to become invisible. What would you do if you could become invisible?**

6. **What kind of friend will help you to do good as well as to feel good? What are the characteristics of such a person?**

7. **Why did George Washington say, "It's better to be alone than in bad company"?**

THE Main Things I learned
in this Champion Session are:

_____

_____

_____

_____

_____

CHAMPION Sheet of Deeds

SHEET OF DEEDS:
Only a *brief* description of each action point is provided here. Go to the Think Tank (chapter 5) for complete instructions.

Go to the CHAMPION Sheet of Deeds on page 9 and write down **one thing you will begin to do** in before the next session (and beyond) to apply the main things you learned in session 4.

Check one of the suggestions below for your son to write down as his action point on his CHAMPION Sheet of Deeds for session 4. Descriptions and explanations of these action points are provided in the Think Tank (chapter 5) of this guide.

❏ Have your son list all his friends and then mark down whether they are a good influence, a neutral influence, or a bad influence. Discuss which of his friends he should be spending more or less time with.

❏ Have your son assess whether or not he is a good friend by reviewing the characteristics of a good friend from this session and the critical maneuver.

❏ Create your own unique action point.

Your Mission

Complete your mission and CHAMPION Session prep before you meet for Session 5.

POWER VERSE: 1 CORINTHIANS 15:33

Date memorized: _____

CRITICAL MANEUVER

This will reinforce what you learned today. Obtain your maneuver instructions from your father.

CHAMPION SHEET OF DEEDS

Begin to apply your action point from your Sheet of Deeds.

——— CHAMPION SESSION PREP ———

Reread episode 5 of *Teknon and the CHAMPION Warriors*, and then complete the questions in session 5 in your *Mission Guide* on your own. **Our next CHAMPION Session will be:**

DATE:

_____

TIME:

_____

PLACE:

_____

He who walks with wise men will be wise, but the companion of fools will suffer harm.

Proverbs 13:20

SESSION 5:
ERGONIAN
PRIDE

CHAMPION Characteristc

Attitude

POWER VERSE: PROVERBS 19:20 (NIV)

Listen to advice and accept instruction, and in the end you will be wise.

STORY SUMMARY

In episode 5, Kratos and Teknon emerge from the jungles of Perasmos and enter the luxurious accommodations of the resort community of Ergo. Ergo enjoys a fairly isolated existence on Kairos and is surrounded by a high wall that only opens to the sea. Planning to meet the other team members in Ergo, the two rent a room and meet the arrogant resort manager, Mr. Poroo, who totally discounts Kratos' warning about the threat of an attack by savage beasts called amachos. However, the beasts end up creating havoc and hurting guests in Ergo, and the resort is only saved when Kratos and Matty repel the amachos.

SESSION 5 OVERVIEW:

In this session, you and your son will explore the importance of teachability. As Mr. Poroo illustrates, an arrogant person who refuses to listen to wise counsel will eventually suffer— or at least the people around him will. The book of Proverbs contains many verses that describe the wisdom of being teachable.

Your son will be challenged to recognize the value of listening to the counsel of his parents and, even more importantly, to his Heavenly Father, who has given us His words in the Bible.

QUESTION #1 TIP:

Ask these questions to gauge the effectiveness of your son's activities:
1. Are you making the critical maneuvers and deeds a priority?
2. Is there enough time between the sessions to complete them?
3. Do you find the maneuvers we are using helpful?

QUESTION #3 TIP:

If your son successfully memorized the verse, have him date the verse in session 4 of his *Mission Guide*.

DISCUSSION TOPICS

Uncovering the danger of pride
Learning the importance of a teachable attitude
Listening to wise counsel

MISSION DEBRIEF

1. Discuss your mission from session 4. What did you learn from your maneuver? How is what you learned affecting your thinking or behavior?

2. Did you start applying your new action point from the Sheet of Deeds? If so, how is it going?

3. Recite your power verse (1 Corinthians 15:33) from session 4.

4a. If you are spending time with people who influence you in bad ways, what steps should you take to change that situation? (Remember, the CHAMPION's Ring from session 1 contains those areas that you can and should control.)

4b. Are you are worried about any other people's perception of you? Is it difficult for you to trust God with those perceptions and your concerns? If so, why do you think that is? (This is part of God's Ring, the area that only He can control and that we need to release to Him.)

QUESTION #4 TIP:
Help your son think through which of his friends are "bad company," and why. Encourage him to take some action if required. Also, discuss what it means to be a good friend (encouraging, strong character, dependability, flexibility, willing to challenge a friend's action or behavior for the good of that friend, etc.).

5. Try to recite all of the CHAMPION Warrior Creed from memory (see page 5).

RECONNAISSANCE

1. Review the Map of the Mission on page 8 and determine the team's location in episode 5. Trace the steps the team has covered thus far, reviewing story highlights and main topics discussed.

    Answer: (1) overcoming fear of the unknown and the Rings of Responsibility (2A) enemy assessment and embracing the mission (2B) effective stewardship (3) sexual purity (4) discernment, choosing friends, and consequences.

QUESTION #5 TIP:
By this time, your son should able to recite the CHAMPION Warrior Creed. God will use this creed and his power verses to direct your son's thinking.

2. What is the CHAMPION definition of **Attitude**? (Refer to the CHAMPION Code on page 6.)

    Answer: "I will cultivate a disposition of humility. I will assume a correct and hopeful view of myself as a member of God's family. I will improve my ability to manage anger and discouragement. I will develop and enjoy an appropriate sense of humor."

3. **What kind of attitude did Mr. Poroo have toward Kratos? Why?**

   Answer: Poroo displayed an attitude of arrogance, especially when Kratos recommended that the manager take precautions against the amachos. Poroo reacted this way because he was prideful and not teachable.

4. **Why did Kratos say, "That attitude might be his undoing"?**

   Answer: Kratos knew that Poroo's prideful response to the warning would come back to haunt him. An unwillingness to listen to good counsel can lead to one's downfall. Poroo was not very teachable.

5. **What occurred as a result of Mr. Poroo's attitude?**

   Answer: The amachos entered Ergo, caused a great deal of fear and destruction, and injured several guests.

6. **In what ways might Mr. Poroo have responded differently to Kratos' suggestion? How would the outcome have been different ?**

   Answer: Poroo could have listened and considered Kratos' warning. The guests and hotel facility would have been spared injury and damage.

7. **What does the word "teachability" mean to you? Be specific!**

   Answer: One possible definition is the willingness to consider wise counsel and to change one's behavior as a result of that counsel. It also means that you are humble and open to learning new things.

   Gleukos was the socially acceptable intoxicant consumed by the resort guests at Ergo. Kratos explained why the guests used this substance: "This is a place to escape. For a few days, all these people want to do is to forget about their lives at home. Sun, fun, eating, and drinking gleukos is what this place is all about."

8. What do you think about teens drinking alcohol? What about adults?

STRATEGY AND TACTICS

EASY MISTAKES

Have you ever acted like you knew it all? We all have. Let's say you're facing an important decision, like buying a new sound system. You see one you like, but don't really know how good it is. You know your neighbor is an expert on these systems and could provide you with excellent information to help you decide which one to buy and might even know the best place to buy it. But you have your pride and don't want to reveal your lack of "surround sound, high density, bass-enriched" expertise. So you don't ask anyone for advice, especially your expert neighbor. What do you do? You buy an overpriced player that breaks down within three months. Of course, the warranty is only good for 30 days.

A few days later, you're over at a new friend's house on a rainy day. Your friend is a proud owner of a new, streamlined dirt bike. He tells you there's no better time to dirt bike than on a rainy day; in fact, the wetter the better. He tells you that if you haven't ridden a dirt bike before, he'd be more than happy to give you a quick lesson. You've never ridden anything more tenacious than a 10-speed, but that's a well-kept secret. *Nothing doing*, you say to yourself. You're not about to look "mechanically challenged" around your buddy. What do you do? You jump on, rev the engine and pop the clutch. Thirty feet of mud and a compound fracture later, you're wondering why you didn't take your friend up on his free introductory lesson.

After you get out of the hospital, your dad expresses concern about one of your new friends. He's bothered that this new acquaintance encourages you to watch dirty movies, tell lies, and use vulgar language. You immediately respond by defending the friend and declaring that your dad is intolerant and that he's

QUESTION #8 TIP:

Discuss your stand on alcohol with your son. While abstinence is clearly the best safeguard and prevention of struggle and addiction, opinions of God's standard in this area vary. Regardless of your position, you can discuss the danger of using alcohol as an escape from reality and the ease of becoming addicted and enslaved to it. Also, share the clear biblical mandate from Ephesians 5:18: " ... do not get drunk with wine for it is dissipation, but be filled with the Spirit."

EASY MISTAKES:

Does your son respond well to instruction? Or does he bristle at even the implication of a helpful hint? This session focuses on several key issues concerning pride. Why, for instance, is it important to receive and apply the advice of godly, wise people? How can a prideful attitude get us into trouble? Ultimately, of course, pride is a spiritual issue because it results in a rebellious attitude toward God.

overreacting. Basically you ignore the whole discussion. A couple months later, you're using profanity, struggling with pornography, and lying to your parents to cover it up.

Life would be much easier if we were teachable, wouldn't it?

1. What does Proverbs 19:20 say about being teachable?

   Answer: "Listen to counsel [advice] and accept discipline [consider instruction], that you may be wise the rest of your days."

2. What happens if you are not teachable? (Read Proverbs 29:1.)

   Answer: "A man who hardens his neck [remains stubborn and unchanged] after much reproof will suddenly be broken beyond remedy."

   Read Proverbs 16:18-19 and Proverbs 18:12.

   3a. What kind of attitude creates the greatest barrier to becoming teachable and leads to your destruction in the end?

   Answer: Pride, which the Bible also calls a "haughty spirit."

   3b. What kind of attitude makes us teachable and leads to honor?

   Answer: Humility or lowliness of mind or spirit. This does not mean that we have a poor opinion of ourselves, but rather that we don't think more highly of ourselves than we should, especially in relation to our awesome God.

4. According to Psalm 50:15, who should we call on first if we need help or have a big decision to make? How will He respond?

   Answer: God will rescue us if we call on Him. He will rescue us so that we will acknowledge and honor Him in our lives.

   If you have invited Jesus into your life as your Savior and Lord, you are a child of God. God loves it when His children call on Him. When we seek God, we honor Him. Jeremiah 29:11-13 (TLB) says, "For I know the plans I have for you," says the Lord. "They are plans for good and not for evil, to give you a future and a hope. In those days when you pray, I will listen. You will find me when you seek me if you look for me in earnest."

God knows what is best for us. When we reject God's wisdom and direction in our decisions, we are trying to do His job. When we aren't teachable, we don't pay attention to God's Word. We also don't listen to people whom God puts into our lives to give us advice and counsel—like our parents, pastors, and teachers. We saw what happened to Mr. Poroo when he didn't listen to Kratos' advice. Make sure you are seeking God with a teachable heart so that He can reveal how to live your life for Him.

5. Do you think your friends (name a few) are teachable? Why or why not?

Read Proverbs 6:20-23

My son, observe the commandment of your father and do not forsake the teaching of your mother; bind them continually on your heart; tie them around your neck. When you walk about, they will guide you; when you sleep, they will watch over you; and when you awake, they will talk to you. For the commandment is a lamp, and the teaching is light; and reproofs for discipline are the way of life ... .

6a. What are the some of the benefits of listening to your parents?

6b. Has this discussion changed your view about the importance of your parents' advice and discipline? How so? Do you need to adjust your attitude in this area?

IMPORTANT NOTE: This would be a good time to highlight the importance of some spiritual disciplines for your son. Help him understand that by developing a habit of daily Bible study and prayer, he will see his relationship with God grow stronger, and he will become more teachable as a result. Encourage him to trust that God will prosper him in many ways as he pursues God in this way.

QUESTION #5 TIP: This question gives your son a third-party reference point to discuss teachability. It temporarily takes the focus from him so that he can discuss it objectively.

Success isn't forever, and failure isn't fatal.

Don Shula

QUESTION #6 TIP: These verses highlight specific practical benefits of listening to the advice of parents, as well as to the Lord.

If needed, help your son by suggesting some key truths that he should have learned during this session, such as the danger of pride, the importance of teachability, and seeking wise counsel.

Teachability is a man's capacity for growth.

Howard Hendricks

SHEET OF DEEDS:

Only a *brief* description of each action point is provided here. Go to the Think Tank (chapter 5) for complete instructions.

THE Main Things I learned in this Champion Session are:

_____

_____

_____

_____

_____

CHAMPION SHEET OF DEEDS

Go to the CHAMPION Sheet of Deeds on page 9 and write down **one thing you will begin to do** before the next session (and beyond) to apply the main things you learned in session 5.

Check one of the suggestions below for your son to write down as his action point on his CHAMPION Sheet of Deeds for session 5. Descriptions and explanations of these action points are provided in the Think Tank (chapter 5) of this guide.

- ❏ Ask your son to identify one area where he needs to become more teachable. Gently help him make adjustments and praise him for making the effort.
- ❏ Ask your son to commit to a daily time of Bible reading and prayer. Have him keep a journal for new insights, passages read, prayer requests, and answers.
- ❏ Create your own unique action point.

Your Mission

Complete your mission and CHAMPION Session Prep before you meet for session 6.

POWER VERSE: PROVERBS 19:20

Date memorized: _____

CRITICAL MANEUVER

This will reinforce what you learned in this session. Obtain your maneuver instructions from your father.

CHAMPION SHEET OF DEEDS

Begin to apply your action point from your Sheet of Deeds.

CHAMPION SESSION PREP

Reread episode 6 of Teknon and the CHAMPION Warriors, and then complete the questions in session 6 in your Mission Guide on your own. **Our next CHAMPION Session will be:**

DATE: _____

TIME: _____

PLACE: _____

CRITICAL MANEUVER: Go to the Think Tank (chapter 5 of this guide) and select one of the critical maneuvers listed under session 5 to accomplish with your son.

Spend less time worrying who's right, and spend more time deciding what's right!

Life's Little Instruction Book

Session 6:
A Storm
of Dishonor

Champion Characteristics
Honor and Attitude

Power Verse: Romans 12:10

Be devoted to one another in brotherly love; give preference to one another in honor.

Story Summary

In this episode Kratos and his team take to the seas, riding an elaborate luxury ship named the *Ergonaut* toward the city of Sarkinos. During the trip, Teknon meets two overindulged young men named Pikros and Parakoe, who constantly bicker, complain, and demonstrate a disrespectful attitude toward their father. Their disrespect helps Teknon to realize his own neglect in honoring his sister, Hilly.

Magos finally surfaces in this episode. He is a self-created cyborg, a former partner of Kratos, and the team's evil foe. He can observe almost any occurrence on Kairos from his fortress, through the eyes of his androids and transmission technology. Able to influence the planet's weather conditions, Magos creates a sudden, hurricane-force storm that hammers the *Ergonaut* and forces the team members to use all of their powers to save the ship and its passengers. During the storm, Teknon acts bravely to rescue the father of Pikros and Parakoe.

Mission Debrief

Session 6 Overview:
In this session, you will have the opportunity to discuss with your son what it means to honor another person. You will talk about ways in which he can show honor to you, your spouse, siblings, and other people he meets.

1. Discuss your mission from session 5. What did you learn from your maneuver? How is what you've learned affecting your thinking and behavior?

Question #3 Tip:
If your son successfully memorized the verse, have him date the verse in session 5 of his *Mission Guide.*

2. Did you start applying your new action point from the Sheet of Deeds? If so, what are you learning? If not, what would help you to get started?

Question #4 Tip:
It may be difficult for your son to identify an area where he is resisting good counsel. To help him think and talk openly, it would be helpful if you share an example from your life when you were not teachable (perhaps when you were your son's age). Describe any resulting bad choices and unfavorable outcomes.

3. Recite your power verse (Proverbs 19:20) from session 5.

4. Think about any area(s) of your life in which you need to be more teachable. What are they? What will you change to become more teachable? (Attitudes and actions like these, which you control, are within the CHAMPION's Ring.)

5. Try to recite all of the CHAMPION Warrior Creed from memory (see page 5). Say it slowly and think about which characteristics mean the most to you.

RECONNAISSANCE

1. Review the Map of the Mission on page 8 and determine the team's location in episode 6.

2. What is the CHAMPION definition of **Honor**? Of **Attitude**? (Refer to the CHAMPION Code on page 6.)

   Answer for Honor: "I will honor God by obeying Him and acknowledging Him as the complete source of my life, both now and through eternity. I will treat my parents, brothers/sisters, friends, and acquaintances with respect. I will appreciate the strengths and accept the weaknesses of all my 'team members.'"

   Answer for Attitude: "I will cultivate a disposition of humility. I will assume a correct and hopeful view of myself as a member of God's family. I will improve my ability to manage anger and discouragement. I will develop and enjoy an appropriate sense of humor."

3. How did Pikros and Parakoe treat their father? What did they reveal about their relationship with him?

   Answer: The brothers' actions revealed a complete lack of respect for their father. They were disobedient and they responded to their father with insolent speech.

4. How did Pikros and Parakoe treat each other?

   Answer: With impatience, anger, and selfishness.

QUESTION #5 TIP:
By this time, your son should able to recite the CHAMPION Warrior Creed. God will use this and his memory verses to direct his thinking. This creed will also be an effective passage for him to recite during his celebration at the completion of his training.

5. How did Teknon feel as he observed the boys' attitudes toward their father? Why did he feel this way?

Answer: He was disturbed by their attitudes. Because Teknon had been raised to exhibit love and respect for Kratos, he could not imagine treating his father in such a manner.

Kind words do not cost much ... yet they accomplish much.

Blaise Pascal

Optional Questions

6. In the Greek, *pikros* refers to acting bitterly. Pikros was disrespectful to his father and bitter about their relationship. Why do you think Pikros was bitter about the relationship with his father?

Answer: Pikros felt neglected by his father.

Question #7 Tip:
Ameleo in the Greek refers to being neglectful or careless.

7. Ameleo said, "I try to give them [my sons] everything they want." Why didn't this help Pikros and Parakoe to develop a better attitude toward their father? What did they really need and want?

Answer: Ameleo had not spent much time with his sons over the years. The boys really needed and wanted their father's time, attention, and discipline. He had indulged them with material things, but did not provide direction in their character development. Help your son understand the dangers of being "spoiled" and overindulged.

Important Note:
This would be a good time to ask your son how he feels about your level of involvement in his life. Listen to his feelings and don't be defensive. Do what you can to improve any problem areas he identifies.

8. What did Kratos mean when he said, "No matter what we accomplish or who we impress, if we don't treat our family and friends with respect, we have nothing to offer"?

Answer: Chuck Swindoll describes the home as the place where "life makes up its mind." If we fail to show honor and respect to those in our closest relationships, namely family, we have no example to offer those around us.

9. How did watching Pikros and Parakoe affect Teknon's attitude toward his sister Hilly?

    Answer: Teknon recognized that he was not really treating his sister well. He did not want his relationship with Hilly to deteriorate to the level of disrespect between these two brothers. He knew he needed to show more honor to his sister.

10. Do you think Teknon shows respect toward his father and mother? Why do you think so?

    Answer: Help your son identify examples in the story when Teknon, by his speech and actions, has shown respect for Kratos and Paideia (there are examples near the end of episodes 2, 3, and 4). Even though he has made some bad decisions, Teknon does listen to his parents' counsel. As a family, they have actively worked at relationships and character development.

STRATEGY AND TACTICS

Honor and respect seem to be lost virtues in our society. We suffer from what has been called "a toxic atmosphere of cynicism" throughout the schools and boardrooms of our country. A newspaper article entitled "Nasty as We Wanna Be" lamented our current attitudes by stating that:

> The old values of courtesy, politeness, and respect have been trampled under. We, as men, need to communicate to our sons what it means to show respect and esteem to the individuals God brings into our lives. The indignities of the road are compounded with further indignities at work, at the movies, on the radio, from the profane mouths of strangers, and in battles between neighbors. Pretty soon, you've got more than a headache. You've got a crisis on your hands.
>
> If we, as Christians, don't lead the way toward honoring people and treating them with dignity as individuals created by God, who will?[1]

> *The deepest principle in human nature is the craving to be appreciated.*
>
> William James

An Honorable Attitude:

We, as fathers, need to communicate and model for our sons what it means to show respect and esteem to the people that God brings into our lives.

Most of us, swimming against the tides of trouble the world knows nothing about, need only a bit of praise or encouragement—and we'll make the goal.

Jerome P. Fleishman

An Honorable Attitude

Read Exodus 20:12. This is one of the Ten Commandments.

1a. **What does this commandment say about the attitude young people should have toward their parents?**

Answer: Honor your father and mother.

1b. **What does God promise the results will be if we obey His commandment?**

Answer: He promises that you will "live long in the land the Lord your God has given you." In other words, He promises that your life will go better and that you will live a long, full life. (See also Ephesians 6:1-3 where Paul quotes these words.)

2. **What are some practical ways in which you can show honor to your parents? (Remember the CHAMPION's Ring involves your attitude and behavior.)**

Some examples include:

· Speak respectfully to them.

· Speak respectfully of your parents when you are not with them.

· Obey them quickly and with a good attitude when they ask you to do something.

3. **What does Galatians 6:9-10 say about how young people should treat their brothers and sisters?**

Answer: They should not grow weary in treating siblings well. Over time, treating siblings with respect will cause them and us to mature; it will "reap a harvest" in all of our lives. God says that we should be especially kind and loving to other Christians and our own family members.

4. **Read Romans 12:10. How can we "do good" within our family?**

Answer: Be devoted to each other and give preference to others. This means setting aside our own desires and serving others as Jesus did throughout his life. God calls husbands to be servant-leaders (Ephesians 5:25), which requires giving up your own desires and giving others preference. True leaders are unselfish servants.

The Bible says we ought to "do good to all people." That should especially apply to our family members.

5. **How do you view your parents? How about your brothers and sisters? Do you act like Pikros and Parakoe? Or do you view your family, even with their flaws, as valuable people given to you by God?**

The members of your family are valuable gifts that God has given you. Are they always easy to get along with? No way! Are you?

Does what they do always make sense? Absolutely not! Does what you do always make sense? Enough said.

A CHAMPION strives to maintain the right attitudes, no matter what other people do. Read Genesis 37:18-36. Joseph's brothers sold him into slavery because they were jealous of him. Even though his capture was a terrible thing, God used Joseph's captivity in an awesome way to eventually place Joseph as the second most powerful man in the Egyptian empire.

Remember the three R's: Respect for self, Respect for others, and Responsibility for your actions.

Life's Little Instruction Book II

Read Genesis 45 to see how Joseph forgave his brothers even when he had the power to hurt them. Joseph understood that "God causes all things to work together for good to those who love God, to those who are called according to His purpose" (see Romans 8:28b).

6a. **If your brother or sister doesn't show you honor, what should you do?**

Answer: Show honor and respect to them anyway.

6b. **Why should you respond this way?**

Answer: Because God loves them and us no matter what we do. God tells us to love and forgive others, just as He loves and forgives us. If you persist in love, you will reap a "good harvest" in your life and their life as well.

You should honor your parents as God's chosen authority in your life. If you have any brothers and sisters, you should honor them as treasured co-workers and help your family to become all that God wants it to be. Don't end up like Pikros and Parakoe. Remember, you honor God by the way you treat other people. Take steps as a CHAMPION to maintain the right _Attitude_ and show _Honor_ to your family.

7. **What are some practical ways you can you show honor to your mother? How about your brothers and sisters?**

THE MAIN THINGS I LEARNED IN THIS CHAMPION SESSION ARE:

_____

_____

_____

_____

MAIN THINGS:
If needed, help your son by suggesting some key truths that he should have learned during this session, like the importance of honoring others, especially family members.

A man's wisdom gives him patience; it is to his glory to overlook an offense.

Proverbs 19:11 (NIV)

CHAMPION SHEET OF DEEDS

Go to the CHAMPION Sheet of Deeds on page 9 and write down **one thing you will begin to do** before the next session (and beyond) to apply the main things you learned in session 6.

Check one of the suggestions below for your son to write down as his action point on his CHAMPION Sheet of Deeds for session 6. Descriptions and explanations of these action points are provided in the Think Tank (chapter 5) of this guide.

❏ Ask your son to open all doors for your wife and pull out her chair during the next two weeks. Encourage him also to do this for any women or girls he's around. (Remember that children learn best by example.)

❏ If he has siblings, ask your son to pay at least one genuine compliment (no empty flattery) to each of them per week. If he has no siblings, apply this same idea with close friends.

❏ Create your own unique action point.

SHEET OF DEEDS:
Only a _brief_ description of each action point is provided here. Go to the Think Tank (chapter 5) for complete instructions.

Your Mission

Complete your mission and CHAMPION Session Prep before you meet for session 7.

POWER VERSE: ROMANS 12:10

Date memorized: _____

CRITICAL MANEUVER

CRITICAL MANEUVER:
Go to the Think Tank (chapter 5 of this guide) and select one of the critical maneuvers listed under session 6 to accomplish with your son.

This will reinforce what you learned in this session. Obtain your maneuver instructions from your father.

CHAMPION SHEET OF DEEDS

Begin to apply your action point from your Sheet of Deeds.

CHAMPION SESSION PREP

Reread episode 7 of *Teknon and the CHAMPION Warriors*, and then complete the questions in session 7 in your *Mission Guide* on your own. **Our next CHAMPION Session will be:**

DATE:

TIME:

PLACE:

Session 7:
An Excellent Choice

Champion Characteristics

Purity and Integrity

Power Verse: Psalm 101:3

I will set no worthless thing before my eyes; I hate the work [deeds] of those who fall away; it shall not fasten its grip on me.

Story Summary

This episode opens with Kratos and his team disembarking the *Ergonaut* and entering the seductive, underworld community of Sarkinos. They hope to link up with an informant, Pseudes, who will provide strategic information vital to the team's battle plan.

Sarkinos supports an elaborate, highly technical red-light district. Holographic imaging salons abound throughout this section of the city, offering interactive pornography to the paying public. Teknon disobeys his father's instruction to remain in the hotel room and follows one of Magos' disciples, who is plotting an attack on the team. Teknon follows the culprit, named Pseudes, and soon finds himself in the center of the red-light district, where he faces a new type of temptation.

Teknon is coerced to enter an imaging salon by Eros, the salon host. Teknon wisely recognizes the evil there and leaves. He meets up with Arti and Epps, and together they capture Pseudes and take him back to the hotel for interrogation. As the episode closes, Teknon confesses that he made a poor decision in disobeying his father, but he is praised for the most part because he made the right choice to flee the temptation of pornography in the salon.

Discuss with your son the importance of developing a game plan for what material he will and will not allow to enter the window of his mind. This includes movies, videos, TV, music, reading material, videogames, and especially the Internet. Viewing pornographic material will distort how a man perceives and responds to women. For many men the lure of pornography becomes addictive.

The second issue you should cover at the end of this session OR at a separate meeting is masturbation. Many guys struggle with masturbation at times in their lives, so why not help your son learn to deal with this temptation as soon as possible?

NOTES TO LEAD YOU THROUGH THE DISCUSSION ARE INCLUDED AT THE END OF THIS SESSION.

QUESTION #3 TIP:

If your son successfully memorized the verse, have him date the verse in session 6 of his *Mission Guide.*

Discussion Topics

Protecting your mind from inappropriate material
Avoiding temptation
Fleeing from temptation
Establishing your convictions in advance

Mission Debrief

1. Discuss your mission from session 6. What did you learn from your maneuver? How is this affecting your attitude or behavior?

2. Did you start applying your new action point from the Sheet of Deeds? What are some of the things you're learning from this and the previous action points?

3. Recite your power verse (Romans 12:10) from session 6.

4. Describe one situation when you honored your mother and/or father since the last CHAMPION Session? Describe one way you have honored your brothers/sisters or other family members? (Remember that honoring others is part of the actions and attitudes in the CHAMPION's Ring.)

5. Recite all of the CHAMPION Warrior Creed from memory (see page 5).

Reconnaissance

1. Review the Map of the Mission on page 8 before beginning this section. Identify where the team is located in episode 7.

2. Review the CHAMPION definition of **Purity** and of **Integrity** (refer to the CHAMPION Code on page 6.)

   Answer for Purity: "I will train myself to keep the temple of my body and mind uncorrupted mentally, emotionally, and physically. I will commit to avoid and flee sexual temptation."

   Answer for Integrity: "I will seek to acquire a clear understanding of who I am in Christ so that I may have a deeper comprehension of what I believe, what I stand for, and how I can live out those convictions in the most difficult circumstances, whether I am alone or with others. I will allow other people to hold me accountable to standards of excellence."

3. *Epios* is a Greek word that refers to someone who shows patience and gentleness to other people. What does Epios (Epps) do to live up to his name?

   Answer: He is sensitive and caring. He shows patience and gentleness in dealing with other people. Epps is the mentor who initiates personal, instructive conversations with Teknon, e.g., later in episode 10 he does this during Kratos' absence. Even his gloves, which can aid in healing wounds, compliment his gentle and caring nature.

4. What did Eros try to get Teknon to do? Why?

   Answer: Eros tried to get him to see images of naked women. Eros knew that if Teknon started watching the sexual images, he would stay and see more. If Teknon stayed, Eros would make money through tempting him with a free look.

QUESTION #4 TIP:
Praise your son for any steps he has taken in honoring other people. Life habits grow from a series of small actions.

QUESTION #5 TIP:
For a change, you should take the initiative to recite the CHAMPION Warrior Creed to set an example for your son.

QUESTION #3 TIP:
In session 2, you were introduced to the concept of four different temperaments lived out through Teknon's mentors. In session 14 your son will have an opportunity to identify his own temperament by reading about how Tharreo, Epios, Artios, and Mataios are put together.

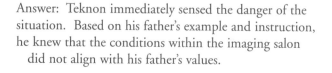

5. **Why do you think Teknon chose not to stay in the image salon and look at the images?**

Answer: Teknon immediately sensed the danger of the situation. Based on his father's example and instruction, he knew that the conditions within the imaging salon did not align with his father's values.

6. **Why do you think Kratos said that looking at pictures of nude women gives a distorted view of women, love, and sex?**

Answer: The images degrade women and give a false and sinful perspective on sexual intimacy. Pornographic images burn themselves into the memory of those who choose to view them.

7. **Why were Kratos and the mentors so excited about Teknon's decision to leave the imaging salon?**

Answer: Because he made the right choice when faced with a serious temptation. He practiced strong discernment and self-control to avoid polluting his mind.

8. **Even though Teknon made an excellent choice at the imaging salon, when did he make a bad choice?**

Answer: Teknon made a bad choice when he left the hotel room and disobeyed his father. By attempting to track Pseudes, Teknon put himself in the very vulnerable position to be exposed to pornographic images in the salons. Even if Teknon's decision was for a good cause, it did not justify his disobedience and could have started him on a destructive course. Partial obedience is still disobedience.

Epps helped Teknon to see the danger that surrounded him when he said, "You [Teknon] took a big chance when you decided to go out on your own and walk past those places. All of us are tempted to look at bad material like that, but we can't afford to take those kinds of risks. We've got to stay as far away from them as possible."

IMPORTANT NOTE:
Emphasize the importance of making the decision to avoid temptations by completely avoiding compromising situations, if at all possible.

STRATEGY AND TACTICS

DON'T PET THE T-REX!

Several years ago, my daughter and I went on a lunch date. After enjoying a great meal in the restaurant, we decided to walk through some nearby stores.

As soon as we entered a pet store named Fishes of the World, we knew that we had discovered a great place to explore. Exotic pets from around the world filled its cages and aquariums. We were surrounded by eels, fish, spiders, and snakes. One glass case was filled with very cute lizards— that's right cute lizards. They were about five inches long and had big, friendly eyes—almost like a Labrador Retriever. Just take my word for it: they were cute.

When the store's owner saw us pausing to look at the lizards, he took one out for us to hold. It snuggled in my hand and almost purred as my daughter and I petted it. "What's the name of this type of lizard? I asked.

"It's a Savannah Monitor," the owner said.

"Is this as big as it gets?" I asked, still petting the calm lizard.

"Oh, no," he responded. "In fact, there's a grown Savannah over there." We followed him around the corner to a much larger cage encased with thick wire. Inside was a reptile about four feet long that looked like it was on loan from the movie "Lost World." When my daughter and I stepped closer, the big lizard whipped around and snapped at the front of the cage.

"Yep," said the owner, "you can walk one around on a leash when it gets this size, but it'll drag you around a bit. You'd have to close in your backyard, of course." Then he added, "I wouldn't let children walk back there, though."

I found it hard to believe that the little, purring reptile I'd held in my hand a few minutes earlier could one day look at my children the way I look at a cheese pizza!

Bad habits are a lot like that cute little lizard. At first a bad habit seems harmless, and we don't believe there is any way it could hurt us. We get comfortable with it, feed it, and soon it begins to grow. Before long, it consumes more time and effort than before. In fact, the habit can become so strong that it is difficult to control. *Soon, it gets so powerful that it can start to control us and drag us around.*

Viewing pornography—sexually explicit material—is one of the most dangerous habits you can develop. It can be compared to petting a baby T-Rex and bringing it into your home. Why in the world would you want to pet a T-Rex *or* bring it into your home? You could never tame it, and you sure couldn't control it.

1. **What are some of the sources of pornography in our society? (Hint: Think about what you see and hear.)**

   Answer: Movies, videos, cable television, some video games, magazines/books, some music, and especially the Internet.

2. **What do you think pornography does to a person's mind?**

   Answer: It distorts the true picture of God's gift of sex for oneness and enjoyment in marriage. It also creates a desire to see more and increasingly explicit images. In effect, it creates an addiction to this type of material. Pornography hurts us spiritually as we focus our minds on sexual fantasy and shut ourselves off from a relationship with God.

Our minds act like computers and also like cameras. Just as a computer's response is based on the data programmed into it, whatever data we put into our minds will affect how we view the world and how we respond to it. It's not quite this simple because our minds are far more complex than any computer in the world, but the basic principles work the same way.

You have probably heard the phrase, "garbage in, garbage out." When we allow ourselves to view sexually explicit material, it's like downloading a computer virus into the hard-drive of our minds. Those images start to corrupt our thinking and how we react to other people.

Our minds are also like a camera because, when we look at a pornographic picture or movie, our minds record it—and store it to be brought back again and again.

3a. What does Romans 12:2 mean by "do not be conformed to this world"?

Answer: J.B. Phillips translates these words as "don't let the world around you squeeze into its own mold". We either conform ourselves to the world's mold or we conform to the mold of Jesus Christ that we see through God's Word and the empowering of the Holy Spirit.

3b. What do you think "renewing of your mind" means?

Answer: The Greek word for *transform* is the root word that we derive the word "morph" from. God wants to morph us, to change us. Morphing comes from the inside out. Our thinking is greatly shaped by our family and our culture. In order to be conformed to the image or mold of Jesus, our way of thinking and of viewing the world needs to be renewed or remolded to line up with God's perspectives. Our part (the CHAMPION's Ring) is to trust God, study His Word, spend time with Him in prayer and obey Him moment by moment. God's part (God's Ring) is to remold our thinking throughout our life.

As we choose to draw near to God and yield our lives to the power of His Holy Spirit, He will give us the power NOT to conform to this world. As we allow God to reshape our defective thinking to align with His mind, our attitudes and actions will change. Life-change occurs from the inside out.

4. What do you think this phrase means: "let us throw off everything that hinders and the sin that so easily entangles" (Hebrews 12:1b NIV)?

Answer: The analogy of a race is used here to give us a picture of our lives. Imagine a runner trying to win a race while carrying a boom box on his shoulder. If he wants to win the race, he's going to have to chuck the box. Another good picture of a "hindrance" is the ball and chain like prisoners once wore attached to their ankles. If we're going to win the race, we have to ditch the ball and chain. Weights in our lives can either be (1) distractions from our goals or (2) sins that trip us up.

Embracing temptation and viewing pornography is sin. Like other sins, it will weigh us down in every aspect of our lives. Did you know that pornography could easily become addicting, just like drinking alcohol or snorting cocaine? Addictions can kill you spiritually, mentally, and physically. The best way to avoid becoming addicted to something dangerous like pornography is to stay away from it altogether.

But that's not easy is it? Pornography is easily available today. Suddenly an ad comes on TV with a sexy woman wearing little of anything. Some of your friends bring a picture or magazine to school and ask you to look at it. You visit someone's house, only to find out that they plan to watch an 'R' rated movie that includes sexual scenes. Maybe a friend wants to show you a sex site on the Web.

5a. What would you do if something like this happened to you?

5b. Have any kids at school brought dirty pictures to school? Do any of them talk about seeing naked women on the Internet? What do you do when they say that?"

Do not offer the parts of your body to sin, as instruments of wickedness, but rather offer yourselves to God, as those who have been brought from death to life; and offer the   parts of your   body to Him as instruments of righteousness.

Romans 6:13
(NIV)

6. According to Psalm 101:3, what should your stand be on pornography or any explicit images that tempt you?

Answer: To hate those hindrances that weigh us down in the race of life and to set no worthless or vile thing before our eyes so that it will not take hold.

7. What does God promise to offer you if you are willing to trust Him when you face a temptation (read 1 Corinthians 10:13)?

Answer: God is faithful. He will ALWAYS provide a way of escape in a temptation. We will be tempted, but we don't have to walk into a trap. God will always give us a way out, but we must choose to take His escape route. We have to work with God to retrain our minds so that we come to hate those things that drag us down. Then we must take God's escape route every time out of temptation. IF we don't move quickly toward the escape hatch, we will be likely to get sucked into the trap!

 *Hoplon* is a Greek term that refers to armor or weapons of warfare. Just as Teknon and Kratos need their armor to protect them in the battle, Christians also need armor—spiritual armor. The Bible describes this armor of God in Ephesians 6:10-18.

8. What makes up the spiritual armor that God provides for us? How could this armor help you to gain more self-discipline in what you watch, listen to, and read?

Answer:

◆ Belt of truth (our integrity and honesty)

◆ Breastplate of righteousness (doing the right things in obedience to God)

◆ Shoes of readiness (being fully trained)

◆ Shield of faith (our trust in God no matter what is fired our way)

◆ Helmet of salvation (our salvation through Jesus Christ will guard our minds)

◆ Sword of the Spirit (the Word of God—the Bible is our only offensive weapon)

These physical objects are metaphors representing God's gifts of protection and spiritual weapons that will help us in the battle against temptation. We need to put on God's full armor or we will not be ready to do battle with Satan. We must trust God and make the right choices in what we see, think, and do.

When you put on the armor of God, it's almost like Kratos putting on the Hoplon. God gives you all of the weapons you need to fight your enemy, Satan. Satan would like nothing more than for you to start a habit of looking at the pornographic or sensual material so that your relationship with God and other people would be hindered.

9. What do you think are some of the benefits of not looking at pornography?

    Answer: A clean mind, more self-control, no guilty feelings, a pure relationship with your future wife, and a closer relationship with God are just a few benefits of using self-discipline concerning porn.

Let's get practical. Here are some suggestions that will help you gain control over this area of your mind, now and in the future. But, to gain control of your mind, you have to make the right choices, even when you're alone.

Movies. Set a standard for what movie rating levels you will not watch. Using the movie rating standards is tough because some "R" rated films are not as bad as some of those rated "PG-13" or even "PG". But, remember, a film that carries a "PG-13" or "R" rating does so for a reason. You can save yourself a lot of headaches and uncomfortable situations with your friends, by telling them you have decided to stay away from these ratings. You can and should check with your father about which movies are acceptable to watch. The real standard you need, God's standard, is found in Philippians 4:8.

Dwell or think only on things that meet God's standard—the PHIL 4:8 standard:

Whatever is:

- true
- honorable
- right
- pure
- lovely
- admirable
- excellent
- worthy of praise

QUOTE TIP:
John Wooden is the most successful college basketball coach of all time. When he coached he was committed to train and prepare players to be the best they could be.

Ask your son: "Why is preparation ahead of time so important to making right decisions?" Use this question to reinforce the need of thinking through media boundaries ahead of time so that we don't make wrong choices when opportunities present themselves.

Videos. The same suggestions apply here. This category is far more available and will require integrity on your part, especially when you are at a friend's house and his parents are gone.

Magazines. Obviously, you need to avoid pornographic magazines like the plague. But, you also need to be careful of publications that are not openly focused on sex, yet talk a lot about it. Reading these magazines and looking at the pictures can entice you to look at something worse. Remember the Shocktech problem—"Error increases with distance."

Cable Television. With more channels comes more opportunity to watch the wrong stuff. Plan ahead of time, which shows you will watch, and which ones you won't. Channel surfing is a dangerous sport; don't play it!

Internet. Every computer needs neon signs around it that flash, "Beware, hazardous roads ahead!" Before you start 'surfing' on the 'Super Highway', do yourself a favor and have your parents set the controls to prevent entry to the bad sites. Be purposeful. Decide which information you need, get it, and get out. The Internet has already ruined many men's minds because of careless surfing. And be careful of chat rooms. Even chat rooms geared toward young people can take off in a sexual direction without advance notice.

Music. What you hear can influence you as much as what you watch. Stay away from music that describes sexual intimacy and violence. And don't let yourself get drawn into the trap of watching music videos on cable channels.

Video Games. Whether at home or at the arcade, video games are becoming more violent and more sexually suggestive. Don't let yourself get sucked into the never-ending spiral of destructive competition that these games offer.

Setting high standards for what you watch, read, and listen to is a lot like racing toward that cliff Kratos described a few episodes ago. The best time to put on the brakes is when you know the cliff *is* ahead. The danger from pornography, like the cliff, is ahead. Remember your part in the CHAMPION Ring and take the responsibility to set high standards. Decide to put on your brakes now by refusing to look at any of pornography. Also trust God to give you the strength to turn away from this material and to encircle you with his ring of protection even before the pictures or words cross your path. Ask your father or mother, and one of your trusted Christian friends, to pray for you and make sure you are holding the line in this area.

PHIL 4:8 STANDARD: Encourage your son not only to avoid the "bad stuff," but also to seek out the "good stuff." Media that meets the "PHIL 4:8" standard can have a strong influence for good in his life. As a parent, you should preview movies or read reviews and screen movies to protect your children. Check out the Think Tank section (chapter 5) for Internet sites and periodicals that will provide you with solid reviews.

YOUR BOUNDARIES: Be ready to discuss what your boundaries are in these areas—and why these boundaries are so important. Some fathers, for example, agree not to watch anything that they would not want their kids to watch.

Take heart if you have already failed or even developed a bad habit in this area. Remember that God loves you and is waiting for you to seek His forgiveness. Don't let the guilt that so often comes with this habit overtake you and make you depressed. You can restore fellowship with God today and draw on His strength to help you kick the habit. Jesus said, "I have overcome the world" (John 16:33). Since He has overcome the world, He can help you overcome your habits and tendencies. Be courageous enough to share your difficulties with your father today and ask him to help you.

Don't pet the T-Rex of pornography. At first, it may purr like a kitten, but sooner or later it will bite like a Savannah Monitor.

THE MAIN THINGS I LEARNED IN THIS CHAMPION SESSION ARE:

_____

_____

_____

_____

_____

CHAMPION SHEET OF DEEDS

Go to the CHAMPION Sheet of Deeds on page 9 and write down **one thing you will begin to do** before the next session (and beyond) to apply the main things you learned in session 7.

Check one of the suggestions below for your son to write down as his action point on his CHAMPION Sheet of Deeds for session 7. Descriptions and explanations of these action points are provided in the Think Tank (chapter 5) of this guide.

❏ Develop a proactive media plan with your son. Based on this session, work together to devise a set of parameters that both you and your son will commit to.

❏ Focusing on the armor of God in Ephesians 6, ask your son to evaluate whether each piece of his armor is strong or weak. Develop a plan to improve weak areas and maintain strong areas.

❏ Create your own unique action point.

SHEET OF DEEDS:
Only a *brief* description of each action point is provided here. Go to the Think Tank (chapter 5) for complete instructions.

ACTIONS FOR DADS:
Check your special action points under session 7 in the Think Tank (chapter 5):
• Read about teen sexuality
• Use movie review sites on the Internet
• Subscribe to a reliable movie review magazine.

CRITICAL MANEUVER:

Go to the Think Tank (chapter 5 of this guide) and select one of the critical maneuvers listed under session 7 to accomplish with your son.

IMPORTANT NOTE:

This would be a good time to help your son to get used to the concept of having an accountability partner. Let him know that *you* are his accountability partner during his CHAMPION Training, but that in the future he should set up an accountability partner or small group.

Later … help your son find a strong partner or develop a small group with a few young men for accountability. When it's time, suggest that as accountability partners, the guys should meet regularly to share issues, pray for each other, and specifically ask each other about this area of purity and other areas of growth and commitment. Just as they are for you, ongoing accountability and support are very important for your son.

Complete your mission and CHAMPION Session Prep before you meet for session 8.

POWER VERSE: PSALM 101:3

Date memorized: _____

CRITICAL MANEUVER

This will reinforce what you learned in this session. Obtain your maneuver instructions from your father.

CHAMPION SHEET OF DEEDS

Begin to apply your action point from your Sheet of Deeds.

—— CHAMPION SESSION PREP ——

Reread episode 8 of *Teknon and the CHAMPION Warriors*, and then complete the questions in session 8 in your *Mission Guide* on your own. **Our next CHAMPION Session will be:**

DATE: _____

TIME: _____

PLACE: _____

SPECIAL TOPIC NOTE PAGES

*Notes to help you in the discussion
of masturbation with your son*

If you haven't already talked with your son about the topic of masturbation (or self-stimulation) then this session has provided an excellent springboard for that discussion. This is a sensitive subject and tough to discuss. But most guys struggle with masturbation at various times in their lives, so why not help your son learn to deal with this temptation as soon as possible?

While some Christians believe masturbation is acceptable within certain boundaries, the following perspective from Dennis Rainey, Executive Director of FamilyLife is one you should strongly consider sharing with your son. This outline is taken from Passport to Purity ©1999 by FamilyLife and used with permission.[2]

What the Bible Says

- The Bible is silent about the specific topic of masturbation, but the Bible is not silent about the subject of sex.

- Nowhere do we find God blessing sex done in solo (by yourself).

- Sex was designed to be enjoyed by a husband and wife in marriage.

- Sex is about focusing on pleasing your spouse, but masturbation is about focusing on yourself and what feels good to you (self-centered).

Problems from Masturbation

- You are tempted during masturbation to think about what you should not be thinking about.

- Masturbation can lead to the use of pornography as well as other gripping sexual addictions.

- Masturbation is often tied to engaging in sexual fantasy— the sin of adultery in the mind.

Self-Control

- God wants you to practice self-control.

- You need self-control now to stay pure and keep your relationship with God growing stronger.

- You will need self-control in the future to stay pure to your wife, so begin now to develop self-control.

What Do I Do With Sexual Desires?
(ideas to share with your son)

- Talk with your dad (or a trusted Christian man) so he can listen, pray with you and give you godly advice from the Bible and his experience.

- Don't feed lustful thoughts by looking at or reading anything that arouses you sexually.

- Diligently guard your heart and mind.

- Practice self-control.

What If I Fail?

- Realize that God loves you and that there's plenty of grace and forgiveness at the cross of Jesus Christ. (See 1 John 1:9.)

- Understand that your dad and mom will keep on loving you.

- Don't give up! Use this as another opportunity to give Jesus Christ first place in everything. Recover, recover, recover.

Recommended Resources

Temptations Men Face, by Tom L. Eisenman (Intervarsity Press, 1992)

Passion and Purity, by Elisabeth Elliot (Fleming H. Revell, 1984)

If we confess our sins, He is faithful and righteous to forgive us our sins and to cleanse us from all unrighteousness.

1 John 1:9

SESSION 8: FACED WITH FEAR

CHAMPION Characteristic

Courage

POWER VERSE: JOSHUA 1:9 (NIV)

Have I not commanded you? Be strong and courageous. Do not be terrified; do not be discouraged, for the Lord your God will be with you wherever you go.

STORY SUMMARY

After leaving Sarkinos, the **CHAMPION** team resumes its search for their informer by hiking toward a small mining village. A band of Magos' footsoldiers ambushes them on the trail. All the combined powers of the team members are required to win the brief, but fierce, battle. Teknon hides during a crucial moment of the battle and then blames himself for shrinking away when he was afraid. He believes he failed his team members when they needed him most.

After the battle is over, a figure suddenly appears from the darkness, unnoticed. Scandalon, an android from Magos' elite fighting force called kakos, surrounds the team with a dangerous energy field that will vaporize them within an hour. Only Teknon escapes, and therefore must assume responsibility for rescuing his companions. Because of his earlier response to the footsoldiers, however, Teknon shrinks in fear from such a daunting task. The episode ends with Kratos telling Teknon that he is their only hope for survival.

STORY NOTE: After reading episode 8, your son's first response might be, "If I were Teknon, facing the footsoldiers for the first time, I would have hidden behind the rock too!" Certainly we can't blame Teknon for his response. His companions did not offer accusations, but Teknon felt a deep remorse because he did not join in the battle when the team needed him.

Overcoming fear of rejection and fear of failure
Learning to recover from failure—part 2

Mission Debrief

In this session, you have the opportunity to help your son distinguish between successful failure, and unsuccessful failure. In *successful failure*, you persevere under difficult circumstances after you fail to accomplish a worthwhile task, and then you manage to recover from that failure and try again. In *unsuccessful failure*, you face the same situation and don't put forth your all, thus giving up or only partially achieving your potential. Unsuccessful failure is usually the result of bad choices or disobedience to God. Your son needs to know the difference between successful and unsuccessful failure, and understand that he can experience successful failures in his life.

Question #3 Tip:
If your son successfully memorized the verse, have him date the verse in session 6 of his *Mission Guide*.

Question #4a Tip:
Help your son identify some practical actions he, and you, can take to prevent sexual temptations.

1. Discuss your mission from session 7. What did you learn from your maneuver? How is what you've learned affecting your attitude or behavior?

2. How will you continue to apply all of your action points from the Sheet of Deeds thus far? The goal for these is to see some habit patterns changing in your life. Are any changes occurring as you continue to apply all your various actions points?

3. Recite your power verse (Psalm 101:3) from session 7.

4a. Have you been more aware of areas where you need to be more careful in what you set before your eyes or hear with your ears? What are you doing to protect yourself in the following areas? (Exercise your responsibility within the CHAMPION's Ring.)

- ■ Movies
- ■ The Internet
- ■ Video games
- ■ Television
- ■ Music
- ■ Magazines

4b. When you are faced with an opportunity to look at pornography, what will you do to gain God's strength to resist that temptation? (What's in God's Ring?)

QUESTION #4B TIP:
Remember the "way of escape" from 1 Corinthians 10:13 and the "full armor of God" from Ephesians 6.

5. Recite the CHAMPION Warrior Creed. Say it as you would to a group of people; speak slowly and clearly.

RECONNAISSANCE

1. Review the Map of the Mission on page 8 and determine the team's location in episode 8.

2. Review the CHAMPION definition of **Courage**. (Refer to the CHAMPION Code on page 6.)

Answer: "I will cultivate bravery and trust in God. I will break out of my comfort zone by seeking to conquer my fears. I will learn to recover, recover, and recover again."

3. What happened to Teknon during the team's fight with the footsoldiers?

Answer: When the footsoldiers attacked, Teknon froze in fear. Kratos got hurt while protecting Teknon during the attack.

4. Why do you think Teknon responded the way he did during the battle?

Answer: He allowed his fear to control him.

Quote Tip:

Ask your son why President Roosevelt said the credit belongs to the man who is actually in the arena.

Answer: We learn and achieve by stepping out. Only those who step forward to take risks by faith, trusting God to provide the strength and resources for accomplishing great things ... will receive the satisfaction and reward God intended.

---

5. **How did Teknon feel about his performance during the battle? Why?**

   Answer: He felt embarrassed and guilty. He felt that he had let his team down by deserting them while they were so courageously protecting him in the battle.

6. **How did the footsoldier manage to hurt Kratos?**

   Answer: Kratos left himself vulnerable to attack when he diverted his full attention and resources to protecting Teknon.

Optional Questions

7. **Could Kratos have prevented getting injured by the footsoldier? If so, how?**

   Answer: By focusing on protecting himself, instead of saving Teknon.

8. **The CHAMPION Warriors worked well as a team. When you face problems, why is teamwork so important?**

   Answer: Each member of the team has unique strengths and weakness. As they work together, they can support each other. The power of any effective team is stronger than the power of each individual battling alone.

---

9. **What did Epps mean when he said, "It takes time to learn how to respond correctly in battle."?**

   Answer: Learning how to live successfully in any area of life takes time and effort.

10. **Epps also coached Teknon that, "You learn by doing." How does this apply to Teknon?**

    Answer: As Teknon takes risks and tries new things, he may initially fail, but if he presses on and continues to try, he will learn and begin a lifelong process of mastering different areas of his life.

Strategy and Tactics

The size of a person is determined by what it takes to stop him.

Dr. Howard Hendricks

Failure is an essential part of life. It can also be an expensive part of life. At the end of the movie "Apollo 13," actor Tom Hanks quotes his character, astronaut Jim Lovell with this statement: "They called Apollo 13 a successful failure. We didn't make it to the moon, but we returned safely."

Gene Krantz, mission control specialist of Apollo 13, vented his frustration at two other NASA officials after hearing them discuss the potential, impending disaster to the space program after this setback. "Excuse me gentlemen," he barked. "I believe this will be our finest hour."

Failure has two faces. There are *successful* failures, and there are *unsuccessful* failures. Apollo 13 was a successful failure. Not only did the astronauts return home safely under incredibly difficult circumstances, they also exercised a high level of creative output and genuine teamwork over a period of only five days that rivals any single human endeavor of the century.

Learning to Recover

Dave Simmons, former linebacker of the Dallas Cowboys, had an interesting football philosophy that applies to the rest of life too. He said, "Every play is a game; learn to recover, recover, recover."

Simmons explained in his seminar *Dad the Family Shepherd* that every play during a football game is like a game in itself. The team plans for the play, gets information for the play, and then executes the play. Usually the play is a success. Sometimes it's not. Whether or not the play is successful, the team must come back and execute again.

Let's say it's second down and ten yards to go. The quarterback throws a short pass over the middle. His eyes widen because it's almost intercepted. If it had been intercepted, the cornerback on the other team would have run for a touchdown. After the play, the quarterback is back in the huddle. What is he going to think? What is he going to do?

Through successful failure your son can learn and grow when he falls short. When he fails as a result of working hard to complete a worthwhile task, remind him he cannot lose—he can only makes mistakes. Dr. Paul Brand, in his book, *Pain—the Gift Nobody Wants* reveals that pain experienced from failure and other sources enables us to grow and learn. Your son needs to understand that, at times, he will need to embrace the successful failures he experiences so that he will grow as a result of those failures. But he also needs to learn that he can recover from unsuccessful failure too.

In great attempts, it is glorious even to fail.

Vince Lombardi

The quarterback has to do three things. (1) He must learn from his mistake of throwing the ball late. (2) He must decide what he is going to do on the next play. (3) He must recover from the mistake and move on to the next play! The more he plays, the less he will make that mistake again. What would happen if he said to himself, *Gosh, I shouldn't have thrown that pass; it was almost intercepted. I guess I just shouldn't play football.* Nonsense!

There are times when failure is a natural consequence of living. In fact, God often uses trials and failures as a learning process in our lives. When He does this, we learn, as Epps said, by doing. In James 1:2-4 the NIV Bible tells us, "Consider it pure joy, my brothers, when you face trials of many kinds, because you know that the testing of your faith develops perseverance. Perseverance must finish its work so that you may be mature and complete, not lacking anything."

There are times, however, when we fail because we run from responsibility. Sometimes we run because we aren't prepared for the challenge we face. Sometimes we run because we fear the criticism we might receive from our peers as a result of taking the responsibility. And sometimes we run because we fear the possibility of failure.

Failure, Forgiveness, and Fortification

Failure can have another name—sin. Sin, simply put, is falling short of God's perfect standard, which results in broken fellowship with Him. Whether we sin by active disobedience or rebellion, or by passive indifference, the result is the same. But we can recover from this type of failure and make it successful.

When we avoid responsibility, we must get back into the game as soon as possible. The recovery progresses in three stages:

I. **Failure:** We make the wrong decision, do the wrong thing, or find ourselves unable to succeed in a task.

II. **Forgiveness:** If sin is involved, we seek to restore fellowship with God by asking His forgiveness for our mistake. Then we forgive ourselves for our poor choice and weakness. We also seek forgiveness from people we have hurt.

III. **Fortification:** We recognize God's forgiveness for our failure and His grace for our limitations, learn from our mistakes, and try again.

If we confess our sins, He [God] is faithful and righteous to forgive us our sins and to cleanse us from all unrighteousness.

1 John 1:9

The Bible describes how the apostle Peter recovered after failing Jesus several times.

1. Check out Matthew 16:21-23. How did Peter respond toward Jesus and his prediction of his own suffering and death? How did Jesus respond to Peter?

Answer: Peter rebuked Jesus and insisted that Jesus would not be killed. Then Jesus scolded Peter, referred to him as Satan, and told him he was a stumbling block to the work of God.

QUESTION #1 TIP: Ask your son: How would you feel about being "chewed out" by Jesus face-to-face?

2a. According to Luke 22:54-62, what did Peter do when Jesus was on the verge of being crucified?

Answer: Peter denied three times that h... knew Jesus or was one of his disciples.

2b. What do you think Peter's responsibility was to Jesus in this situation?

Answer: Peter could have stood up and acknowledged his connection with Jesus, he could have encouraged Jesus in this difficult time, and he could have spoken to the chief priest on Jesus' behalf.

2c. Why do you think Peter ran from responsibility and failed Jesus in His time of need?

Answer: He let fear control him and abandoned Jesus. He did not trust Christ to do what He promised because the circumstances did not seem to be going in his favor.

The early teen years are a particularly rough time for boys to feel good about themselves. Be sensitive and encouraging for your son. Encourage him that you believe in his ability to recover from a failure.

Even though large tracts of Europe have fallen or may fall into the grip of the Gestapo and all the odious apparatus of Nazi rule, we shall not flag nor fail. We shall go on to the end, we shall fight in France, we shall fight on the seas and the oceans, we shall fight with growing confidence and growing strength in the air, we shall defend our island, whatever the cost may be ... we shall never surrender.

Winston Churchill (before Parliament in June 1940)

3. Read John 21:15-19 and Acts 2:38-47. Was Peter able to recover from his failures to obey and follow Christ? How do you know?

Answer: Jesus forgave Peter for denying him and then encouraged him to continue his mission of teaching and caring for others. Peter went on to lead many people to faith in Christ and was a key leader in the rapid growth of the early church.

Peter was one of Jesus' closest friends. In fact, Jesus referred to Peter as the "Rock" because of his faith and strength of character. When Jesus told Peter that all of His friends would eventually deny him, Peter promised that he would never do such a thing. And yet, Peter ran from his responsibility on the night Jesus was crucified. When asked about his friendship with Christ, Peter denied that he even knew Jesus three times!

"What a cowardly failure Peter was!" we might say. How could he recover from such a mistake? Well, he not only sought forgiveness from God for his mistake, but he went on to become one of the most powerful preachers the world has ever known. Peter recovered!

4. Have you ever felt like a failure the way Teknon felt after the battle? Do you think God understands that you aren't perfect?

5. Read Psalm 103:13-14 and 1 Corinthians 1:25-27. What do these verses teach us about our own strength and God's understanding of how we're put together?

Answer: God created us so He knows our weaknesses and failures. And yet, God still has compassion on us as a loving father would. Our awesome God loves you in all your weakness and wants to use you to help build His kingdom and bring glory to His name!

God knows that we make mistakes. He knows us better than we know ourselves because He created us. If you've made a mistake you can recover. If you've run from responsibility, you can recover. If you've been criticized, you can recover. God has unlimited power to enable you to recover, recover, and recover again. Remember, successful failure is not a bad thing. But if your failure is a sin, you must admit your failure to God, choose not to make the bad choice again, and return to walking with God. If you do these things, He promises to restore you.

6. When, in your life, have you experienced a successful failure? How did you learn from, and recover from, that failure?

QUESTION #6 TIP:
This would be a good place to share a couple of your own stories about when you recovered from successful failures.

7. Describe one or two or your unsuccessful failures? How did you learn from, and recover from the failure?

QUESTION #7 TIP:
Again, share one of your own stories of unsuccessful failure, but be careful not to share anything too personal or degrading that would reduce your son's respect for you.

8. As a result of what you've learned in this session, how will you handle successful and unsuccessful failures differently in the future?

IMPORTANT NOTE:
Remind your son that if he has invited Jesus Christ into his life, he has access to God's forgiveness for his unsuccessful failures. When he sins, he should confess it to God, turn away from that attitude or behavior (repent), and recover by moving on with the assurance that God has forgiven him. Confession and repentance will immediately restore his fellowship with God.

Do you think that Teknon will learn how to recover and get back into the battle? Press on to episode 9 of the story.

If needed, help your son by suggesting some key truths that he should have learned during this session. For example, ask your son to discuss the difference between successful and unsuccessful failure and how to deal with each type. Or, you might highlight the importance of facing fears and of learning how to recover.

THE Main Things I learned in this Champion Session are:

_____

_____

_____

_____

_____

CHAMPION Sheet of Deeds

SHEET OF DEEDS:

Only a *brief* description of each action point is provided here. Go to the Think Tank (chapter 5) for complete instructions.

Go to the CHAMPION Sheet of Deeds on page 9 and write down **one thing you will begin to do** before the next session (and beyond) to apply the main things you learned in session 8.

Check one of the suggestions below for your son to write down as his action point on his CHAMPION Sheet of Deeds for session 8. Descriptions and explanations of these action points are provided in the Think Tank (chapter 5) of this guide.

❏ Ask your son to identify one of his fears that you would like to help him overcome. Then help him to set up an activity where he can face that fear.

❏ Ask your son to make a full list of his sins, failures, and shortcomings. Then review 1 John 1:9 highlighting confession, repentance, and God's promise of forgiveness and cleansing. Encourage him to seek forgiveness and then destroy the list (which God promises to remember no more).

❏ Create your own unique action point.

Your Mission

Complete your mission and CHAMPION Session Prep before you meet for session 9.

Power Verse: Joshua 1:9

Date memorized: _____

Critical Maneuver

This will reinforce what you learned today. Obtain your maneuver instructions from your father.

CHAMPION Sheet of Deeds

Begin to apply your action point from your Sheet of Deeds.

—— CHAMPION Session Prep ——

Reread episode 9 of *Teknon and the CHAMPION Warriors*, and then complete session 9 in your *Mission Guide* on your own. **Our next CHAMPION Session:**

Date:
_____

Time:
_____

Place:
_____

Critical Maneuver:
Go to the Think Tank (chapter 5 of this guide) and select one of the critical maneuvers listed under session 8 to accomplish with your son.

◆ Teknon and the CHAMPION Warriors ◆

Session 9:
Recover,
Recover, Recover

Champion Characteristics
Courage and Mental Toughness

Power Verse: Psalm 56:3-4

When I am afraid, I will put my trust in You. In God, whose word I praise, in God I have put my trust; I shall not be afraid. What can mere man do to me?

Story Summary

Teknon's apprehension spills over into episode 9 as he realizes that he must act to save his father and friends. Matty gives Teknon a crash course in leadership, coaching him in how to enlist the aid of other people. Teknon hesitates because he does not want to enter a situation where he may not be accepted. But, he realizes the magnitude of the situation and is forced to break out of his comfort zone. He runs to get help in the nearby mining village.

Help comes in the form of a stocky, little fellow named Phileo. Phileo belongs to a race of people know as the Phaskos. Even though Teknon is barraged with negative mental messages from Scandalon on his way to the Phasko village, the urgency of the situation helps him overcome his lack of confidence and his inhibitions. He convinces Phileo and the other Phaskos to help him. On their return trip to where the team is entrapped, Teknon comes face to face with Scandalon, who inflicts a gash on Teknon's arm before Phileo comes to his aid.

After the rescue is complete, his team members congratulate Teknon for his courage in overcoming his fears and in gaining the help they needed. Then Kratos and Phileo, nicknamed Phil, acknowledge a long-term friendship. Phil is the informant they've been seeking.

In this session, you and your son will explore what it means to live courageously—facing fears, getting out of comfort zones, and standing for what is right. You will also discuss the importance of seeking respect from other people rather than doing things for their acceptance. Finally, you will discuss the potential paralysis of discouragement, as well as the importance of recovering from failure. Session 12 will delve deeper into the topic of managing discouragement.

QUESTION #3 TIP:
If your son successfully memorized this verse, have him date the verse in session 8 of his *Mission Guide*.

QUESTION #4 TIP:
Refer back to sessions 1 and 8 for previous discussions around the topic of fear and ways to overcome it.

Discussion Topics

Breaking out of your "comfort zone"
Being respected vs. being liked
Recovering from failure—part 2: not giving in to discouragement

Mission Debrief

1. Discuss your mission from session 8. Did you complete your maneuver? If so, what did you learn? If not, why not?

2. What are some habits you are successfully forming as you apply your action points from your Sheet of Deeds? Any areas of struggle?

3. Recite your power verse (Joshua 1:9) from session 8.

4. What is your greatest fear from among those you identified during your mission from session 8? What are some things you could do to overcome it (remember, the CHAMPION's Ring includes areas where you can make a difference)? What things do you need to trust to the Lord (responsibilities that rest in God's Ring)?

5. Recite the CHAMPION Warrior Creed out loud. Pause before you say the lines about courage and mental toughness.

RECONNAISSANCE

1. Review the Map of the Mission on page 8 to determine the team's location in episode 9.

2. Review the CHAMPION definitions of **Courage** and **Mental Toughness** (refer to the CHAMPION Code on page 6).

   Answer for Courage: "I will cultivate bravery and trust in God. I will break out of my comfort zone by seeking to conquer my fears. I will learn to recover, recover, and recover again."

   Answer for Mental Toughness: "I will allow God to direct my thinking toward gaining common sense and wisdom. I will use discernment when making hard decisions. I will desire respect from others rather than compromise my convictions for acceptance or approval."

OPTIONAL QUESTIONS

3. What were Matty's three main instructions to Teknon?

   Answer: He told Teknon to (1) meet the people with confidence and authority, (2) analyze the people while trying to determine any unmet needs, and (3) state the problem in a clear and concise manner.

4. How did Teknon motivate the Phaskos to join him?

   Answer: He determined their need (the missing children) then described how they could achieve a set of mutual objectives by saving Kratos and the mentors.

---

5. **Why did Teknon hesitate to go to the village? What was he afraid of?**

   Answer: He was afraid of confronting people and trying to motivate them to help him. He was also afraid of the rejection he might experience from those people after presenting his plea for help.

6. **Why did Tor tell Teknon not to worry about being liked by the Phaskos? What did Tor say about respect? What did he mean?**

   Answer: Tor told Teknon that the only thing that matters is that the Phaskos respect his position. He essentially told him that it was far more important to be respected than to be liked.

7. **Look back at episode 4 where Teknon meets the Harpax. Do you think Teknon liked being liked? Why do you think acceptance by the Harpax was so important to Teknon?**

   Answer: He wanted to be liked by the Harpax until he realized their intentions. Teknon's desire for acceptance is the same as it is for most teenagers—he wants to fit in and be a part of the group. He wants others to be recognized and viewed as a worthwhile person by his peers.

8. **What did Scandalon do to Teknon on his way to the village? Why?**

   Answer: Scandalon tried to deceive and discourage Teknon in order to dissolve the youth's confidence, keep him from accomplishing his objective, and eventually convert him to Mago's way of thinking.

9. **What did Teknon recognize about the strange voice he heard while he was leading the Phaskos back to the team?**

   Answer: Teknon finally recognized that the discouraging voice was fabricated, and that the messages were lies intended to deceive and discourage him.

10. Why did Teknon respond differently to Scandalon's voice on the way back to the clearing?

Answer: With renewed confidence, Teknon listened more closely and once he identified the source of the voice, his insecurity subsided and he changed his focus.

11. Why did Teknon want to keep the scar on his arm?

Answer: Teknon kept the scar as a reminder of the lessons he learned during the experience of rescuing his father and mentors. Tor described it as a badge of courage because Teknon faced his fear and conquered it.

QUESTION #11 TIP: Sometimes we need to remember the battle scars, emotional and spiritual, that we have received during difficult times in our lives. These scars have helped us to grow as men. Share with your son about a time when God led you through a difficult experience and what you learned from it.

12. Do you think Teknon recovered from his failure in episode 8? If so, how?

Answer: Teknon moved beyond his failure and refocused his efforts on his objective instead of on himself and his failure. With a renewed focus, he proceeded to the Phasko village where he succeeded in his objective to get help. He recovered!

Strategy and Tactics

Be on the alert, stand firm in the faith, act like men, be strong.

1 Corinthians 16:13

Break Out of the Zone!

Have you ever heard an athlete say, "I was in the zone"? For an athlete, being "in the zone" refers to playing a sport far beyond what he considers his normal ability. If you've had that experience, you know how good it feels to experience that kind of achievement. There's another zone, however, that also feels good, but for another reason. It's called the "comfort zone."

In the comfort zone, you feel good because you feel comfortable. The comfort zone is a place where you do things because it's the way you've always done them.

Let's say you are becoming a skilled trumpet player. One

BREAK OUT TIP: To a young man it's not just the task of accomplishing something he fears that concerns him. He probably also struggles with the desire to be accepted and liked. In this section you will also have the opportunity to explore with your son how to deal with his longing to be liked and accepted by his peers.

morning the bandleader says to you, "How about playing a solo during our next concert?"

"No way," you blurt out. "I like playing with the other trumpet players just fine, thank you very much." There you are in the center of your comfort zone. You have an opportunity to grow, but you don't want to risk breaking out.

QUESTION #1 TIP:
Assure your son that if he's experienced fear, he's not alone. Everybody has been afraid at one time or another. But we don't have to remain trapped in our fears. This might be a good place to share an example of your own fear that you eventually overcame.

1. Have you ever been afraid to take on a particularly difficult task, to work closely with someone who really seems not to like you, or to ask for the help of someone who you are afraid to approach? Jot down a couple of examples.

We break out of our comfort zone by conquering our fears. When we conquer fears with God's help, we experience personal, emotional, and spiritual victory.

We will examine some important factors to remember when you want to break out of your comfort zone.

Every noble work is at first impossible.

Thomas Carlyle

GOD PROVIDES THE POWER TO BREAK OUT OF THE ZONE

2a. What does King David tell you about who God is and what He does for you in Psalm 27:1,13-14?

Answer: God is his light (dispelling anxieties and dangers), his salvation (guaranteed victory), and his defense (stronghold against any assaults). With God on his side, he has nothing or nobody to dread. Verse 13 highlights that God is good. He is always looking out for your son's good, no matter how things may seem.

2b. What does Psalm 27:1,13-14 tell you not to do? What does it tell you that you should do?

Answer: DO NOT fear or dread things or people. DO NOT despair because God is good. DO believe in God's goodness. DO wait for the Lord and His direction and timing of events. DO be strong and let your heart take courage.

Breaking Out of the Zone Is Profitable but Not Always Popular

Often, the biggest barrier to leaving the comfort zone is our own fear of what others might say. Nobody likes to be criticized, and nobody likes to be misunderstood. When we do something outside our comfort zone, like giving a speech or sharing our faith in God with someone else, we put our egos at risk. Let's face it: we like to be liked. But it is not always necessary to be liked by everyone. At times, people are going to misunderstand us. At other times, people will also become angry with us even when we do the right thing!

3. Read Psalm 56:3-4. If you trust in God, what can others do to you?

   Answer: The psalmist asks, "What can mere man do to me?" The answer is obvious: nothing! The real question is, do we really believe this? In Romans 8:31b Paul asks, "If God is for us, who is against us?" Our God is awesome in His power.

4. What does Jesus warn us about living in this world in John 15:15-16? How should we expect to be liked and accepted if we are His friends and follow Him?

   Answer: Jesus said we shouldn't be surprised if the world hates us (His followers and friends), because it hated Him first. We must expect that people in this world will not always accept us if we choose to follow God.

On May 20-21, 1927, Charles Lindbergh accomplished something many people thought was impossible. In fact, many people didn't understand why the young pilot would even attempt to fly solo across the Atlantic Ocean from New York to Paris. Today hundreds of planes fly transatlantic every day, but prior to 1927 several other pilots had met their deaths in similar transatlantic attempts. People tried to convince Lindbergh that death was waiting for him somewhere in the icy waters of the Atlantic. Many became angry and called him crazy. Fortunately, Lindbergh ignored his critics and showed the world that he and his famous plane, "The Spirit of St. Louis," had the right stuff. Today we recognize him as an American hero because of his unwillingness to allow circumstances or criticism to discourage him from reaching his dream.

In the same way, Scandalon hit Teknon with discouraging comments on his way to the village when he was trying to recover from failure. Our enemy (Satan) can use this tactic very effectively to keep us from recovering,

5. Do you ever hear voices like this from other people or in your own thoughts? Underline the following comments that sound familiar.

- Don't tell me you're going to speak in front of the class today. Are you nuts?!

- Forget trying out for the team. You don't stand a chance.

- Why do you want to make good grades? No one else does.

- You mean you haven't kissed a girl yet? What are you, some kind of freak?

- Share your faith? What if the person laughs at you?

Any others? Write them here:

As Teknon returned to the clearing, he recognized that Scandalon's voice was a trick. He determined that the voices he heard were a lie and did not apply to him. Then he changed his mental course by ignoring those false messages.

6. What does 2 Timothy 1:7 say about fear?

Answer: God did not create us to be fearful and timid about carrying out the tasks He gives us, but rather to draw on His power to live courageously by faith. We also need to draw on His love and seek a sound mind to focus on His truth instead of the lies of the devil.

7. What does Jesus say about the truth (God's Word) in John 8:32?

Answer: Jesus tells us that if we abide in His Word and learn the truth, then knowing and living by the real truth revealed in God's Word will set us free from sin and the lies of the devil.

When you hear false voices, replace them with the truth of God's Word. If you have invited Christ into your life by faith, you are child of the King. Neither people nor Satan's messengers can intimidate you unless you let them.

According to Henry Blackaby and Claude King, authors of *Experiencing God*, God is working all around us. When we seek to develop our personal relationship with Him, which began when we invited Him into our lives by faith, He provides opportunities to join Him where He is working. These invitations usually take us out of our comfort zone. But if we step outside the zone (remember the CHAMPION's Ring on the Hoplon) and allow God to accomplish what only He can (God's Ring), we grow as individuals as well as in our relationship with Him.

BREAKING OUT OF THE ZONE IS WORTH THE RISK

At times, God asks us to step out of our comfort zone to obey His will. We may not know how we are going to accomplish it, but we know that He wants it done. That's when God expects us to trust in Him by faith and watch Him bring about the results.

> *We all are faced with a series of great opportunities brilliantly disguised as impossible situations.*
>
> Charles Swindoll

QUOTE TIP:
Ask your son what this quote means. Then, give your son an example from your life when you faced what appeared to be an impossible situation, but God worked through it and turned it into a great opportunity.

8. Read Matthew 17:20. If we have faith in God, what does He say that we can do? How much faith do we need in order to see God do mighty things?

Answer: If you have faith as small as a tiny mustard seed, God can even move a mountain. Without faith, it is impossible to please God, but with a little faith nothing is impossible if God wants to do it for you.

We can have faith in God is because He is faithful. He is all-powerful and loves you unconditionally. If God provides you an opportunity to leave your comfort zone, He will give you the power to break out of it. Philippians 4:13 reminds us that "I can do all things through Him [Jesus Christ] who gives me strength."

We grow by taking the risk to trust God in our daily lives. God loves us and wants us to grow—in our relationship with Him, in our understanding of ourselves, and in our relationships with other people. Just like Teknon received help to accomplish his rescue mission, we can trust God to provide the power to accomplish whatever mission He gives us when we ask for His help. We may not always see His answer right away. Sometimes God wants us to wait patiently; He wants us to learn through waiting, even though it's difficult. But we can always be confident that He knows our concerns and wants the best for us.

Remember when Tor told Teknon to look at his scar often, and never to forget what he had learned that night? Faith often involves risk—risk to our self-esteem and maybe even to our friendships. Sometimes we have to risk getting hurt by other people. But when we conquer our fears, step out of our comfort zone, and trust God through the experience, we will receive a feeling of exhilaration and a memory of victory that will stay with us forever!

9. Name three activities that would take you out of your comfort zone.

(1)

(2)

(3)

THE Main Things I learned in this Champion Session are:

_____

_____

_____

_____

_____

CHAMPION Sheet of Deeds

Go to the CHAMPION Sheet of Deeds on page 9 and write down **one thing you will begin to do** before the next session (and beyond) to apply the main things you learned in session 9.

Check one of the suggestions below for your son to write down as his action point on his CHAMPION Sheet of Deeds for session 9. Descriptions and explanations of these action points are provided in the Think Tank (chapter 5) of this guide.

- ❑ Develop a list of his comfort zones and activities to challenge those zones.
- ❑ Choose one significant activity to help him to face a fear.
- ❑ Create your own unique action point.

Check the *dads-only action* (listed under session 9 in the Think Tank): Read chapter 6 in the book *Telling Yourself the Truth* by Will Backus and Marie Chapman for a description of how your son can begin to manage his need to be accepted by others.

MAIN THINGS:
If needed, help your son by suggesting some key truths that he should have learned during this session, such as the importance of breaking out of his comfort zone when God leads him to new opportunities and challenges. You may want to remind him of the three important factors for breaking out of comfort zones: (1) God provides the power to break out of the zone, (2) breaking out of the zone is profitable but not always popular, and (3) breaking out of the zone is worth the risk.

SHEET OF DEEDS:
Only a *brief* description of each action point is provided here. Go to the Think Tank (chapter 5) for complete instructions.

You gain strength, courage, and confidence by every experience in which you really stop to look fear in the face ... You must do the thing you think you cannot do.

Eleanor Roosevelt

Complete your mission and CHAMPION Session Prep before you meet for session 10.

POWER VERSE: PSALM 56:3-4

Date memorized: _____

CRITICAL MANEUVER

CRITICAL MANEUVER:
Go to the Think Tank (chapter 5 of this guide) and select one of the critical maneuvers listed under session 9 to accomplish with your son.

This will reinforce what you learned today. Obtain your maneuver instructions from your father.

CHAMPION SHEET OF DEEDS

Begin to apply your action point from your Sheet of Deeds.

CHAMPION SESSION PREP

Reread episode 10 of *Teknon and the CHAMPION Warriors*, and then complete the questions in session 10 in your *Mission Guide* on your own. Our next CHAMPION Session will be:

DATE:
_____

TIME:
_____

PLACE:
_____

SESSION 10: GOOD ENOUGH

CHAMPION Characteristics
Attitude and Integrity

POWER VERSE: 1 CORINTHIANS 9:24-25A

Do you not know that those who run in a race all run, but only one receives the prize? Run in such a way that you may win. Everyone who competes in the games exercises self-control in all things.

STORY SUMMARY

Phil joins the warriors as they travel to the Northron Peninsula. "Laid back" are the best words to describe the people and lifestyle of this tropical paradise. Unfortunately, Northrons have abandoned all desire to rise above a life of leisure. They have settled into a mindset of mediocrity, which is characterized by their oft-spoken motto: "good enough." Because Northrons refuse to improve themselves and their surroundings, they have neglected the vital foundations of their lives.

The team uses Northros as a temporary base before entering the mountainous region to challenge Magos in his fortress. Kratos and Matty leave their companions to perform reconnaissance of enemy territory, while the remaining team members stay in Northros. During their stay, the warriors engage in a fierce battle with a creature called a leviathan. This confrontation results from the apathetic negligence of the Northrons. In the battle, the team saves a young woman named Paranomia. During the struggle, one of the Northron men abandons the young woman and stands by aimlessly. Tor, greatly frustrated by the Northron's attitudes and lifestyle, unleashes his temper by throwing and injuring the young man, whom Epps later heals. Afterward, Tor's conscience gets the best of him and he asks forgiveness from the young man.

Help your son to under-
stand that he can set the
pace within the mire of
mediocrity in our cul-
ture by being a good
example. This episode
offers an opportunity to
discuss with your son
what it means to "rock
the boat" by setting a
high standard in every
area of his life.

In addition, use Tor's
angry outburst and
actions as a springboard
to discuss what factors
caused his anger to
build and explode.
Tor's example will also
enable you to discuss
with your son proper
ways to handle anger
and seek forgiveness.

QUESTION #3 TIP:
If your son successfully
memorized the verse,
have him date the verse
in session 9 of his
Mission Guide.

QUESTION #4 TIP:
Sometimes bullies make
life difficult through
their cowardly threats
and oppression. This
question gives you the
opportunity to deter-
mine if there are bullies
in your son's life. If
there are, provide guid-
ance on handling his sit-
uation and remind him
that you are there to
help him work through
this.

DISCUSSION TOPICS

Pursuing excellence and resisting mediocrity
Managing your anger

MISSION DEBRIEF

1. Discuss your mission from session 9. What was the most important thing you learned from your maneuver?

2. Name one key thing that you have learned so far by applying your action points from the Sheet of Deeds.

3. Recite your power verse (Psalm 56:3-4) from session 9.

4. This power verse reveals that we should not fear people. Is there any person or group of people you fear? Why? What can you do to face this fear?

   Answer: There isn't anyone we should fear in this world. There are those we should respect and obey—our parents and other authorities God has placed in our lives, for example. There are also those we should approach with caution or even those we should avoid, but none we should fear.

5. Recite the CHAMPION Warrior Creed together from memory (see page 5).

RECONNAISSANCE

1. Review the Map of the Mission on page 8 to determine the team's location in episode 10.

2. Review CHAMPION definition of **Integrity**.

    Answer: "I will seek to acquire a clear understanding of who I am in Christ so that I may have a deeper comprehension of what I believe, what I stand for, and how I can live out those convictions in the most difficult circumstances, whether I am alone or with others. I will allow other people to hold me accountable to standards of excellence."

3. What does the phrase "I will allow other people to hold me accountable to standards of excellence" mean to you?

    Answer: We will only achieve that for which we aim. With God's direction and strength, combined with the encouragement of those we love and respect, we can accomplish great things.

QUESTION #3 TIP: The purpose of this session is to illustrate to your son the importance of setting high standards and goals in our lives, as well as the danger of settling for mediocrity or "good enough" results.

4. Phil said that the Northrons enjoyed mediocrity. How is this revealed in their lives?

    Answer: Through their actions and speech. Northrons showed no motivation to improve themselves or their environment. They also showed no interest in helping each other.

5. Tor said that the Northrons "have no vision ... no purpose ... no plan." He said, "Where there's no purpose, there's no passion for living." Why is it important to have vision, purpose, and a plan in our lives?

Answer: Over time, God, through our relationship with Him, gives us the vision He has for our lives. From this vision we gain the full, meaningful passion for living that only He can provide. From this passion, we have a sustained, productive, and exciting purpose in everything we do. Personal integrity involves taking the responsibility (CHAMPION's Ring) to pursue excellence and exercise discipline in every area of our lives so that God's can accomplish His exciting purpose through us.

Optional Questions

6. *Northros*, a Greek term, refers to being slothful, sluggish, or lazy. Why was this community called Northros?

   Answer: The people living in Northros are not only lazy, but also irresponsible and negligent.

---

7. Why did Tor lose his temper?

   Answer: Tor was angered because of the Northrons' lack of initiative, especially when it concerned helping each other. Tor was especially angered by the young man's cowardly response to saving the young girl from the leviathan.

8. Do you think that Tor had a right to get angry? Why or why not? Was it right for him to hurt the Northron? Why do you see it that way?

   Answer: The Bible tells us we can be angry for the right reasons, but we still should not sin (see Ephesians 4:26). Tor sinned when he lost control of his emotions and hurt the Northron.

9. How did Tor feel after he lost his temper? What did he do after he hurt the Northron? Why?

   Answer: He felt guilty because he recognized his lack of self-control. After he regained his composure, Tor went back to the Northron and asked his forgiveness for the attack. The CHAMPION Warrior Code states: "I will improve my ability to manage anger." Tor knew that the teachings of Pneuma included the principle of managing anger effectively.

Hold yourself responsible to a higher standard than anyone else expects of you. Never excuse yourself.

Henry Ward Beecher

10. **What did Epps say was a sign of true strength in Tor? What did Epps mean by that?**

Answer: The sign of true strength was Tor's willingness to humbly ask for forgiveness. Epps meant that it takes strength of character to humble yourself, admit that you are wrong, and ask another person for forgiveness.

11. ***Tharreo*** **is a Greek word that refers to having courage, confidence, and boldness. Tor is a task-driven leader; one who likes to be in authority. How does he show his courage?**

Answer: Tor has risked his own safety on several occasions for the sake of his team and the completion of the mission. For example, in episode 6, he saves many of the passengers aboard the *Ergonaut*. Tor also reveals his courage in the stand he takes for Pneuma and the CHAMPION cause against Magos and his evil schemes.

STRATEGY AND TACTICS

RAISE THE BAR, ROCK THE BOAT, BUT DON'T ROLL WITH THE TIDE

You decide to make better grades this semester. To make this happen, you will need to work harder and pay more attention in class. When your friends find out what you're doing, what might they say?

"JUST CHILL OUT!"

You choose to get into excellent physical shape. You will have to run and work out with weights three times a week. Some of your friends who don't exercise hear about this. What might they say?

"JUST CHILL OUT!"

You sense that God wants you to share your faith with some non-Christians. But in order to do that, you'll need to learn how to share your testimony of how you became a Christian, as well as how to lead another person into a relationship with Jesus.

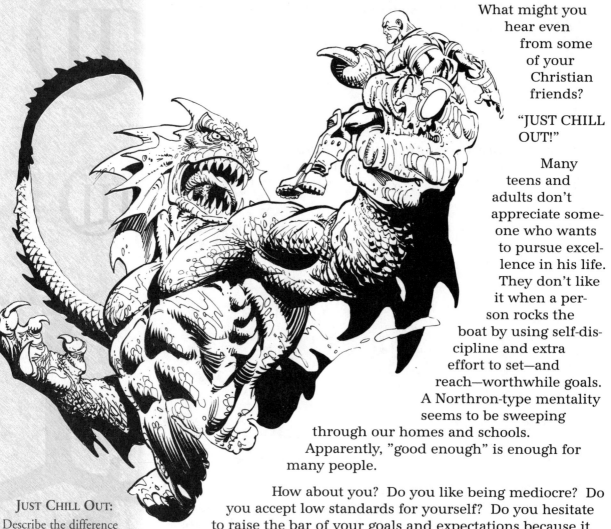

What might you hear even from some of your Christian friends?

"JUST CHILL OUT!"

Many teens and adults don't appreciate someone who wants to pursue excellence in his life. They don't like it when a person rocks the boat by using self-discipline and extra effort to set—and reach—worthwhile goals. A Northron-type mentality seems to be sweeping through our homes and schools. Apparently, "good enough" is enough for many people.

How about you? Do you like being mediocre? Do you accept low standards for yourself? Do you hesitate to raise the bar of your goals and expectations because it will set you apart from others? Or is it just too much effort to be better than "good enough"?

JUST CHILL OUT:
Describe the difference between a thermometer and a thermostat. A thermometer only records the temperature. A thermostat, on the other hand, determines and activates the level of the temperature in its surroundings. Encourage your son to be a thermostat, rather than a thermometer, within his sphere of influence.

1. Revelation 3:15-16 describes the church at Laodicea. What kind of attitude is Jesus describing here? And what is His response toward this type of attitude?

   Answer: Jesus says their deeds are neither cold nor hot. Jesus is describing the attitude of being lukewarm or indifferent to God's principles, compromising, accommodating, and "on the fence." This is the attitude that says, "I don't care; it's good enough." This attitude is so disgusting to the Lord and so damaging to His purposes that He says it makes Him feel sick!

2a. According to Ephesians 5:15-17, how should we use our time?

Answer: The NIV translates this as follows: "Be very careful, then, how you live—not as unwise but as wise, making the most of every opportunity, because the days are evil. Therefore, do not be foolish, but understand what the Lord's will is." We need to be wise and careful in how we live. We must live our lives with God's vision, purpose, and plan for our lives.

2b. What do you think it means to "make the most of every opportunity"?

Answer: We must always be ready (training) and available (attitude) to be used by God whenever He provides an opportunity.

Let us run with endurance the race that is set before us.

Hebrews 12:1b

3. Read Luke 2:40-52. In what ways was Jesus growing as a person even though He was only 12 years old?

Answer: Verse 52 says, "And Jesus kept increasing in wisdom and stature, and in favor with God and men." He was assuming greater levels of responsibility in His life. He was growing mentally (wisdom), physically (stature), spiritually (favor with God), and socially (favor with men).

God expects us to be thankful for the talents and opportunities He gives us. He also expects us to make the most of the life and gifts He has provided. The story in Luke 2 declares that Jesus grew and kept increasing in stature (physically), in wisdom (mentally), in favor with men (socially), and in favor with God (spiritually). Jesus was a good steward of what God the Father had entrusted to Him. He set an example for us to keep increasing in our maturity by avoiding mediocrity in our lives.

4. In Matthew 19:26 what does Jesus say is possible with God?

Answer: Although Jesus is talking here about salvation and entering heaven, He also points out that this (and many other things) is impossible for men, but ALL THINGS are possible with God.

5. Read Philippians 4:13. If we are Christians, what can we do as a result of God's power working through us?

Answer: "I can do all things through Him [the Lord] who strengthens me."

Average is your enemy.

Pearce "Rocky" Lane

QUOTE TIP:
Ask your son, "What does this quotation mean? Why would 'average' be your enemy? How do you fight this enemy?"

If you accept "average" you will never rise above mediocrity. You fight average by continually challenging yourself. You can't lower your standards to meet those around us.

If nothing is impossible with God, and you can do all things through Him as He gives you His strength, how should you approach your activities? Ask yourself these questions:

- Am I trying to learn everything that I can at school?
- Do I do my chores at home completely, without grumbling?
- Am I exercising and being careful what I eat?
- Am I reading good books on a regular basis?
- Am I learning how to interact well with people and treating them kindly?
- Am I consistent in spending time with God in prayer and Bible reading?
- Do I know how to share my faith?
- Do I look for opportunities to share my faith?

These questions refer to attitudes and behaviors that are your responsibility within the CHAMPION's Ring (see session 1). You can and should take responsibility to make the right choices in areas such as study, work, exercise, learning, and so on.

Don't allow yourself to fall into the Northron "good enough" mentality and don't be afraid to rock the boat of mediocrity. God will do His part (God's Ring), so trust Him to help you raise the bar in the different areas of your life. You don't have to roll with the tide of what everybody else is doing. "Aim high," as the Air Force says. Pursue excellence and let someone else do the chilling out!

USE YOUR HEAD; DON'T LOSE YOUR HEAD!

Do you have a short fuse? When people disagree with you or fail to meet your expectations does your response resemble the fireworks display at Walt Disney World? How often do you lose your patience or "blow up" with other people?

It's almost fashionable to have a short fuse, isn't it? More and more people seem to be adopting the attitude of "I'm mad and I'm not going to take it anymore!" as their creed for social interaction. Even violent anger is recognized as the status quo.

OPTIONAL QUESTIONS

6a. What makes you angry? How do you handle it when it erupts?

6b. Does any particular person make you angry? Why? How do you handle it when this person makes you angry?

7. Review the CHAMPION definition of Attitude (refer to "The CHAMPION Code" on page 6).

   Answer: "I will cultivate a disposition of humility. I will assume a correct and hopeful view of myself as a member of God's family. I will improve my ability to manage anger and discouragement. I will develop and enjoy an appropriate sense of humor."

---

8. How do you think a person learns to manage anger?

   Answer: We learn by deepening our relationship with God, living according to His principles, and following Christ's example so that we become "conformed to the image of Christ" (Romans 8:29-30). Then, we draw on His strength to control our emotions.

The Bible talks about the process of managing anger as a key component of self–control. Self-control is one of the outward expressions of Christ's presence in our lives as we learn to trust our lives to Him. The Bible calls these characteristics the "fruit of the Spirit."

USE YOUR HEAD: Anger and violence is becoming much more the norm for teens in our culture. Cultural restraint is eroding as people turn away from God's truth. The level of frustration and anger is rising because of disintegrating family structures. This is the arena in which your son must participate every day. And yet, God makes it clear that He wants us to exercise self-control when it comes to anger. In this section, you will explore biblical truths with your son that provide the solution for anger prevention and, ultimately, long-term anger management. Help your son to understand that anger is a normal, God-given emotion, but that it must be controlled.

9. Read Galatians 5:22-23. What is the fruit of the Spirit?

Answer: The fruit of the Spirit is a collection of nine characteristics produced by the Spirit in those who walk in dependence on Him (see verse 5:16). The collection is: love, joy, peace, patience, kindness, goodness, faithfulness, gentleness, and self-control.

Uncontrolled anger, like so many other things, can become a habit. Once you get used to "losing your head" it becomes easier to let it happen the next time. Tor had a habit of losing his temper until he decided to become a CHAMPION Warrior. He knew that self-control was a key characteristic of a CHAMPION and didn't want to accept "good enough" in his life.

If you are a Christian, God expects you to overcome a bad temper by drawing on His power. We plug into His strength by being filled with His Spirit. When you are filled with the Holy Spirit, you start displaying the fruit of the Spirit. It is one thing to hate evil and become angered by its presence in the world. It's another thing to take out frustrations on others. When we do that, we disobey God. If you sense that you have disobeyed God through a fit of bad temper, remember 1 John 1:9 and confess your anger to Him. He will forgive you and reestablish His line of communication and power with you.

But we could spend our lives trying to manage anger after it has erupted. How do we keep from losing our temper ahead of time? The book of James describes an effective formula for anger prevention.

10. Read James 1:19-20. What three things should we do to keep from losing our temper?

Write the formula here:

God's Power + _Quick to Hear or Listen_ + _Slow to Speak_

\+ _Slow to Anger_ = Anger Management

Emmett John Hughes, a friend of former President Eisenhower gave him this advice: "Never miss an opportunity to keep your mouth shut."

Keeping our mouths shut is one of the hardest things in the world to do when we get upset. It's also one of the most effective tools in anger management. A spoken word is like a football right before it's intercepted. As much as the quarterback wants it back, he can't get it back. If there is any question whether or not you should say something, listen to what Mr. Hughes said to the president. DON'T SAY IT!

Instead of being quick to speak, use the other highly effective tool in anger management. Learn to listen. Author Stephen Covey says, "Seek first to understand, then to be understood." Listen not only to what's being said, but also to what isn't being said. Try to put yourself in the other person's shoes so you can better understand his or her position.

God knows that you get angry; He created anger to alert you that something is wrong. But when you get angry, draw on His strength to remain calm and under the control of His Spirit. Use your head; don't lose your head!

If needed, help your son by suggesting some key truths that he should have learned during this session, such as the importance of pursuing excellence rather than settling for "good enough" in different areas of his life, and the formula for anger management.

Don't fly into a rage unless you are prepared for a rough landing.

Anonymous

SHEET OF DEEDS:

Only a *brief* description of each action point is provided here. Go to the Think Tank (chapter 5) for complete instructions.

THE Main Things I learned in this Champion Session are:

_____

_____

_____

_____

_____

CHAMPION SHEET OF DEEDS

Go to the CHAMPION Sheet of Deeds on page 9 and write down **one thing you will begin to do** before the next session (and beyond) to apply the main things you learned in session 10.

Check one of the suggestions below for your son to write down as his action point on his CHAMPION Sheet of Deeds for session 10. Descriptions and explanations of these action points are provided in the THINK TANK (chapter 5) of this guide.

❏ Identify one area where your son is just getting by and then develop a plan with him so he can raise the bar in that area.

❏ Help your son use the anger management formula for a specific situation in his life.

❏ Create your own unique action point.

Your Mission

Complete your mission and CHAMPION Session Prep before you meet for session 11.

POWER VERSE: I CORINTHIANS 9:24-25A

Date memorized: _____

CRITICAL MANEUVER

Your father will give you instructions for your maneuver.

CHAMPION SHEET OF DEEDS

Begin to apply your action point from your Sheet of Deeds.

CRITICAL MANEUVER: Go to the Think Tank (chapter 5 of this guide) and select one of the critical maneuvers listed under session 10 to accomplish with your son.

CHAMPION Session Prep

Reread episode 11 of *Teknon and the CHAMPION Warriors*, and then complete the questions in session 11 of your *Mission Guide* on your own. **Our next CHAMPION Session will be:**

DATE:
_____

TIME:
_____

PLACE:
_____

SESSION 11:
THE ELEMENT
OF DOUBT

CHAMPION Characteristics

Integrity and Purity

POWER VERSE: 1 THESSALONIANS 5:21-22

But examine everything carefully; hold fast to that which is good; abstain from every form of evil.

STORY SUMMARY

Magos takes full advantage of Kratos' absence from the rest of the team in episode 11. The evil cyborg speaks to Teknon through a holographic image and confuses Teknon about his belief in the CHAMPION principles and way of life. Assailed by doubts Magos has created in his mind, Teknon becomes mentally and emotionally vulnerable. As he grapples with his own uncertainty, he seeks a temporary diversion to relieve his frustration and stress.

He finds his escape in the company of Pary, the young woman rescued by the team in episode 10. Teknon spends the better part of three days with Pary enjoying leisurely activities around the Northron Peninsula. While Teknon views his time with Pary as fun and diverting, Pary interprets his interest in her as more than platonic.

Epps warns Teknon about miscommunicating his intentions to Pary, yet Teknon is surprised and alarmed when Pary discloses her feelings for him. At first, Teknon is overcome with embarrassment as Pary storms off deeply hurt. Then, Teknon experiences regret as he realizes the effect of his insensitivity to Pary.

The episode ends with the return of Kratos and Matty from their reconnaissance of Mago's fortress.

Around the emblem (circular text): Courage · Honor · Attitude · Mental toughness · Purity · Integrity · Ownership · Navigation

Does your son know who he is as a Christian and what he stands for? Does he have strong assurance of his position in Christ and an understanding of personal integrity?

In this episode, you and your son will have the opportunity to discuss the importance of maintaining personal convictions and understanding the emotional side of relationships—particularly between a young man and young woman. Although Teknon does not engage in a physically sexual relationship with Pary, except to hold her hand, he still carelessly manipulates her emotions and treats her insensitively. He uses her to meet his needs for relaxation and to hide from his inner doubts and confusion, while leading her on emotionally. Take this opportunity during your son's CHAMPION training to start preparing him for the inevitable challenges to his faith that he will face as he grows.

QUESTION #3 TIP:
If your son successfully memorized the verse, have him date the verse in session 10 of his *Mission Guide.*

DISCUSSION TOPICS

Knowing who I am and what my personal convictions are
Living out my convictions
Avoiding romantic relationships and entanglements

MISSION DEBRIEF

1. Discuss your mission from session 10. What was the most important thing you learned from your maneuver?

2. What changes are happening in your life as you apply your action points from the CHAMPION Sheet of Deeds? Share some victories you are seeing.

3. Recite your power verse (1 Corinthians 9:24-25a) from session 10.

4. Name at least one area in which you have executed self-control since your last CHAMPION session.

5. Recite the CHAMPION Warrior Creed from memory. If you can, invite two or more people to be in the room when you say it.

1. Review the Map of the Mission on page 8 before beginning this section. Identify where the team is located in episode 11.

2. Review the CHAMPION definitions of **Integrity** and **Purity** (refer to the CHAMPION Code on page 6).

   Answer for Integrity: "I will seek to acquire a clear understanding of who I am in Christ so that I may have a deeper comprehension of what I believe, what I stand for, and how I can live out those convictions in the most difficult circumstances, whether I am alone or with others. I will allow other people to hold me accountable to standards of excellence."

   Answer for Purity: "I will train myself to keep the temple of my body and mind uncorrupted mentally, emotionally, and physically. I will commit to avoid and flee sexual temptation."

3. How did Magos try to confuse Teknon?

   Answer: Magos tried to convince him that Kratos had not been entirely honest. Magos also implied that the mission to retrieve the Logos was misguided.

4. What did Magos offer Teknon?

   Answer: A new, improved, flawless body that he could design, which would last forever.

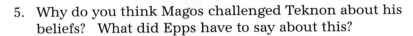

5. **Why do you think Magos challenged Teknon about his beliefs? What did Epps have to say about this?**

Answer: (Epps speaking): "Magos wanted to create doubt in your mind about your beliefs so that you would feel frightened and insecure. He knows that you're young in your convictions, and he wants to take advantage of that. … Magos knows that if he can confuse and tempt you, your father will become concerned … distracted, and more open to attack."

Magos wanted to place the element of doubt into Teknon's mind about his convictions and mission. He used this tactic to try to turn Teknon to his way to thinking as well as to distract Kratos and make him more vulnerable to attack.

> *Magos wanted to create doubt in your mind about your beliefs, so that you would feel frightened and insecure.*
>
> **Epps**

6. **Why did Teknon enjoy spending time with Pary?**

Answer: Because Pary offered Teknon an enjoyable escape from the pressure and stress he was experiencing on the mission.

7. **In what way(s) did Teknon's encounter with Magos affect his decision to see Pary again?**

Answer: He wanted to forget, at least temporarily, about the confusion Magos had caused concerning his beliefs. Pary provided Teknon with an avenue to escape from the stress of his mission as well as the need to face doubts about the CHAMPION principles and goals.

8. **Describe how Teknon treated Pary during the three days they spent together.**

Answer: Teknon was friendly, but he also led Pary to believe that he cared for her romantically. He used her emotionally to meet his needs for relaxation, to have a fun time with a young woman his age, and to mentally escape from his inner doubts and confusion.

9. **After his conversation with Epps, what did Teknon realize that he had done wrong?**

Answer: He realized that he had communicated incorrect intentions to Pary. Instead of treating her like a friend, he had carelessly encouraged her to have an emotional attachment to him.

10. **How did Pary respond when Teknon talked with her that last morning on the beach? Why did she react this way?**

Answer: She was surprised and hurt. She reacted angrily because she thought Teknon felt the same way that she did. Teknon's miscommunication through his words and actions reinforced her distrust of people, which was based upon her previous experiences with the Northrons.

11. **How could Teknon have prevented this from happening and still maintained his friendship with Pary?**

Answer: He could have been more careful in his speech. He also could have refrained from physical contact. It would have been wise for him to have included other people in their daily trips so that the two were not alone for extended periods of time.

STRATEGY AND TACTICS

Failure to prepare is preparing to fail.

John Wooden

IMPORTANT NOTE

Does your son know who he is, as a Christian, and what he stands for? Does he have strong assurance of his position in Christ and an understanding of personal integrity? These are big questions for a young man. But the sooner he starts thinking through the details of his values and convictions, the less likely he will be to stray from those tracks during the years ahead. We live in a cynical world, one in which skeptics enjoy any opportunity to challenge the claims of a committed Christian with the element of doubt.

Ultimately, of course, your own personal example, as his dad, will provide the greatest evidence to your son that you have a personal relationship with Jesus Christ. But challenges will come. And when they do, we, as Christians, should be prepared to provide a response. It is important, therefore, to know what we believe and why we believe it. You can help your son clarify many potential issues. During the coming years your son may be challenged on such issues as:

- ❏ **His assurance of salvation.** "How can you know that you're going to heaven?" a skeptic might ask. Help your son realize that he can know with certainty that he has a future residence in heaven.
- ❏ **The attributes of God.** "How can you believe in one God, who is all-powerful, all-knowing, perfectly just, and merciful?" is another common question. God's attributes are unchanging, indicative of who He is.

❏ **His actions in accordance with God's plan for his life.** "How can you believe that you should live your life according to the teachings of a bunch of men, written down thousands of years ago? What makes you think that you can know God's will?" How would your son answer questions like this?

Take this opportunity, during your son's CHAMPION Training, to start preparing him for the inevitable challenges to his faith that he will face throughout his teen and early adult years.

Be Willing to Get a Bloody Nose

Several years ago, a guy in his twenties named Brad got a job with a medical company selling surgical equipment. He spent the first six weeks training with that company in Chicago, learning everything he could about how to sell his company's products to hospitals and surgeons. One day during training, the vice-president sat down with Brad in the cafeteria. Trying to make conversation, Brad asked, "What would you do if you were starting out as a salesman again?" The executive's response was simple:

"I'd get out in the field and get my nose bloody. That's the way you learn this business."

What was he saying to Brad? Did the vice-president mean that his new salesman should go back and try to start fights with doctors? No, he didn't have enough insurance for that! The executive was telling the young salesman that he needed to talk with his customers, try to meet the customers' needs, face stiff competition from other salesmen, allow himself to get challenged about what he had learned in training, and be willing to fail a few times as he started his new career. The vice-president knew that challenge isn't a bad thing. Challenge is a good thing.

1. Have you ever felt overly confident about a particular subject or task?

Author and speaker Stephen Covey often says, "Confidence is what you have before you understand the problem." It's important for each of us to realize that when we start out doing something new and important, we'll probably be challenged. Even if we feel confident about what we are learning, we don't know how *little* we know until we get *challenged* about what we know. When we get challenged on a topic, like Magos challenged Teknon, we have a great opportunity to reaffirm what we believe about that topic and to identify the things we don't know about it. Once we learn what we don't know, we can go and find the answers we need.

An expert at anything was once a beginner.

H. Jackson Browne

Magos gave Teknon a "bloody nose" by confusing him about his beliefs and convictions. Teknon became flustered and upset because he allowed Magos to inject the element of doubt into his mind. And because Teknon didn't immediately have an answer for Magos, he lost his confidence. Could Teknon have prevented Magos from frightening him like that?

A temptation to compromise your standards often comes when your beliefs are challenged. Let's look at another person who was challenged and offered a proposition by someone evil like Magos.

2a. Read Luke 4:1-13. Who was challenged? —and by whom?

Answer: Jesus was tempted and challenged by the devil himself.

2b. Considering that Jesus ate nothing during His time in the desert (verses 1-2), how do you think He felt when He was being challenged?

Answer: He must have felt tired and very hungry after 40 days of wandering in the desert without food.

2c. How did Jesus respond to the temptations and challenges made to Him?

Verses to consider	Temptation/Challenge	Jesus' response
Luke 4:3-4	*Are you the Son of God? Prove it by turning this stone into bread!*	*He quoted from the Bible (Deuteronomy 8:3) that man does not live on bread alone.*
Luke 4:5-8	*Just worship me, and I'll give you all the kingdoms of this earthly world.*	*He quoted from the Bible (Deuteronomy 6:13) that you are to worship and serve only the Lord.*
Luke 4:9-12	*Are you the Son of God? If so, jump off from here. God promises to use angels to care for you, so you won't get hurt.*	*He quoted from the Bible (Deuteronomy 6:16) that you should not put the Lord your God to the test.*

Jesus was very tired and hungry when Satan challenged His beliefs. But instead of becoming unsettled when Satan tried to use the element of doubt, Jesus quoted Scripture to strengthen his position. He confidently relied on the words of His Heavenly Father.

If you have accepted Jesus as your personal Savior by faith, sooner or later you will get challenged about why you believe in Jesus. If that happens, great! You will have the opportunity to go back to the Bible to find the answers to the challenges given to you. By doing that, you will fuel your confidence and reinforce your position in Christ! If you need help, ask your parents, your pastor, or someone else whom you respect to point you to Bible verses and other Bible-based materials that apply to your situation.

Better yet, even when someone else is *not* challenging you, spend time reading and studying the Bible now so that you will become more knowledgeable about what it means to be a Christian and apply God's truth each day.

3. Most everyone has asked himself or herself, "What will my friends think if I stand up for what I believe?" Why is that such an important question to us?

Answer: It can seem easier to do whatever it takes to be liked and accepted by our peers, while it seems quite difficult to obey God and to do what people in authority over us (including our parents) tell us to do.

Build your character based on what God's Word has to say about His character. Don't get rattled like Teknon. He got stressed out over Magos' challenge, decided to take a break from reality in order to make himself feel better, and hurt himself and Pary in the process ... which leads us to our second topic.

Avoid the Gush!

Here's what God says about relationships:

"Learn to love appropriately. You need to use your head and test your feelings so that your love is sincere and intelligent, not sentimental gush." Philippians 1:9-10 (The Message)

Avoid the Gush!

When most of us think of an early "romantic relationship," we visualize two high school seniors trying to figure out if they should keep dating over the summer before attending separate universities. But early teens?! Romantic relationships? Many teenagers are involved in romantic relationships—before they really even understand what romance is about and how dangerous it can be. A lot of hurt can happen in a scenario in which two teenagers claim to "like" each other.

This segment will give you the opportunity to discuss romantic relationships with your son. What should he consider before encouraging a girl to "like" him? What are the potential consequences of attaching himself to a young lady at this stage in his life? What does it mean to show honor and respect to the opposite sex? These are important issues. And if you haven't already discussed them with him, Dad, it's time!

4. It's nice when a girl shows you affection, isn't it? What could be more pleasant than when she calls you on the phone and tells you how great you are? It makes you feel good, doesn't it? But when you feel that way, whose needs are you meeting—yours or hers? Are you being sincere and intelligent, or are you giving in to sentimental gush?

Answer: Flattery, especially from a young woman, is like soothing balm on a wound for a young man. If your son is not careful, he can let his motivations become self-centered; then the sentimental, romantic gush will begin. When that happens, the Bible says he is loving inappropriately.

QUESTION #4 TIP:
Share your own thoughts with your son about how he might apply the thrusters ahead of time to avoid driving over a cliff into the sentimental gush of a romantic relationship (recall Kratos' illustration of the transtron racer in episode 3).

Emotions can be weird and funny things. When emotions get involved in a relationship between a young man and a young woman, friends start to become more than friends. Often at that point people start getting hurt.

5a. Read 1 Timothy 5:1-2. How are you supposed to treat young women if you will honor her and honor God?

Answer: God's Word instructs us to treat older women as mothers, but to treat younger women as sisters. The verse adds the emphasis "in all purity" just to make sure we get the point.

5b. Is it wise for me to be anything other than a friend to what the Bible calls my sisters in the Lord? Why or why not?

Answer: In the illustration of the Shocktech during episode 3, Kratos explained to Teknon that "error increases with distance." If he allows himself to become romantically involved with a young woman, even a Christian young woman, at this stage of his life, then where will he let his emotions take him in his late teens and early 20s? Making a decision to avoid teenage boyfriend-girlfriend relationships is obviously counter-cultural, but it is worth the investment. When, and if, the time comes for God to bring him a wife, she will be just the right person and will meet him in just the right context. Once they are married, they can share with integrity all the emotion and romance he and she have to offer.

QUESTION #5B TIP:
Challenge your son to set some boundaries in the area of romantic relationships. Help him with ideas and help keep him accountable.

In his excellent book, *I Kissed Dating Goodbye*, Joshua Harris has this to say about romantic relationships:

> "I've come to realize that I have no business asking for a girl's heart and affections if I'm not ready to back up my request with a lifelong commitment. Until I can do that, I'd only be using that woman to meet my short-term needs, not seeking to bless her for the long term."

A lifelong commitment??? Wait a minute! you may be thinking. *I'm not talking about a lifelong commitment! I just want to talk on the phone for a while. Or go to the movies. Or out to eat. Just have a little fun.*

Sounds crazy doesn't it? But even now, if you're not careful, you can misuse a romantic relationship with a young woman in order to meet your short-term needs instead of blessing her for the long term. Remember Teknon and Pary? Teknon just wanted to get away from it all for a few days. But instead, a "perceived" romantic relationship was created and Pary was hurt as a result.

The pressure to start dating and to begin relationships is occurring earlier in life than ever before. Don't allow yourself to start something romantic that you can't and shouldn't finish. Instead, seek to treat young women as cherished sisters, friends whom you can encourage. Don't get caught up in the gush because there is so much more to enjoy at this point by being friends. This delayed gratification (waiting for what I want until God gives it to me at the right time) will become tougher as the years go by, but God will bless you for making the right decisions. And your effort will be greatly rewarded—beyond whatever you could ask or think! God promises this in Ephesians 3:20. Check it out.

6. What do you think would cause a girl to like you?

7. Describe what you think a friendship with a girl should be like?

QUESTION #7 TIP:
This question will give you the opportunity to give input as you help your son define a healthy relationship. You can also talk with him about avoiding what the Bible calls "every form of evil" or "every appearance of evil." It is wise to set personal convictions and boundaries that help him to avoid even the appearance of evil (such as allowing himself to be in a one-on-one situation with a young lady that would tarnish her reputation and his).

THE Main Things I learned in this Champion Session are:

_____

_____

_____

_____

_____

CHAMPION SHEET OF DEEDS

Go to The CHAMPION Sheet of Deeds on page 9 and write down **one thing you will begin to do** before the next session (and beyond) to apply the main things you learned in session 11.

Check one of the suggestions below for your son to write down as his action point on his CHAMPION Sheet of Deeds for session 11. Descriptions and explanations of these action points are provided in the Think Tank (chapter 5) of this guide.

❏ If your son has invited Jesus Christ into his life, help him to write out his personal testimony of coming to faith in Christ.

❏ If your son has an unhealthy romantic relationship with a young woman, discuss the struggles and potential pitfalls ahead. Encourage him to make the tough phone call to end the relationship.

❏ Create your own unique action point.

MAIN THINGS:
If needed, help your son by suggesting some key truths that he should have learned during this session, such as the importance of avoiding romantic relationships with young women until the appropriate time (when he is older and ready for marriage), or the importance of studying God's Word to establish and defend his own beliefs.

SHEET OF DEEDS:
Only a *brief* description of each action point is provided here. Go to the Think Tank (chapter 5) for complete instructions.

The gem cannot be polished without friction, nor man perfected with scars.

Chinese Proverb

Your Mission

Complete your mission and CHAMPION Session Prep before you meet for session 12.

Power verse: 1 Thessalonians 5:21-22

Date memorized: _____

Critical Maneuver

This will reinforce what you learned in this session. Obtain your maneuver instructions from your father.

CHAMPION Sheet of Deeds

Begin to apply your action point from your Sheet of Deeds.

── CHAMPION Session Prep ──

Reread Episode 12 of *Teknon and the CHAMPION Warriors,* and then complete the questions in Session 12 in your *Mission Guide* on your own. **Our next CHAMPION Session will be:**

Date: _____

Time: _____

Place: _____

For Dads Only:

It is very important for you to completely read Joshua Harris' book, *I Kissed Dating Good-bye.* You will benefit from this material as a father, now and in the years to come.

Critical Maneuver:

Go to the Think Tank (chapter 5 of this guide) and select one of the critical maneuvers listed under session 11 to accomplish with your son.

Important Note:

Dad, it's time to start working out the details of your son's Celebration Ceremony if you haven't done so already. Refer to chapter 4 for instructions and helps. If you intend to use correspondence from friends, notify them as soon as possible. Give them a target date to return their input to you.

SESSION 12:
NOTHING MORE,
NOTHING LESS,
NOTHING ELSE

CHAMPION Characteristic

Attitude

POWER VERSE: 1 CORINTHIANS 15:57-58

But thanks be to God, who gives us the victory through our Lord Jesus Christ. Therefore, my beloved brethren, be steadfast, immovable, always abounding in the work of the Lord, knowing that your toil is not in vain in the Lord.

STORY SUMMARY

The episode begins as the team splits into two groups when they reach the Thumos Mountains. Teknon, Phil, and Kratos begin to set up camp; the others scout out the trails ahead. Suddenly a huge seismos enters the campsite, eats the team's food, and moves to attack Teknon and Kratos. Phil uses his unique digging abilities to create a hole to capture the beast. The three salvage what gear they can and move to a different clearing. There, Phil digs a cave complete with stone beds, chairs, and a table. As the three settle in for the night, Kratos and Phil pray for the return of the other team members. Teknon's attitude worsens as he becomes discouraged, and frustrated with his circumstances.

At the end of episode 12, Teknon awakens in a very dangerous predicament. He has slept soundly, recovering from the traumatic battle the night before that he survived due to the heroic efforts of Kratos and their new team member, Phil. He still hasn't recovered from the failure he had a few days ago. He awakens fatigued, famished, and frightened as he realizes that he's all alone! It appears that Phil and Kratos have been injured or worse. Alone, hungry, confused, tired—and ready to give up—Teknon finds the Hoplon in the snow.

This episode focuses on how to manage discouragement. During the next few years, your son will have the dubious pleasure of heading into an uncharted territory known as young adulthood. While piloting his way through peer pressure, relationships with young women, school's challenges, and other rigors of daily life, he may be "shot down" in the enemy territory of discouragement. Your son's emotional health may be affected by many factors, including his family, friends, diet, sleep patterns, and, of course, his relationship with God. Discouragement can send him into a downward spiral.

QUESTION #2 TIP:

Help your son through his struggles and remind him that God can and will put obstacles in our path, even on worthwhile projects, in order that we may learn some character lessons that He has designed for us.

QUESTION #3 TIP:

If your son successfully memorized the verse, have him date the verse in session 11 of his *Mission Guide*.

DISCUSSION TOPICS:

Managing discouragement

Keeping circumstances and self-perception in proper perspective

Drawing on God's strength and wisdom

MISSION DEBRIEF

1. Discuss your mission from session 11. What did you learn from your maneuver? Has your attitude or behavior changed as a result of your maneuver?

2. Are you experiencing any struggles as you apply your action points from the CHAMPION Sheet of Deeds? If so, please share these.

3. Recite your power verse (1 Thessalonians 5:21-22) from session 11.

4. Our last session explored the topic of romantic relationships. Do you have a romantic relationship with a young woman right now? If so, should the relationship continue as it is? Why or why not?

5. Recite all of the CHAMPION Warrior Creed from memory (see page 5).

RECONNAISSANCE

QUESTION #5 TIP:
If you son really has it memorized and is tiring of the repetition, don't force the issue. Be flexible; pick it up again in a future CHAMPION Session.

1. Review the Map of the Mission on page 8 and determine the team's location in episode 12.

2. Review the CHAMPION definition of **Attitude** (refer to the CHAMPION Code on page 6).

Answer: "I will cultivate a disposition of humility. I will assume a correct and hopeful view of myself as a member of God's family. I will improve my ability to manage anger and discouragement. I will develop and enjoy an appropriate sense of humor."

3. **What were some of the reasons Teknon became frustrated and angry?**

Answer: He felt guilty about the incident with Pary and how it ended. He was also feeling discouraged at this point about his overall performance on the mission.

4. **What were some of the things that contributed to Teknon's discouragement?**

Answer:

- The way he mishandled the situation with Pary.

- His weakness in allowing Magos to confuse him about the mission and his convictions.

- The difficulties and dangers he experienced during the mission.

- His fatigue and hunger after the encounter with the seismos.

- He was tired of making mistakes.

5. How did Teknon act when he became discouraged? Be specific.

Answer: He became irritable and began to doubt the importance of the mission.

6. What, according to Kratos and Phil, is the way to overcome discouragement?

Answer: They told Teknon to stay focused on completing the mission and to gain strength from the Warrior King, Pneuma.

7. Phil told Teknon, "Even when our emotions tell us otherwise, we must stay focused on trusting Pneuma to help us make the right choices." Do you think our emotions are dependable? Why or why not?

Answer: Our emotions are good indicators of problems, but they are not dependable. Developing the ability to control and deal with emotions, especially in the midst of discouragement, is a mark of maturity.

STRATEGY AND TACTICS

Former fighter pilot, Charlie Plumb says that it was the parachute packers in his life who pulled him through the loneliness and discouragement he faced during his six years as a prisoner of war during the Vietnam conflict. Charlie, now a popular seminar speaker, states that he is continually thankful for the man who carefully assembled his parachute aboard the USS *Kittyhawk* on the day his airplane was shot down over enemy territory.

But Charlie is quick to add that he is even more thankful for his cellmates in the concentration camp who carefully helped him pack his emotional, mental, and spiritual parachutes. Due to the constant help and encouragement that these extraordinary men provided, Charlie not only survived his imprisonment but also returned home a stronger person.

Soon, you will have the dubious pleasure of "flying" into an uncharted territory known as young adulthood. While you pilot through peer pressure, relating to young women, school challenges, and the other struggles of daily life, you may be "shot down" by discouragement. Your emotional health may be affected by a number of things, including your family, friends, diet, sleep patterns, and, of course, your relationship with God.

Discouragement can become a big gaping hole in your spiritual parachute. At some point, you will probably need a spiritual "parachute packer" who can encourage you as you face the enemy fire of confusion, isolation, and discouragement during your teens and into young adulthood. Use this opportunity to build a stronger relationship with your father. You can also ask your dad or pastor to identify men who could encourage you during your teenage years. Remember, they've been there, so they know what it's like to be shot down, to regroup, and then to take off again.

1a. List those people who are emotional and spiritual "parachute packers" in your life.

1b. How do these people support you?

QUESTION #1A TIP:
You may have to give some examples in your own life to help your son get started. If he is not able to identify his "parachute packers," offer suggestions of close family members, teachers, his friends, and close adults.

QUESTION #1B TIP
At some point, your son will need someone who can encourage him through the battle zone of young adulthood. Use this opportunity to build a stronger relationship with him. Also, identify other men who can encourage him during his teen years, when he may need it the most (see chapter 4 about choosing and enlisting mentors).

THE POWER OF HOPE

A few years ago, scientists conducted an experiment on hope. They took a common rat and put it into a large bowl of water. Then they watched as the rat swam around the edge of the bowl for days, staying afloat and trying to find a way to get out.

Then the scientists started the second phase of the study. They removed the first rat and put another rat into the same bowl of water, but this time they turned off all the lights in the room. Left to swim in total darkness, the second rat drowned in only a few hours, greatly surprising the scientists. Why did this rat die so quickly? The scientists concluded that it simply gave up hope. Without visual contact, the second rat had no vision of the outside world—and thus had lost all hope of survival.

Can you identify with the second rat? Have you ever felt as if you were swimming for your life in a dark bowl full of peer pressure, challenging relationships, and stressful activities? As if you could barely keep your head above water? If so, you're not alone. Many people face the darkness of discouragement.

> *Victory belongs to the most persevering.*
>
> Napoleon

2. **List some of the possible characteristics of a discouraged person.**

   Answer:

   1. sad

   2. always tired

   3. insecure; critical of others

   4. has sudden outbursts of anger

   5. withdrawn from people; lonely

3. **List some things that you think would cause someone to feel discouraged.**

   Answer:

   1. failure or difficulties (in school or otherwise)

   2. guilt; shaming by parents or other people

   3. rejection; negative feedback from friends

   4. stressful relationships (at home or elsewhere)

   5. becoming overtired

   Other Answers: a bad diet, not taking care of yourself physically, or lack of time with God

Many things can cause us to feel discouraged and cause us to start going downhill emotionally. The more we get discouraged and lose hope, the farther down we go. Let's look at several categories of downhills that can cause discouragement.

Category 1: Health Downhills

▲ **Lack of sleep.** Former President Teddy Roosevelt said, "Fatigue makes cowards of us all." If we don't get enough sleep, we can become irritable and start to "cycle down."

▲ **Bad diet.** Too much sugar, caffeine, and fat can wreak havoc on our minds and our emotional stability.

▲ **Lack of exercise.** When we exercise, blood pumps oxygen into our blood and sends hormones called endorphins through our bodies to make us feel alert and energetic. When we spend too much time being a couch potato, we feel and act like sedated slugs.

Category 2: Head Downhills

▲ **Criticism from peers.** Overly critical people can have a negative effect on our attitudes and actions.

▲ **"Successful" failure.** We can become discouraged when we fail at doing the right things, like trying our best but still losing the game.

▲ **Stress.** Too much activity makes us feel like we're under the pile and unable to dig out.

Category 3: Heart Downhills

▲ **Unresolved conflict.** If we haven't reconnected with friends or family after an argument, we will experience a lack of closure until the problem is resolved.

▲ **"Unsuccessful" failure.** When we make a bad choice and disobey God (sin), we will feel miserable.

▲ **Unconfessed sin.** When we don't acknowledge to God that we have sinned and ask His forgiveness, guilt and discouragement will follow.

Teknon's discouragement related to all three of these categories. He was tired and hungry. He had unresolved conflict with Pary. In addition, Magos had confused him with criticism of the CHAMPION principles, causing him to doubt his beliefs and to have a bad attitude toward Pneuma and their mission. All of these circumstances prompted him to lose hope and start riding the downhill of discouragement.

A real leader faces the music, even when he doesn't like the tune.

Unknown

4. How might Teknon have avoided becoming discouraged?

5. What kind of things get you down emotionally or spiritually?

QUESTION #6 TIP:
If your son gets discouraged, he may be experiencing guilt from an unconfessed sin. Help him to talk through this and confess it to God as this session continues.

6. Is there anything bothering you that you need to discuss with God? If so, what do plan to do?

There's a lot you can do to dodge discouragement. To avoid the health downhills, you need to eat right, get enough sleep, and get on a regular exercise program. *To avoid the head downhills*, you should try not to spend too much time with negative people. You should also recover when you have an "unsuccessful" failure and prioritize your time by involving yourself in only a few activities at a time.

As for avoiding the heart downhills, you should make sure that you are doing what you can to clear up unresolved arguments with others. Most importantly, you need to remember the importance of staying in communication with Jesus Christ. If you have unconfessed sin in your life, the phone lines are cut between you and God. You need to remember how to reconnect those communication lines through confession and turning away from your sin and toward God (repentance).

7a. Remember 1 John 1:9? What does that verse say we need to do if we have disobeyed God?

Answer: Confess our sin to Him.

7b. What does God promise to do in return?

Answer: God promises to forgive our sin and cleanse us from all unrighteousness.

The longer we ride the downhill of discouragement, the more we take our eyes off the One who can help us. Soon, we start losing hope and forgetting about the big picture. God doesn't want us to become discouraged.

8. You looked at Hebrews 12:1-2 in an earlier session. Look at it again, but this time focus on the first part of verse 2: "fixing our eyes on Jesus, the author and perfecter of faith ... " These verses talk about how we run the race of life that God has marked out for us and how we run to win. What is the big key to success that you find in verse 2?

Answer: These verses plead with us to throw off everything that hinders, especially sin (through confession and repentance). Then the passage encourages us that we can run our race with endurance and hope IF we keep our eyes fixed on Jesus instead of on our problems.

9a. According to John 10:10, what kind of life does He want us to live?

Answer: "I [Jesus] came that they may have life, and have it abundantly [or to the full]."

9b. **What does the concept of abundant life or life lived to the full mean to you?**

Answer:

Following are a few of the characteristics of a person living life abundantly or to the full.

- Has a positive outlook through faith in God's love and sovereignty.
- Has a high confidence level (his confidence is really in Christ, not himself).
  - Has a close relationship and open communication with God.
    - Arguments with other people are resolved quickly (keeps short accounts and is a peacemaker).
    - Keeps anger, anxiety, and stress under control.
    - The power of God flows in and through his life.

God wants each of us to live a meaningful, significant, maximum kind of life. He understands when you become discouraged, but He also knows that you don't have to stay that way. Take the right steps to get off of the downhill, and start riding the Abundant Life Express transport that God has for you!

THE MAIN THINGS I LEARNED IN THIS CHAMPION SESSION ARE:

_____

_____

_____

_____

_____

CHAMPION SHEET OF DEEDS

Go to the CHAMPION Sheet of Deeds on page 9 and write down one thing you will begin to do before the next session (and beyond) to apply the main things you learned in session 12.

Check one of the suggestions below for your son to write down as his action point on his CHAMPION Sheet of Deeds for session 12. Descriptions and explanations of these action points are provided in the Think Tank (chapter 5) of this guide.

- ❏ Ask your son to identify which of the three categories in the downhills of discouragement affects him the most. Then help him develop ways to improve his situation or his response in that area.
- ❏ Explain to your son how to apply the truths of 1 John 1:9 (confession) and John 10:10 (abundant living) using an exercise called "spiritual breathing."
- ❏ Create your own unique action point.

Your Mission

Complete your mission and CHAMPION Session Prep before you meet for session 13.

POWER VERSE: I CORINTHIANS 15:57–58

Date memorized: _____

CRITICAL MANEUVER

CRITICAL MANEUVER: Go to the Think Tank (chapter 5 of this guide) and select one of the critical maneuvers listed under session 12 to accomplish with your son.

This will reinforce what you learned in this session. Obtain your maneuver instructions from your father.

CHAMPION SHEET OF DEEDS

Begin to apply your action point from your Sheet of Deeds.

CHAMPION SESSION PREP

Reread episode 13 of *Teknon and the CHAMPION Warriors*, and then complete the questions in session 13 in your *Mission Guide* on your own. **Our next CHAMPION Session will be:**

DATE:

_____

TIME:

_____

PLACE:

_____

Champion Characteristics

Mental Toughness and Navigation

Power Verse: Philippians 3:13b-14

Forgetting what lies behind and reaching forward to what lies ahead, I press on toward the goal for the prize of the upward call of God in Christ Jesus.

Story Summary

As episode 13 opens, we find Teknon reeling from the peculiar disappearance of his father and Phil. He is not sure whether he should return to the safety of Northros or travel up the unknown mountain path in the hope of finding someone familiar. The only thing on Teknon's mind at this point is his own survival.

It takes an ambush by a charging amacho to jolt Teknon back into the realization that he has a larger purpose to accomplish. He handily defeats the creature, and determines to take up the team's original cause of retrieving the Logos.

A pivotal event in Teknon's life takes place when he connects on a truly personal level with Pneuma, the Warrior King, for the first time. Teknon pledges his life to carry out Pneuma's mission. Teknon's new relationship gives him an inner peace and sense of purpose that he has not known before. Later, he triumphs over his old enemy, Rhegma, which further builds Teknon's confidence and strengthens his resolve to focus on the mission at hand. During the scuffle, Teknon discovers that he is able to utilize the features of the Hoplon that he found on the ground back by the cave. Teknon uses the shield to fly to the outskirts of Magos' fortress. He investigates a bright light and is astonished to see his father and the rest of the team waiting for him.

Using the choices Teknon made in this session as a launching point, you will have the opportunity to encourage your son to focus on completing worthwhile tasks as he progresses toward manhood. If he is starting to lose his enthusiasm for completing his CHAMPION Training, remind him of your original purpose in starting it with him. Explain that one of the key traits of manhood is the ability to persevere through difficult times. Remind him, too, that he is nearly finished with his training, his celebration ceremony is close at hand, and you will soon formally recognize him as a young man.

QUESTION #3 TIP:

If your son successfully memorized the verse, have him date the verse in session 12 of his *Mission Guide*.

QUESTION #4 TIP:

If your son experienced discouragement recently, remind him of the three types of "discouragement downhills" from session 12 and help him to determine how to improve his particular situation.

Discussion Topics

Choosing to focus on the mission
Learning to persevere even in difficult circumstances
Connecting with God and drawing on His power

Mission Debrief

1. Discuss your mission from session 12. What did you learn from your maneuver? How is what you've learned affecting your attitude or behavior?

2. Did you start applying your new action point from your Sheet of Deeds? If so, what have you learned? If not, when do you plan to get started?

3. Recite your power verse (1 Corinthians 15:57-58) from session 12.

4. In our last session, we discussed the topic of discouragement. Have you dealt with any discouragement this week? If so, how did you handle it? If not, what helped you to avoid feeling discouraged?

5. Recite the CHAMPION Warrior Creed (see page 5).

RECONNAISSANCE

1. Review the Map of the Mission on page 8 and determine the team's location in episode 13.

2. Review the CHAMPION definition of **Mental Toughness**.

    Answer: "I will allow God to direct my thinking toward gaining common sense and wisdom. I will use discernment when making hard decisions. I will desire respect from others rather than compromise my convictions for acceptance or approval."

3. **Why did Teknon decide to complete the mission on his own after he defeated the amacho?**

    Answer: The incident with the amacho gave Teknon renewed confidence in his training and helped him to refocus on his purpose and his objective of completing the mission.

4. **Why do you think Teknon decided to talk with Pneuma?**

    Answer: He realized that he could not complete the mission in his own strength. This pushed him to recognize his own inability to save himself and his need for a dependence on the Warrior King. He finally understood some of the reasons a relationship with Pneuma was so important.

5. **How did Teknon make the Hoplon fly?**

    Answer: First, he had to take a step of faith (literally!) to step onto the shield. Then, he focused his thoughts with the goal of completing his mission, and maintained self-control as he flew.

Teknon really learned to focus in this episode, didn't he? He focused in order to get back on the track of completing his mission. Did you notice how much more confident Teknon became after using his training to defeat the amacho and Rhegma? Did you notice his resolve and inner strength after he finally connected with Pneuma on a personal level?

Strategy and Tactics

The Power of Focus

In the early 1900s, the United States needed a capable athlete to compete in the pentathlon, the most difficult track-and-field event of the fifth Olympiad. After much debate, the Olympic committee chose an unlikely candidate for an unlikely reason. The competitor they chose was a young army lieutenant who had displayed marginal competence in only one of the five events needed to win the pentathlon. What he lacked in ability, however, he made up with intensity. He was chosen to compete because of his determination and his focus.

He had one month to prepare for the event. During that short period of time, the focused army officer trained with unbridled passion. He forced his body to perform far beyond its normal limitations. He made it his mission to represent his country in an admirable fashion. Amazingly, he almost won a medal competing against the greatest athletes in the world. The name of the young lieutenant was George S. Patton, future four-star general of the American Armed Forces. He later became famous for his focus and determination as the leader of the Third Army that helped to defeat Hitler during World War II.

1. Are you able to focus so that you can complete a task even under stressful conditions? Would you say you are strong or need to improve a little, or need to improve a lot? Why do you say that?

A Mark of Maturity

Pastor and author Dr. Joel Hunter says that one of the most telling marks of maturity in a person is his ability to focus on the completion of a worthy task. The ability to focus is becoming a lost art for many young people today. For the most part, our fast-paced, entertainment-obsessed society does not see the need nor are they equipped to develop this important character trait.

Three primary things can disrupt our focus as we attempt to accomplish worthwhile objectives:

1. **Complications.** These are the problems and obstacles that come our way.

2. **Criticism.** Negative and severe judgments can come from other people or from ourselves. Criticism is an occupational hazard for a person who sets high standards for himself.

3. **Circumstances.** Usually these focus-busters come in the form of opposition against a worthwhile objective.

In the movie "October Sky," high school student Homer Hickam gazed up with amazement into a clear West Virginia night. His eyes were fixed on *Sputnik I*, the world's first orbiting satellite that was shooting across the atmosphere at 17,000 miles per hour. At that moment, he made a decision that would affect the rest of his life. He decided to build rockets.

The idea seemed impossible to everyone who knew him. Homer grew up in a small coal-mining town in which most men spent long working days a hundred feet below the earth's surface. Homer and his friends were expected to follow the same career path into the mines as soon as they graduated from high school. But Homer had a different set of dreams to pursue.

Homer and his three companions decided to build a miniature rocket in the hope of winning the national science fair. They dedicated themselves to learning physics, math, and chemistry. Step by step, enduring failure after failure, Homer and his friends moved closer to their goal. In 1957, against incredible odds, the "Rocket Boys," as they were later called, came in first place in the national science fair and went on to achieve what they wanted most. They all continued to work hard and graduated from college.

What was so special about the Rocket Boys? Why did they succeed in achieving their dreams—overcoming all the obstacles that stopped others? It's because they took responsibility to do what they could do, and they focused on completing their objectives under very difficult conditions.

The Rocket Boys studied, worked hard, and never took their focus off of their objective. That's why Homer Hickam went on to train astronauts for NASA.

2. Look up the word "focus" in the dictionary. How would you define focus in your own words?

    Answer: The American Heritage Dictionary defines "focus" as having the ability to concentrate, to converge at a point of focus, or the center of interest or activity." The key to focusing is concentrating your interest, resources, and energy.

When a person can maintain his concentration and direct his efforts long enough to complete an important task regardless of the obstacles, he is revealing a mature mark of manhood. He's acting like a CHAMPION by doing all he can within his own CHAMPION's Ring and trusting God for the results.

Remembering the Lion and the Bear

The Bible tells about a young man who also focused in order to complete his mission under difficult conditions. His name was David and his "super-sized" mission was defeating a giant named Goliath.

Read 1 Samuel 17:1-54

3a. Describe Goliath (verses 4-11 and 43-44).

    Answer: Goliath was a champion for the Philistine people and stood over nine feet tall. He was heavily armed and known to be vicious in speech and action.

REMEMBERING THE LION ...

Your son has probably heard the story of David and Goliath since he was a toddler, but encourage him to look at it from a fresh perspective. Ask him to read the story from the perspective of staying focused on your mission.

3b. How did David view Goliath (verse 26 and 46)?

Answer: David viewed Goliath with loathing and disdain because the giant chose to defy the armies of the living God. David did not appear intimidated whatsoever.

3c. Why did David believe that he could defeat Goliath (verses 34-37 and 47)?

Answer: David knew that he was well-trained and prepared. But, more importantly, he was very aware of God's past faithfulness in his life. God had already given him strength to kill a lion and a bear. David knew that the same God who had given him victory over the lion and the bear would also give him victory over this Philistine.

3d. Why did David refuse to wear King Saul's armor (verses 38-40)?

Answer: David was not used to wearing armor; it was clumsy and slowed him down. Besides, he knew that he would not need the armor to defeat his opponent. David was convinced that God would deliver Goliath into his hands.

3e. According to 1 Samuel 17:45-47, how did David feel about completing his mission? Circle the number on the following scale that best describes his level of confidence.

0   1   2   3   4   5   6   7   8   9   10

Very Worried   Very Confident

3f. What did David use to defeat Goliath (verses 40 and 47-50)?

Answer: David defeated Goliath by using a method and tools common to him as a shepherd. With a common sling, he hurled a stone, which was delivered under God's power directly into Goliath's forehead. The Bible calls attention to the fact that there was no sword in his hand. David didn't have a weapon, but he had something much more powerful—the almighty and living Lord of Hosts.

David was willing to face Goliath because he—a shepherd boy—remembered how God had delivered him from the lion and the bear in the fields of Israel. David knew that God was watching over him and protecting him.

Success seems to be largely a matter of hanging on after others have let go.

Will Feather

Do you realize that God is watching over you 24/7 (24 hours a day, 7 days a week) to protect you? Psalm 121:7 gives you a great promise: "The Lord will protect you from all evil; He will keep your soul."

How to Focus

Let's use David's example to discover some practical steps you can use to focus on completing important missions in your life.

- ■ **Target your objective.** David targeted Goliath as the adversary he had to defeat for God and his country.
- ■ **Train yourself for the mission.** David trained himself by conditioning both physically and spiritually during his time as a shepherd.
- ■ **Think of the resources** you will need to complete the mission. David carefully chose his method and the tools he needed to ensure Goliath's defeat.
- ■ **Trust that God will use and empower you** to complete any mission that He has given you. David acknowledged at an early age that his strength came from the Lord.
- ■ **Thank God** for His faithful commitment to provide for you so that you can complete the mission. It is very important to remember how God has been faithful to you in the past. David expressed his gratitude to God for delivering him from the lion and the bear and then from Goliath.
- ■ **Take action to complete your mission.** David acted upon his trust in God by stepping onto the battlefield. Once he made the first step to confront Goliath, there was no turning back. The Bible says that David actually charged toward Goliath on the battlefield.

It's easy to become distracted from doing the important things in our lives. Sometimes even good things can prevent us from doing the best things—those things that will make the greatest long-term impact. For example, too many basketball games or too much time with friends might prevent us from spending time reading the Bible or finishing our homework.

To become a CHAMPION, you must learn to prioritize your objectives wisely. Then you must focus your mind, your time, and your resources to complete the most important objectives before moving on to the other ones. It won't be easy. But when

The will to win is important, but the will to prepare is vital.

Joe Paterno

you look at guys like David, or Homer Hickam, you can see the benefits of learning how to focus.

4. What if you don't want to complete an important objective? How do you get it done if you just don't feel like it?

QUESTION # 5C TIP: Guide your son through the six Ts of how to focus. In addition, share with him about an important objective that you completed even though you didn't have the "want to." Encourage your son that it is often the objectives we don't want to finish that God uses to provide the greatest growth in our lives.

Sometimes you need to have the "want to" when it comes to completing a worthy objective. Sometimes, however, God directs you to achieve an important objective that is not fun or pleasant. If maturity can be identified by your ability to focus, then you show your level of maturity by your willingness to trust God, even through a task that offers little enjoyment through the process of completion.

5a. Which important objectives do you have that you find pretty easy to accomplish?

5b. Which ones are tough and demand all the focus you can muster in order to get them done?

The greatest honor we can give Almighty God is to live gladly because of the knowledge of His love.

Julian of Norwich

5c. In what ways might God be able to help you face—and achieve—difficult objectives in your life?

If needed, help your son by suggesting some key truths that he should have learned during this session, such as the importance of focus when it comes to completing an important objective or use of the six T's when he needs to focus.

IMPORTANT NOTE:

This session may provide another chance to talk with your son about inviting Jesus Christ into his life (if he has not already taken this step). Consider walking your son through the exercise entitled "Just Do It!" in the appendix. If your son has already made this step, this session also provides a good opportunity to challenge him to allow Jesus to be the Lord of his life, giving Him first place in everything (Colossians 1:18).

SHEET OF DEEDS:

Only a *brief* description of each action point is provided here. Go to the Think Tank (chapter 5) for complete instructions.

THE MAIN THINGS I LEARNED IN THIS CHAMPION SESSION ARE:

_____

_____

_____

_____

_____

CHAMPION SHEET OF DEEDS

Go to the CHAMPION Sheet of Deeds on page 9 and write down one thing you will begin to do before the next session (and beyond) to apply the main things you learned in session 13.

Check one of the suggestions below for your son to write down as his action point on his CHAMPION Sheet of Deeds for session 13. Descriptions and explanations of these action points are provided in the Think Tank (chapter 5) of this guide.

❏ Ask your son to identify one important objective or task that he has continued to put off. Help him to work through the six Ts of how to focus in order to accomplish that objective.

❏ Encourage your son to keep a journal to capture specific instances where God has delivered him or provided for him in challenging circumstances. This is a great way to honor God and to build your son's confidence in God's faithfulness.

❏ Create your own unique action point.

Your Mission

Complete your mission and CHAMPION Session Prep before you meet for session14.

POWER VERSE: PHILIPPIANS 3:13B-14

Date memorized: _____

CRITICAL MANEUVER

This will reinforce what you learned today. Obtain your maneuver instructions from your father.

CHAMPION SHEET OF DEEDS

Begin to apply your action point from your Sheet of Deeds.

CHAMPION SESISON PREP

Reread episode 14 of *Teknon and the CHAMPION Warriors*, and then complete the questions in session 14 in your *Mission Guide* on your own. **Our next CHAMPION Session will be:**

DATE:

_____

TIME:

_____

PLACE:

_____

CRITICAL MANEUVER:
Go to the Think Tank (chapter 5 of this guide) and select one of the critical maneuvers listed under session 13 to accomplish with your son.

SESSION 14: BACK TO BACK

CHAMPION Characteristics

Integrity and Attitude

POWER VERSE: PSALM 139:14

I give thanks to You [Lord], for I am fearfully and wonderfully made; wonderful are Your works, and my soul knows it very well.

STORY SUMMARY

In this final battle between Magos and the CHAMPION Warriors, Teknon finally participates as a vital member of the team. Teknon now personally owns the mission and realizes that Pneuma is his ultimate source of strength and protection. Teknon finds out that the Hoplon he used in episode 13 is actually a duplicate designed for him by Kratos. After receiving Kratos' final briefing, the team heads for Sheol, the enemy fortress. Magos throws everything he has at them: energy fields, footsoldiers, kakos, land mines, deadly energy beams, hidden panels, poisonous gas, doubt, deception, and scorn. Teknon has an opportunity to demonstrate what he has learned—about fighting, about himself, and about Pneuma. The team uses the varied strengths of each member to overcome challenge after challenge. Teknon overcomes Scandalon and then faces Dolios, who takes the form of his worst fear. Magos nearly defeats Kratos, but the team prevails and Teknon retrieves the Logos as the team narrowly escapes Sheol before it self-destructs.

**SESSION 14
OVERVIEW:**

This session will give you an opportunity to discuss how our unique God-given bents contribute to the power of the team. We each have strengths and weaknesses. Yet God gave each of us different bents, or temperaments, so that we can all contribute in unique ways to accomplish His mission in the world. During this session, help your son to understand that he is a valuable part of God's team—and your team. Both you and he need to accept that God has given him strengths and weaknesses for a reason, and that we all need to function together in unity to be most effective.

Discussion Topics

**Embracing the strengths and weaknesses of other people
Understanding my own unique bent and value to God's team
Harnessing the power of a diverse team to complete a mission**

Mission Debrief

1. Discuss your mission from session 13. What did you learn from your maneuver? How is what you've learned affecting your thinking or behavior?

2a. As you approach the end of your CHAMPION Training, which of your action points have you been applying from your Sheet of Deeds?

2b. Which of your action points have been difficult for you to apply?

   It will be important for you to put even greater focus on continuing to apply all of your action points after your CHAMPION Training is complete. Over the next few years, you will have the opportunity to use your action points to develop powerful habits that will advance your development toward courageous manhood. Don't stop the process! Remember what you have learned and continue the process of growth.

3. Recite your power verse (Philippians 3:13b-14) from session 13.

4. Is there an important objective or task that you need to complete? Look again at David's example and the six T's from session 13. Which of these will help you to focus so you can accomplish your objective? Circle them.

   ▲ Target your objective
   ▲ Train yourself for the mission
   ▲ Think of the resources you will need
   ▲ Trust that God will use and empower you
   ▲ Thank God
   ▲ Take action

5. Recite the CHAMPION Warrior Creed (see page 5).

RECONNAISSANCE

1. Review the Map of the Mission on page 8 and determine the team's location in episode 14. They have finally achieved their objective of retrieving the Logos and defeating Magos! But success required tremendous team effort, a great deal of character, and dependence on Pneuma.

2. Review the CHAMPION definitions of **Integrity** and **Attitude**.

   Answer for Integrity: "I will seek to acquire a clear understanding of who I am in Christ so that I may have a deeper comprehension of what I believe, what I stand for, and how I can live out those convictions in the most difficult circumstances, whether I am alone or with others. I will allow other people to hold me accountable to standards of excellence."

   Answer for Attitude: "I will cultivate a disposition of humility. I will assume a correct and hopeful view of myself as a member of God's family. I will improve my ability to manage anger and discouragement. I will develop and enjoy an appropriate sense of humor."

3. **Why do you think Kratos waited so long to let Teknon use his Hoplon?**

   Answer: Teknon was not ready to receive it earlier in the mission. He needed to grow in important areas of his life before Kratos could entrust it to him.

QUESTION #4A TIP:
Remind your son that each member of any team (sports, family, church, etc.) must believe in—or own— the mission that they strive to fulfill. Although we are most effective when we work together, a true CHAMPION is willing to take responsibility to complete the mission, even when he must act alone.

Tor explained to Teknon what it means to own the mission: "You gained the head knowledge about becoming a CHAMPION, but not the conviction of heart. For that, you had to face the possibility that no one else would retrieve the Logos unless you stepped in. When you did, the mission not only belonged to us, but to you as well."

4a. **What do you think it means to "own" a mission? Is being God's CHAMPION more head knowledge for you or have you been gripped by conviction of the heart? Be honest.**

4b. **Do you believe God has a mission for you to own? What do you think that mission might be?**

Optional Questions

5a. **Dolios transformed himself into Teknon's greatest fear in order to defeat him. What was Teknon's greatest fear?**

Answer: Teknon's greatest fear was to see his father as evil—a man with no convictions or purpose.

5b. **Why do you think this was Teknon's greatest fear?**

Answer: Teknon respected his father more than anyone else. He loved his father and believed in his values, his purpose, and his example. Nothing scared Teknon more than to see his father violate that example by compromising his convictions and destroying the relationship they enjoyed.

6. **How did Teknon defeat Dolios?**

Answer: He sought strength from Pneuma to overcome his fear. When Teknon's fear went away, so did Dolios' power over him.

Logos is the Greek term that means "the word." Teknon, his father, and the CHAMPION Warriors risked their lives to retrieve the Logos because of its importance to the people of Basileia. *Logos* is used in the Bible to refer to thoughts and expressions of God Himself delivered in spoken or written form to us. Jesus is also called the Logos because He is the ultimate expression of God's message to man.

7. **Why is God's Word, the Bible, so important to us?**

   Answer: Hebrew 4:12 says that God's Word is "living and active." It is not an ancient book, but rather the living and powerful messages of life given to us directly from the heart of God. The Bible shows us who God is, clarifies His mission, highlights our value to Him, and gives us guidance for our daily lives.

8. **Tor said, "There is great power in a team." What do you think he meant by that?**

   Answer: Help your son to see that God has created each one of us with different strengths and weaknesses, just like each of the CHAMPION Warriors. If we work together as a team, we can compliment each other as we all seek to do His will and accomplish the mission He gives to us.

9. **Kratos instructed the warriors to "watch each other's backs." Why is it important for us to watch out for each other?**

   Answer: The spiritual battle we are in is just as real and just as dangerous as any physical battle. We need every member of the team to stand strong. That's why teamwork and accountability are so important. True friends encourage each other to stay on track in our attitude and behavior. We must hold each other to a high standard, care for one another, and pray for each other's success.

Please fill in this chart.

NOTE:
DO NOT discuss the descriptions of each mentor yet. Wait until later in this session AFTER your son completes the assessment. For now, just get your son's impressions.

Jot down five words you
think describe **Tor:**

1. _____
2. _____
3. _____
4. _____
5. _____

Jot down five words you
think describe **Epps:**

1. _____
2. _____
3. _____
4. _____
5. _____

Jot down five words you
think describe **Arti:**

1. _____
2. _____
3. _____
4. _____
5. _____

Jot down five words you
think describe **Matty:**

1. _____
2. _____
3. _____
4. _____
5. _____

STRATEGY  TACTICS

DIFFERENT IS DYNAMIC

It's no secret that we all have different "bents." You may like to be the point person, positioning yourself in front of the group as the leader. Or maybe you like to be in the background keeping track of details and helping get things done. Maybe you're a natural salesman: motivating, promoting, and trying to present yourself well in the process.

Does it bother you that you're not the life of the party? Do you wish that you could make friends easier? Does it bother you that you're a cautious person or don't feel comfortable leading?

The point is this: it takes different types of players to make a great team. God uniquely designed each one of us with different strengths and weaknesses. And it's a good thing that everybody isn't alike. What would the world be like if everybody was a CEO ... or an engineer ... or a salesperson ... or a farmer ... or a public speaker?! In God's plan, different is dynamic. Your unique differences provide a dynamic contribution to the mission God has for His team here on earth. To accomplish an important mission, it takes people with different bents and strengths that can fill in each other's gaps and accomplish more as a synchronized unit than any one person could accomplish alone. Be yourself and bring your unique strengths to your family, your church, or whatever team you are a part of—and make it more dynamic!

HOW ARE YOU BENT?

1. What do you like best about yourself? What do other people seem to like about you?

DIFFERENT IS DYNAMIC:

Help your son to understand that he is indeed a valuable part of God's team and your team. Your son needs you to tell him that he is uniquely created and blessed with strengths from Almighty God to accomplish His mission here on earth. He needs to know that you love him whether the two of you are very similar or very different.

Coming together is a beginning; keeping together is progress; working together is success.

Henry Ford

2. Describe yourself:

   ▲ Are you organized?
   ▲ Are you the life of the party?
   ▲ Do you like to be in charge?
   ▲ Are you a loyal and dedicated friend?

   Have you ever considered how unique and important your personal traits are in accomplishing God's plan here on earth? Did you know that God designed you specifically with His perfect plan in mind?

3a. How well does God know you? (Read Psalm 139: 1-12.) What does He know about you?

   Answer: God knows everything about you and me. He is intimately acquainted with all of our ways. He knew about us from the beginning of our existence in the womb and even before the foundation of the earth was made.

3b. According to Psalm 139, who created you?

   Answer: God created each of us with a specific purpose and intent.

3c. Describe what Psalm 139: 14-18 reveals about your design and uniqueness in God's eyes.

   Answer: (1) He is fearfully and wonderfully made, (2) He is skillfully designed, (3) He is designed for God's special purpose determined ahead of time, and (4) God put precious thought into his specific design because He cares for him.

   Do you think God makes mistakes? Well, He's God and He doesn't! And according to Psalm 139, God made you just the way you are. And because He made you just the way you are, you are fearfully and wonderfully made in His view! Learn to appreciate who you are and find where you fit on the T-E-A-M.

Let us not give up meeting together, as some are in the habit of doing, but let us encourage one another—and all the more as you see the Day approaching.

Hebrews 10:25
(NIV)

Where Do You Fit On The T-E-A-M?

Complete the following steps to assess your bent and find out where you fit:

Step 1: Under each letter category of the T-E-A-M chart, circle every word or phrase that describes a *consistent* character trait or behavior that you exhibit as you interact *within your family.*

Step 2: Total the number of items you circled in each letter category and write the total in the box at the bottom of each category.

Step 3: Plot the totals from each box on the graph entitled "What's My Bent?" on the next page. Put an "X" on each arrow scale to indicate your score for that category.

Step 4: Discuss your results.

After your son completes his assessment, share the results that you came up with for him from the "Understanding Your Son's Bent" exercise in chapter 6 of your *Mentor Guide.* Discuss similarities and differences in your ratings, but don't assume that either one of you has the full picture. If your son expresses a lot of interest in this assessment, feel free to share more about the four bents with him from chapter 6 of your *Mentor Guide.*

ASSESSMENT TIP:

If your son has trouble identifying his strengths, help him by suggesting things that you see in his life.

T

demanding · adventurous · dominant · strong-willed · decisive · task-oriented · authoritative · wants the bottom line · likes challenge · insensitive · fearless · wants choices · competitive · risk taker · confident · problem solver · likes direct answers · firm · controlling · likes freedom from control

"T" TOTAL

E

tolerant · friendships are very important · good listener · peacemaker · wants to be liked · pleasant or likeable · passive · careful · likes security · sensitive · nurturing · avoids confrontation · likes established work patterns · patient · indecisive · thoughtful · adaptable · wants to please · calm · people-oriented

"E" TOTAL

A

precise · correct · scheduled · calculating · consistent · likes "to do" lists · accurate · competent · analytical · cautious · likes Daytimers™ or electronic organizers · perfectionist · likes support from others · organized · detailed · predictable · likes defined tasks · discerning · practical · factual

"A" TOTAL

M

comes up with ideas · impressive · likes to look good · very verbal · comic · inspiring · enthusiastic · optimistic · prideful · influencer · promoter/marketer · enjoys change · motivator · fun · good mixer in crowds · spontaneous · energetic · enjoys popularity · likes variety · visionary (sees the big picture)

"M" TOTAL

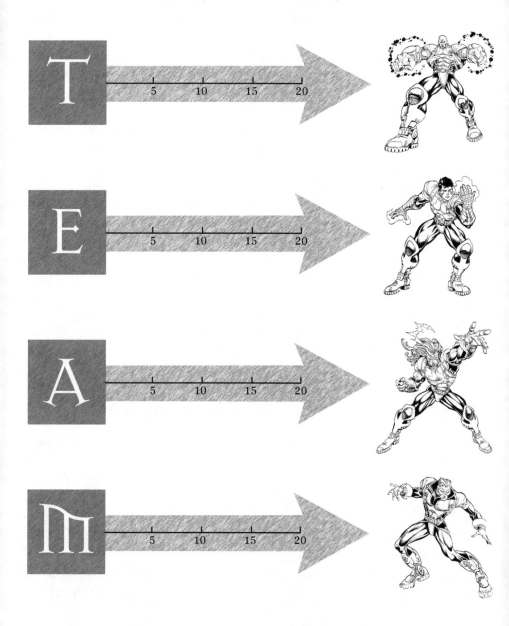

Based on your ratings, you probably notice that you identified with one of the Warriors more than the others. There's a reason for that. Even though we each have mix of traits, God created us with specific bents. For instance, if you are a strong A like Arti, you don't have to worry if you're not the one who makes everybody laugh like a strong M like Matty. As a strong A, you bring value to the team in other ways, such as your ability to get tasks done completely.

If you are a strong E like Epps, you offer a great deal to the team because of your ability to help calm things down and be a peacemaker. You may admire the leadership skills of a strong T like Tor, but it shouldn't bother you that don't always want to be in charge.

The bottom line: God doesn't want a team made up of clones. God blessed you with a uniquely crafted design for His special purpose in your life. Enjoy the design He gave you and use it to be an integral part of God's team. God wants you on His TEAM—and so do your family and your church!

4. After completing your T-E-A-M assessment, what do you see as some of your strengths?

QUESTION #4 TIP: Feel free to help your son identify some of his strengths if he has trouble doing so. Tell him how these strengths (leadership, people skills, analytical ability, servant heart, etc.) can benefit him and others in various situations.

5. Are there strengths or skills that you wish you had? If so, why?

QUESTION #5 TIP: If your son identifies a skill or trait that he would like to have, help him find an avenue to develop it. Also remind him that you accept and love him whether or not he successfully develops that skill or trait.

MAIN THINGS:

If needed, help your son by suggesting some key truths that he should have learned during this session, such as why a team needs people with different strengths or what he learned about his own bent or dealing with other types of people.

In order to have a winner, the team must have a feeling of unity; every player must put the team first—ahead of personal glory.

Paul "Bear" Bryant

QUOTE TIP:

Ask your son, "Why is this true? How could our family work better as a team?"

SHEET OF DEEDS:

Only a *brief* description of each action point is provided here. Go to the Think Tank (chapter 5) for complete instructions.

THE MAIN THINGS I LEARNED IN THIS CHAMPION SESSION ARE:

_____

_____

_____

_____

_____

CHAMPION SHEET OF DEEDS

Go to the CHAMPION Sheet of Deeds on page 9 and write down **one thing you will begin to do** before the next session (and beyond) to apply the main things you learned in session 14.

Check one of the suggestions below for your son to write down as his action point on his CHAMPION Sheet of Deeds for session 14. Descriptions and explanations of these action points are provided in the Think Tank (chapter 5) of this guide.

❏ Ask your son to brainstorm specific ways that he can use the strengths that he highlighted in his T-E-A-M assessment to help his family, friends, or church.

❏ Work with your son to identify weak temperament traits that he needs to strengthen. Help him to develop a plan for building these traits.

❏ Create your own unique action point.

Your Mission

Complete your mission and CHAMPION Session Prep before you meet for session 15.

Power Verse: Psalm 139:14

Date memorized: _____

Critical Maneuver

This will reinforce what you learned today. Obtain your maneuver instructions from your father.

CHAMPION Sheet of Deeds

Begin to apply your action point from your Sheet of Deeds.

CHAMPION Session Prep

Reread episode 15 of *Teknon and the CHAMPION Warriors*, and then complete the questions in session 15 in your *Mission Guide* on your own. **Our next CHAMPION Session will be:**

Date: _____

Time: _____

Place: _____

CRITICAL MANEUVER:
Go to the Think Tank (chapter 5 of this guide) and select one of the critical maneuvers listed under Session 14 to accomplish with your son.

SESSION 15: CELEBRATION

CHAMPION Characteristics

Navigation and Ownership

POWER VERSE: 2 Timothy 4:7-8A

I have fought the good fight, I have finished the course, I have kept the faith; in the future there is laid up for me the crown of righteousness.

STORY SUMMARY

The battle is won. It's time to celebrate! Friends, family, and dignitaries join the victorious team in the multilevel flying mansion of Kratos and his wife, Paideia. The entire team is honored for its heroic efforts against the evil forces that threatened Basileia. Kratos publicly recognizes Teknon as a young man and a valued member of the team. For illustrative purposes, Kratos takes Teknon's shield from him but later returns it to his son to use for Pneuma's glory (and not his own). Admiral Ago officially revives the ancient CHAMPION fighting unit by proclaiming them the New League of CHAMPION Warriors. As the excitement of their celebration winds down, Kratos gets word of another evil uprising detected on Basileia that requires the immediate attention of Kratos, Teknon, Tor, Epps, Arti, Matty, and Phil. It seems Magos survived and he's back. The mission continues.

Completion of the CHAMPION Training begins a new era for you with your son. You have helped him to establish a base set of skills and a level of rapport with you that can now continue. Be his coach and cheerleader during the coming years. Help him to navigate his future course by encouraging him to set high standards in every area of his life and to trust God in all things on a daily basis. Remind him to focus on serving God and other people. Continue to provide opportunities of growth and challenge for him. Refer to the "Ongoing Involvement" section in chapter 4 of your *Mentor Guide* for ideas.

QUESTION #3 TIP:
If your son successfully memorized the verse, have him date the verse in session 14 of his *Mission Guide*.

Discussion Topics

Charting your course and accepting your mission
Earning your "wings" so you can begin to fly on your own
Celebrating victories and giving glory to God

Mission Debrief

1. Discuss your mission from session 14. What did you learn from your maneuver? How has your attitude or behavior changed as a result of your maneuver?

2. One final reminder about your Sheet of Deeds: If you continue to apply all of your action points, it will truly help you to grow toward courageous manhood. Select one of your action points that you will focus on as a priority over the coming weeks. Write it here and put a star by it on your Sheet of Deeds.

3. Recite your power verse (Psalm 139:14) from session 14.

4. Which of the four mentors do you most resemble in temperament? Who came in second on your list? List what you believe to be three of your greatest strengths from the list of temperament traits.

5. Recite the CHAMPION Warrior Creed (see page 5).

RECONNAISSANCE

1. Look again at the Map of the Mission, pause at each location in Teknon's quest, and remember what he learned. Then, review the key things you have learned on your quest for truth. Highlight three important lessons you have learned.

   Answer: (1) overcoming fear of the unknown; the Rings of Responsibility (2A) enemy assessment; embracing the mission (2B) effective stewardship (3) sexual purity (4) discernment; choosing friends; consequences (5) teachability (6) showing honor and respect (7) avoiding sexual temptation (8) overcoming fear; recovering (9) breaking out of your comfort zone (10) resisting mediocrity (11) living your convictions; avoiding romantic entanglement (12) managing discouragement (13) choosing to focus on the mission (14) harnessing the power of the T-E-A-M (15) charting your course and celebrating victories

2. Review the CHAMPION definition of **Ownership**.

   Answer: "I will apply effective stewardship by using my life and the resources God entrusts to me—including my possessions, time, and talents—for His glory. I will seek contentment in God's provision for my needs. I will learn to practice delayed gratification."

3. Why do you think Kratos took Teknon's shield back from him?

   Answer: To illustrate to Teknon that he was only a steward of the shield, not the owner. Notice that it was renamed the Shield of Pneuma, indicating its true owner.

4. Why do you think Kratos returned Teknon's shield to him during the celebration?

   Answer: To complete the illustration that now Teknon should use the shield in Pneuma's service, as a faithful steward to the owner.

IMPORTANT NOTE:
It is extremely important that you continue comitting the time and effort to coach your son through his teen and early adult years. It is also important that you continue to set a good example for him. Let your son know about your intention to stay involved in his life and that you look forward to growing with him in your own relationship with Christ. Remember that your children are the arrows that God has placed into your hands to shoot into the next generation. What do you want your legacy to be?

Kratos is a Greek word that means "power and strength." *Teknon* means "child" or "youth." During the CHAMPION Training, you have seen how much you should draw from your dad's strength of character and example. Take note that if you also strive to know God and draw on His power, as Teknon did with Pneuma, you will move from childhood toward becoming a young man of character and courage.

5. **What did Kratos say to the group about Teknon during the ceremony?**

   Answer: Kratos publicly declared that Teknon had played a vital role in the success of the team's mission, that he had grown in maturity, that he was now a key member of the New League of CHAMPION Warriors, and that he had transitioned from boyhood into young manhood.

6. **Why do you think it was important for the team to celebrate after its victory on Kairos?**

   Answer: It is important to celebrate our God-given victories and the victories of others. While honoring other people is important, the key element of any victory celebration should be giving thanks and praise to God for His provision and faithfulness in our lives.

7. **Why do you think it was important for Kratos to acknowledge Teknon as a young man to his friends and family?**

   Answer: Young manhood is a significant transition that should be prepared for, recognized, and celebrated.

8. **What is the team's continuing mission?**

   Answer: To continue spreading the principles and teachings of the CHAMPION Warriors to the people of Basileia, and to protect them from the sinister strategies of their enemies—Magos and his master, Poneros.

Strategy and Tactics

Earning Your Wings

One of the richest and most significant traditions in our country's history is the awarding of a military pilot's "wings." When a pilot has completed his rigorous training, he is invited to a ceremony and presented with a symbol of the rank, skill, and responsibility that he has earned. When he receives his wings, he is authorized to sit behind the stick of his airplane and fly missions in the service of his country.

But just because he is awarded his wings, a pilot does not stop training. He knows that he must spend his career logging flight time, learning, training, and growing in his knowledge and piloting skills. He wants to become the best pilot that he can be.

Now that you have completed your CHAMPION Training, it's time for you to receive your "wings" and begin the flight into young manhood.

Accept the Challenge

Life was different in the mid-1800s. More than a hundred years ago, Native Americans roamed the plains and mountains of the United States. In those days, teenagers became men almost overnight. Young Indian men knew that when they reached a certain age, they were expected to provide and care for a family. They were also expected to join the rest of the warriors from their tribe in battle.

At what age would you be ready to assume responsibility for a family or be willing to fight an enemy to protect your homeland? If you were a Native American during the mid–1800s, you would have been about 14 years old.

But life is quite different for many teens today. Instead of using their talents and resources to set worthy goals and accomplish great tasks when they're young, they usually settle for trying to get homework done in time to watch TV or get on the Internet. They expect too little of themselves.

Throughout the centuries, there were men who took the first steps down new roads armed with nothing but their own vision.

Ayn Rand

You may not be in this camp, especially after finishing your CHAMPION Training. There are teens who are making a difference in their families and communities. They remember that God is the ultimate source of their talents and resources. They are thankful for what they have and want to be good stewards. They are taking responsibility—helping their parents, working hard at school, reaching out to other people, learning what friendship is all about, setting the right boundaries, and so on. These young people have learned to set high standards for themselves and they are meeting important objectives in life. They seek to know God better and to share Him with others. But remember, there's always room for growth.

An important key to living as a courageous man is to recognize the source of your talents and resources. Once you really grasp Who gave you your abilities and why He gave them to you, your life will never be the same. Let's look at a man in the Bible who learned about the power of God and how God could use him to accomplish mighty things for His people.

WHAT ARE YOU WAITING FOR?

Moses, an Israelite, was adopted by Pharaoh's daughter and raised as a prince in Egypt. But he was enraged about the treatment of his people, who were enslaved and pushed down under the heavy hand of the Egyptians. Initially, he tried to accomplish the mission of freeing his people in his own strength—he killed an Egyptian and had to run away.

Before Moses could become camp counselor to almost seven million people, the leader of the entire nation of Israel, he had to be humbled. He needed time to reflect, to think about who he was, and to learn to depend on God. So God allowed him to shepherd sheep for 40 years in the hills of what became the nation of Israel.

1. According to Exodus 3:1-10, what did God use to get Moses' attention? What did He want Moses to do?

   Answer: God spoke to Moses on top of the mountain of Horeb. His voice came from a bush that was burning but was not being consumed. God wanted Moses to lead the Israelites out of Egypt to freedom.

2. When Moses was afraid to carry out the mission God had given him, what did God promise to do for Moses (see Exodus 3:12-21)?

Answer: God promised to be with him, to empower him, and to guide him every step of the way. God explained to Moses that the success of this mission did not depend upon Moses' power, but upon the hand of God.

As God continued to speak to Moses out of the burning bush to reveal His plan to deliver the Israelites from Egypt, He told Moses to do something very puzzling.

Read Exodus 4:1-5.
3a. What was in Moses' hand?

Answer: His shepherd's staff.

3b. What did God tell Moses to do with it the staff?

Answer: God told him to throw it down on the ground.

3c. What did God tell Moses to do next?

Answer: When the staff became a snake, the Lord told him to pick it up again. When he picked up the snake it became a staff again.

3d. Why do you think God told Moses to do these things (see verse 5)?

Answer: So that the Israelites would believe that God had truly appeared to Moses and had given him the mission of delivering them out of bondage in Egypt. In addition, God wanted Moses to lay down what he depended on and give it to God.

After 40 years of being a shepherd, God told Moses to lay down his staff. A staff was the most important tool a shepherd owned. It was an instrument he used to guide his sheep through the mountains and it was a weapon he used to ward off wild animals that tried to attack the flock. A shepherd valued his staff even more than Tiger Woods values his driver. Over time, Moses' staff had become like an extension of his arm. He seldom went anywhere without it. The staff was also Moses' security. After all, he had been comfortably hiding out in the wilderness for 40 years. God was asking Moses to take a giant step out his comfort zone.

Bring me men to match my mountains. Bring me men to match my plans. Men with empires in their purpose, and new eras in their brains.

Sam Walter Foss

When God asked Moses to lay down his staff, it was like Kratos asking Teknon to return his shield. Moses may not have understood God's reasoning, but he obeyed anyway. God showed Moses the miracles He would perform through the staff and explained that through these miracles the Israelites would know that He had truly appeared to Moses. When God returned the newly designed shepherd's tool to Moses, it was no longer the staff of Moses. It was now the staff of God! The staff became God's instrument to accomplish His mission through Moses.

5. Review the CHAMPION definition of **Navigation**.

Answer: "I will allow God to chart my course by accepting my mission from Him, and I will complete that mission by trusting in Him. I will study the Bible, God's Word, so I can know Him better and gain His strength and direction for my life. I will become goal-oriented by learning to focus my attention on completing worthwhile short-term and long-term objectives."

Have you grasped through your training that God has a mission for each of us? Do you realize that He has given you the talents and resources you need to accomplish the mission He has for you? When you use your talents for God, and depend on His power, you are exercising good stewardship. You are becoming God's instrument on earth to accomplish His mission.

So what are you waiting for? Get involved in God's mission as a CHAMPION. Trust Him to accomplish the impossible in and through you (that's within God's Ring of Responsibility), but make sure that you're taking responsibility to do all that you can to seek God and pursue excellence in every part of your life (that's within your CHAMPION's Ring). Shouldn't you use the abilities and assets that God has given you to accomplish His goals? God's mission will unfold for you day by day if you will commit to follow Him. It's a great adventure!

One more thing ... it's time to celebrate! You've just completed the entire CHAMPION Training adventure. You've read the episodes, answered the questions, discussed many topics with your dad, and completed the maneuvers and action points. Take time to enjoy this victory and any other victories that you've experienced during your CHAMPION Training. God wants to celebrate the wins in your life and He wants you to celebrate with Him. Thank God for what he has done and for what He will do in and through you as you live your life as a CHAMPION.

What kind of man would live where there is no daring? I don't believe in taking foolish chances, but nothing can be accomplished without taking any chances at all.

Charles Lindbergh

QUOTE TIP:
Charles Lindbergh's flight across the Atlantic Ocean was greeted with the same awe and enthusiasm as Neil Armstrong's first step on the moon. If you watched "The Spirit of St. Louis" after episode 9, you realize the chances that Lindbergh took in his mission. Help your son realize the value of stepping out of his comfort zone, trusting God to accomplish even more than he would ask for or imagine. There is no more significant or satisfying mission than joining God's army of warriors.

THE Main THINGS I LEARNED in THIS CHAMPION SESSION ARE:

_____

_____

_____

_____

MAIN THINGS:
If needed, help your son by suggesting some key truths that he should have learned during this session, such as how God can use him as a part of His mission here on earth, why he must focus on continuing to grow, and why it is important to celebrate our wins.

CHAMPION SHEET OF DEEDS

Go to the CHAMPION Sheet of Deeds on page 9 and write down **one thing you will begin to do** before the next session (and beyond) to apply the main things you learned in session 15.

Check one of the suggestions below for your son to write down as his action point on his CHAMPION Sheet of Deeds for session 15. Descriptions and explanations of these action points are provided in the Think Tank (chapter 5) of this guide.

❏ Ask your son to write a brief essay that describes the key things that he learned during his CHAMPION Training. Ask him to read this at his celebration ceremony.

❏ Ask your son to develop a set of goals for the next year based on what he has learned from his CHAMPION Training. Work with him to strengthen his plan and ask how you can support him.

❏ Create your own unique action point.

SHEET OF DEEDS:
Only a _brief_ description of each action point is provided here. Go to the Think Tank (chapter 5) for complete instructions.

And looking at them Jesus said to them, "With people this is impossible, but with God all things are possible."

Matthew 19:26

YOUR MISSION

Complete your mission before you meet for your Celebration Ceremony.

POWER VERSE: 2 TIMOTHY 4:7-8A

Date memorized: _____

CRITICAL MANEUVER

This will reinforce what you learned today. Obtain your maneuver instructions from your father.

CRITICAL MANEUVER:
Go to the Think Tank (chapter 5 of this guide) and select one of the critical maneuvers listed under session 15 to accomplish with your son.

CHAMPION SHEET OF DEEDS

Continue to apply your action points from your Sheet of Deeds.

CELEBRATION CEREMONY

If your dad is planning a celebration ceremony for you, write down the specifics here.

Dad, celebrate your son's accomplishment in completing his CHAMPION Training with a ceremony! Refer to chapter 4 of your *Mentor Guide* for practical tips on putting together an effective ceremony for your son. My Celebration Ceremony will be:

Date: _____

Time: _____

Place: _____

Congratulations on a job well done!

Nike® says it, and we buy into it. You look at the "swoosh," as Nike calls it, and the phrase comes to your mind. You hear it in commercials, you see it on the billboards, and it's plastered on millions of shirts, shoes, and shorts. Over a period of time, we come to believe it only because some well-paid marketing wizards found a creative way to sell more products. Now, why don't we say that phrase all together? Ready, one, two, three:

Just Do It!

If only all of life were as easy as this slogan makes it sound. The truth is, life is a lot harder than selling trendy clothing. In fact, we can't "just do it" on our own when it comes to living a life in which we're unconditionally loved, eternally protected, and fully satisfied.

We need power to do that—a lot of power. Power that can only come from an all-powerful God who wants us to relate to Him on a personal level. Only those people who know Him and seek Him have access to God's unlimited power. He offers it as a free gift that we receive through faith in His Son, Jesus Christ.

God created us to have an abundant life now and for eternity. But He did not create us like androids that would automatically love and follow Him. He gave us a will and freedom to choose or eternal destination. What will you choose?

Are you 100% sure that, when you die, you are going to heaven? Why do you say that?

Mark on the following scale, how sure are you that you have a personal relationship with God, through Jesus Christ?

Not at all sure   1   2   3   4   5   Very sure

How do you know?

_____

_____

Would you like to be 100% fully sure that you have a personal relationship with God that will guarantee your passport to heaven?

_____

_____

God's power is experienced by knowing God personally and by growing in our relationship with Him. God has provided the power necessary to fulfill His purposes and to carry out His mission for our lives. God is so eager to establish a personal, loving relationship with you that He has already made all the arrangements. He is patiently and lovingly waiting for you to respond to His invitation.

The major barrier that prevents us from knowing God personally is ignorance of who God is and what he has done for us. The following four principles will help you discover how to know God personally and experience the abundant life He promised.

1 GOD LOVES YOU AND CREATED YOU TO KNOW HIM PERSONALLY.

a. God loves you.

"For God so loved the world, that He gave His only begotten Son, that whoever believes in Him should not perish but have eternal life." John 3:16

b. God wants you to know Him.

"Now this is eternal life: that they may know You, the only true God, and Jesus Christ, whom You have sent."   John 17:3 (NIV)

What prevents us from knowing God personally?

2 WE ARE SINFUL AND SEPARATED FROM GOD, SO WE CANNOT KNOW HIM PERSONALLY OR EXPERIENCE HIS LOVE AND POWER.

(Author's Note: The word sin *confuses a lot of people. The word* sin *comes from a Greek term that was used in archery. When archers shot at the target, the distance by which their arrow missed the bull's-eye was called sin. That distance represented the degree to which the archer missed the mark of perfection. When we miss God's mark of perfection, it's called sin too. And because of sin, there is a wall that separates us from a perfectly holy God. Through the years, people have tried many things to break through that wall. Money, power, and fame are just a few of the things people have tried. None of them have worked. We all fall short of God's perfection.)*

a. Man is sinful.

"For all have sinned and fall short of the glory of God." Romans 3:23

b. Man is separated.

For the wages of sin is death [spiritual separation from God]. Romans 6:23a

How can the canyon between God and man be bridged?

JESUS CHRIST IS THE ONLY PROVISION FOR MAN'S SIN. THROUGH HIM ALONE WE CAN KNOW GOD PERSONALLY AND EXPERIENCE GOD'S LOVE.

a. God became a man through the Person of Jesus Christ.

> But the angel said to them, "Do not be afraid; for behold, I bring you good news of great joy which will be for all the people; for today in the city of David there has been born for you a Savior, who is Christ the Lord." Luke 2:10-11

b. He died in our place.

> "But God demonstrates His own love toward us in that while we were yet sinners, Christ died for us." Romans 5:8

c. He rose from the dead.

> "Christ died for our sins according to the Scriptures ... He was buried ... He was raised on the third day according to the Scriptures ... He appeared to Peter, then to the twelve. After that He appeared to more than five hundred." 1 Corinthians 15:3b-6a

d. He is the only way to God.

> "Jesus said to him, 'I am the way, and the truth, and the life; no one comes to the Father but through Me.'" John 14:6

It is not enough to know these truths ...

 WE MUST INDIVIDUALLY RECEIVE JESUS CHRIST AS SAVIOR AND LORD; THEN WE CAN KNOW GOD PERSONALLY AND EXPERIENCE HIS LOVE.

a. We must receive Christ.

> "But as many as received Him, to them He gave the right to become children of God, even to those who believe in His name." John 1:12

b. We must receive Christ through faith.

> "For by grace you have been saved through faith; and that not of yourselves, it is the gift of God; not as a result of works, so that no one may boast." Ephesians 2:8-9

c. When we receive Christ we experience a new birth (read John 3:1-8).

d. We must receive Christ by personal invitation.

> "I am the door; if anyone enters through Me, he will be saved ..." John 10:9

Receiving Christ involves turning to God from self (repentance) and trusting Christ to come into our lives to forgive us of our sins and to make us what He wants us to be. Just to agree intellectually that Jesus Christ is the Son of God and that He died on the cross for our sins is not enough. Nor is it enough to have an emotional experience. We receive Jesus Christ by faith, as an act of our will.

These two circles represent two kinds of lives:

Which circle best represents your life?

Which circle would you like to have represent your life?

You Can Receive Christ Right Now By Faith Through Prayer

God knows your heart and is not so concerned with your words as He is with the attitude of your heart. Here is a suggested life-changing prayer:

> Lord Jesus, I want to know You personally. Thank you for dying on the cross for my sins. I open the door of my life and receive You as my Savior and Lord. Thanks you for forgiving me of my sins and giving me eternal life. Take control of the throne of my life. Make me the kind of person You want me to be.

> If you sincerely prayed this prayer, you can know with 100% certainty that Christ is in your life and He is there to stay (Hebrews 13:5). So, you don't have to "just do it". God has already done it for you. You may or may not feel like it now, but this is the most important day of your life. To remember this major event in your life when you joined God's family, sign and date this page.

_____   _____
                  Signature   *Date*

What Are the Results of Placing Your Faith in Jesus Christ?

The Bible says:

1. Jesus Christ came into your life (Colossians 1:27).

2. Your sins were forgiven (Colossians 1:14).

3. You became a child of God (John 1:12)

4. You received eternal life (John 5:24).

5. You have the power to pursue intimacy with God (Romans 5:5).

6. You began the great adventure, the mission, for which God created you (John 10:10, 2 Corinthians 5:17, and 1 Thessalonians 5:18).

CHAMPION
Training Adventure
Program

For other *Teknon and the Champion Warriors* resources check out our Web site at www.familylife.com/teknon for:

▲ Character illustrations and descriptions

▲ Downloadable CHAMPION Creed and Code

▲ Downloadable sample forms

▲ New ideas for CHAMPION Training

▲ Great links and more!

Acknowledgements

Putting together an integrated program with a fiction novel for teens, an interactive training guide, and a comprehensive how-to manual for dads has been quite a challenge. There are a number of people I wish to thank for helping me to make *Teknon and the CHAMPION Warriors* a reality.

I would like to thank Neal and Ida Jean Sapp, Sam Bartlett, Sheri and Jack McGill, Dr. Gilbert Chandler, Martin Shipman, Don Jacobs, Roger Berry, Nick and Amy Repak, Michael Hohmann, Steve Bruton, Sergio Cariello, Rick Blanchette, Donald Joy, and Stephen Sorenson for their invaluable input and encouragement.

I also appreciate the dedicated team at FamilyLife for the theological, editorial, and design direction. This team includes Jerry McCall, Blair Wright, David Sims, Bob Anderson, Anne Wooten, and Fran Taylor.

My heartfelt thanks are extended to Ben Colter who, through his hard work and creative editing expertise, has helped to transform this material into an adventurous, user-friendly training program that we hope will greatly benefit both you and your son.

I want to thank my wife, Ellen, for striving with me to raise our children with strong character and for enduring the process of developing these materials. Last, but not least, I want to acknowledge my children, Katie, Kimberly, Kyle, and especially Casey for giving me encouragement and inspiration during the creative development of the CHAMPION Training adventure program. Thanks, kids!

Notes

Mentor Preparation section

Chapter 1:

Robert Lewis, *Raising a Modern Day Knight* (Colorado Springs: Focus on the Family, 1997).

Mission Guide section

Session 6:

Original source unknown for "Nasty as We Wanna Be" article.

Session 7:

Dennis and Barbara Rainey, Passport to Purity (Little Rock, Arkansas, 1999).

About the Author

Brent Sapp is a first time writer from Orlando. When his older son, Casey, was nearing the teen years, Brent conceived a fun program that he and some friends pursued together with their sons. They called themselves CHAMPION Warriors. The program caught on in Florida and in other areas of the country. From this successful venture, Brent has adapted the key principles of a CHAMPION into a futuristic adventure novel for teen boys. He has also developed an interactive character-building program for fathers to use with their sons as a companion resource to *Teknon and the CHAMPION Warriors*.

Brent and his wife, Ellen, have four children (Casey, 16; Katie, 14; Kimberly, 12; and Kyle, 9). Brent is a graduate of Florida State University and has an MBA from Rollins College. He has worked as a medical sales representative for the past 16 years. When not representing medical and surgical equipment, Brent volunteers with Ellen to help bring the FamilyLife Marriage Conference to Orlando and also to prepare dozens of young couples for marriage each year at Northland Community Church.

About the Illustrator

Sergio Cariello is the talented free-lance illustrator behind the characters of *Teknon and the CHAMPION Warriors*. He also draws such well-known icons as Superman and Batman for DC Comics. In addition, he teaches at the prestigious Joe Kubert School of Cartooning and Animation. Sergio lives in South River, N.J., with his wife, Luzia.